Orkney and Shetland Folklore

COUNTY FOLK-LORE
VOL. III.

PRINTED EXTRACTS No. 5

EXAMPLES OF PRINTED FOLK-LORE

CONCERNING THE

Orkney & Shetland Islands

COLLECTED BY
G. F. BLACK
AND EDITED BY
NORTHCOTE W. THOMAS

A facsimile reprint, 1994,
Llanerch Publishers/Folklore Society.

ISBN 1897853 53 X

Published for the Folk-Lore Society by
DAVID NUTT, 57-59 LONG ACRE
LONDON
1903

INTRODUCTION

The word "folklore" was invented almost 150 years ago, on August 22 1846, when the antiquarian W. J. Thoms appealed in the *Athenæum* for readers to join in recording"... what we in England designate as Popular Antiquities or Popular Literature (though by-the-by it is more a Lore than a Literature, and would be most aptly described by a good Saxon compound, Folk-lore) ...". The word was new, but the subject was not; for two hundred years antiquarians had been fascinated by local and seasonal customs, popular tales, traditions, beliefs which did not conform to official relligion or science. Such material appears sporadically in the writings of William Camden (1551-1623), and far more abundantly in those of John Aubrey (1626-97). Some decades later came Henry Bourne's *Antiquitates Vulgares* (1725), a fierce attack against popular relligious observances such as Christmas carols or visiting holy wells, because they were originally Roman Catholic, "the invention of indolent monks", and so undoubtedly diabolical and heathen. His book, ignored at the time, was incorporated in 1777 into a much larger and more influential work, John Brand's *Observations on Popular Antiquities*. Brand agreed that most folk customs dated from before the Reformation, but he was free from the Puritan intolerance which equated Catholicism with paganism, and he enjoyed historical research for its own sake. He went on gathering material till his death in 1806, mostly by copying from books and journals, but sometimes by personal observation. After he died, his book was reissued in a greatly enlarged edition, incorporating the later notes by Henry Ellis (1815). It had grown into a vast, confused scrapbook: local historians pounced upon it and used it as a model for their own researches.

In the course of the nineteenth century, many

scholars boldly tried to formulate some all-embracing theory which would explain the origin and significance of myths, folktales, superstitions and magical beliefs, and the more picturesque folk customs, especially those connected with agriculture. The explanations offered went far beyond medieval Catholicism. Some suggested origins in pre-Christian Germanic or Celtic cultures; others, noting similarities with beliefs and rituals found among "primitive" non-European peoples, argued that folklore consisted of survivals from a prehistoric "savage" stage in human social development. The debate between these and other conflicting theories was carried on energetically at a high scholarly level, and attracted much public interest. It has been well described in Richard M. Dorson's *The British Folklorists: A History* (1968). And although modern scholars agree that all these Victorian attempts to find "a key to all mythologies" ended in failure, due to oversimplifications of the highly complex topics, some of the theories then launched are still to be found recycled in popular form: prehistoric paganism and Celtic paganism, separately or combined, are currently enjoying a fashionable revival in the mass market.

By the 1890s the Folklore Society, which had been founded in 1878, saw a need for systematic and accurate documentation of traditions within specific localities: huge unwieldy compilations like Brand's would not do. Between 1895 and 1914 seven volumes of *County Folklore: Printed Extracts* were published by the Society. The first covered three counties: *Gloucestershire* by E. S. Hartland, *Suffolk* by Lady Camilla Eveline Gurdon, and *Leicestershire and Rutland* by C. J. Billson. The rest covered one region apiece: *The North Riding of Yorkshire, and the Ainsty* by Eliza Gutch; *Orkney and Shetland Islands* by George Black, ed. N. W. Thomas; *Northumberland* by M. C. Balfour, ed. N. W. Thomas; *Lincolnshire* by Eliza Gutch and

Mabel Peacock; *The East Riding of Yorkshire* by Eliza Gutch; and *Fife* by J. E. Simpkins. The 1914 war then interrupted the project.

These books may seem strange today because, like Brand's, they consist almost entirely of extracts from previously printed books and journals. Fieldwork, i.e. gathering information through interviews or by tape-recording, filming, and personal observation, is central to a present-day folklorist's technique, and was already practised in Victorian times by means of the simple notebook. Yet from these books it is virtually absent; editorial theorising and interpretation are also minimal. It must be stressed that the "Printed Extracts" series was never intended to stand alone, but to be a starting point for further study of the contemporary lore of each area. In his preface to the Gloucestershire volume, Hartland made "suggestions for systematic collection of folklore" to be undertaken by university students, school teachers, clergy, doctors, local historians and others. Plenty of his contemporaries were already working in this way; the purpose of reprinting old material was to provide historical perspectives and a set of securely dated benchmarks, from which to measure later developments, innovations or losses.

Another century has passed, and the County Folklore series is being reprinted in the 1990s, a period of nostalgia for an idealized rural past, seen as a time of idyllic simplicity and closeness to nature. Readers will find ample encouragement for nostalgia here: picturesque accounts of harvest customs, Christmas customs, fairs and festivals; old tales of ghosts, giants, fairies, boggarts, witches, heroes, bandits; healing charms, divinations, omens, spells; customs at marriage, birth or death. It is only too easy to see in all this mere quaintness and charm. To get a more historically balanced picture one needs to remember also the harsh social and economic conditions affecting very many rural workers: one may well wonder, for instance, whether a good harvest supper really compensated for low wages during the other 51 weeks of the year. The "printed extracts", like old photographs, offer facts, but facts selected and presented according to the viewpoint of the observers who recorded them. Now, in the 1990s, we inevitably add interpretative viewpoints of our own, conditioned by the cultural assumptions of our age.

Folklore is an ongoing process, in which every custom, story or belief (if it survives) is constantly remodelled by social pressures so that it remains in some way relevant to changing conditions. Books written a hundred or two hundred years ago are in no sense a final word on the topic, nor are the versions of a story or custom which they contain necessarily "better" than the current ones – they merely pinpoint what it was like in one phase of its existence. Moreover, anything that is passed on through oral tradition exists in multiple versions, each differing in some degree from the next, and each equally valid. What is the "true" story about that haunted tree? What is the "right" way to dispose of Christmas decorations, and on what date? What "should" children do at Halloween? Are black cats lucky (UK), or unlucky (USA)? We shall never find definitive answers to such questions, but it is fascinating to compile our own observations about them, and to compare with writers who went hunting along the same tracks long before us.

Jacqueline Simpson,
President,
The Folklore Society,
1994.

PREFACE.

THE material for the following pages was brought together some years ago by Mr. G. F. Black, and would have been passed through the press by him but for his absence from England. Mr. Black having gone to reside in the United States since he placed his collections in the hands of the Council for publication, the Society is indebted to Mr. N. W. Thomas for undertaking the duty of editing the MSS., as well as for some additional matter, and for the care he has bestowed on the whole work. The Council desire to express their thanks to the compilers of the volume, to Mr. Gilbert Goudie, Mr. A. K. Williamson, and the Rev. Thomas Mathewson, for notes communicated to Mr. Black, and to those owners of copyright works who have permitted extracts therefrom to appear in the ensuing pages.

It may perhaps be well to remind members of the scope and object of the series of County Folklore volumes; namely, to bring together in an accessible form the scattered notices of local folklore which occur in local records, old topographies, travellers' diaries, miscellaneous periodicals, and other such out-of-the-way sources. It is designed to form a record of the past, not a description of the present. Hence information from oral or modern sources is only exceptionally used or quoted in its pages.

The present volume, therefore, borrows nothing from the interesting little work on *Shetland Folklore* by Mr. John Spence, F.E.I.S., of the Schoolhouse, Vassa, Shetland (Lerwick: Johnson and Greig, 1899), reviewed in *Folklore*, XII., 330. The two books illustrate and supplement each other. Besides information about the prehistoric antiquities of the Shetlands, Mr. Spence gives a detailed account of the superstitions and customs connected with fishing, anecdotes of trows, selkies, witches, and Finns, some notices of festival customs, and a good deal on medical magic, with some incantations and word-charms, and upwards of a hundred and fifty proverbs. He informs us (p. 168), that "Forker's Pig," the bowl stolen from the Trows, described by Mr. Edmondston and Mrs. Saxby in the passage quoted *infra*, p. 30, is now in his possession, but he does not mention the belief recorded by them, that the ointment in the "pig" was never exhausted.

One curious point about the folklore of the islands may be noted. With two exceptions only (*infra*, pp. 35, 141), no item of plant-lore has been recorded by any writer consulted.

The Norwegian Earldom of Orkney and Shetland, mainly inhabited by a Scandinavian population since the time of its colonisation from Norway in the ninth century, was not annexed to Scotland till the fifteenth. The Norn language continued to be the ordinary speech of the people during the sixteenth century, lingering in Orkney to the end of the seventeenth, and in Shetland to the middle of the eighteenth. We find the witch-trials of the seventeenth century conducted in the native *Law-ting*, and the *dooms* pronounced by the native *Dempster*, though the official

Preface.

record of the proceedings is couched in literary Lowland Scottish. Even to this day the old Norn Yule-tide festival prevails over the Scottish Hogmanay. With a past so simple, so well ascertained, and differing so entirely from that of any other part of the United Kingdom, the modern parliamentary "county" of Orkney and Shetland affords a singularly favourable field for the investigation of that ethnological side of folklore, to elucidate which is the principal object of the County Series.

By order of the Council.

E. W. BRABROOK, *President* 1901.

⁂ For an account of the Uphelly A' or Yule-tide festival as now celebrated at Lerwick, see *Folklore*, vol. xiv., p. 74.

CONTENTS.

	PAGE
LIST OF AUTHORITIES,	ix

PART I.

SUPERSTITIOUS BELIEFS AND PRACTICES.

INORGANIC NATURAL OBJECTS, - - - - - 1-12
    Holy Places—Stones—Holy Wells and Lochs—Buildings—Sea.

PLANT SUPERSTITIONS, - - - - - - 12

ANIMAL SUPERSTITIONS, - - - - - - 12-20
    Insects—Birds—Animals—Fish and Reptiles—Sponges.

GOBLINDOM, - - - - - - - - 20-50
    Brownies, fairies—Luridan—Wilkie—Poltergeist—Various.

WITCHCRAFT, - - - - - - - - 50-139
    General—Formulae—Trials.

LEECHCRAFT, - - - - - - - - 140-152
    General—Spells—Charms.

MAGIC AND DIVINATION, - - - - - - 153-161
    Ancient Weapons—Storm-raising—Miscellaneous—Spells—Counter Charms—Divination.

SUPERSTITIONS GENERALLY, - - - - - 161-193
    Miscellaneous—Sea and Fishing—Selkies.

Contents.

PART II.
TRADITIONAL CUSTOMS.

	PAGE
FESTIVAL CUSTOMS,	194–205
CEREMONIAL CUSTOMS,	206–216
Wedding—Funeral.	
GAMES,	216–218
LOCAL CUSTOMS,	218–219

PART III.
TRADITIONAL NARRATIVES.

TALES,	220–228
Sagas—Märchen—Cumulative Tales.	
BALLADS, SONGS, AND MUSIC,	228–257
PLACE LEGENDS AND TRADITIONS,	257–262
DRAMA,	262

PART IV.
FOLK SAYINGS.

COUNTING-OUT RHYMES,	263
PROVERBS,	263–265
LOCAL TEE, TUE, OR NICKNAMES,	265–268

APPENDIX.

PHYSICAL CHARACTERISTICS,	269
NAMES,	270
GLOSSARY,	271–277

PRINCIPAL WORKS REFERRED TO.

Abbotsford Club Miscellany. "Trials for Witchcraft, Sorcery and Superstition in Orkney." Printed in *Miscellany of the Abbotsford Club*, v. i. pp. 133-186.

Barry. History of the Orkney Islands, including a view of the Manners and Customs of their ancient and modern Inhabitants, &c. By Rev. Dr. George Barry. 2. ed. with corrections and additions by Rev. James Headrick. London, 1808.

Ben, Jo. "Descriptio Insularum Orchadiarum, in Anno 1529." By Jo. Ben [*i.e.* John Bellenden]. Forms App. vii. of Barry's *History*, 2. ed. pp. 437-50.

Blind, Gentleman's Magazine. "New Finds in Shetlandic and Welsh Folklore." By Karl Blind. Published in *Gentleman's Magazine*, v. cclii. March, April, 1882.

Blind, Nineteenth Century. "Discovery of Odinic Songs in Shetland." By Karl Blind. *Nineteenth Century*, 1879, v. v. pp. 1091-1113.

Blind, Contemporary Review. "Scottish, Shetlandic, and Germanic Water Tales." By Karl Blind. *Contemporary Review*, v. xl. pp. 186-208, 399-423.

Blind, Archæological Review. "A Grimm's Tale in a Shetland Folklore Version." By Karl Blind. *Archæological Review*, 1888, v. i. pp. 346-352.

Blind, New Review. Shetland Folk-lore and the old faith of the Teutons. By Karl Blind. *New Review*, v. xi. pp. 612-623.

Brand. A New description of Orkney, Zetland, Pightland-Firth, and Caithness. By Rev. John Brand. Edinburgh, 1703.

Buckley. Vertebrate Fauna of the Orkneys. By J. A. Harvie Brown and Buckley. Edinburgh, 1894.

Burgess. "Some Shetland Folklore." By J. J. Haldane Burgess. *Scottish Review*, v. xxv. pp. 91-103. Paisley, 1895.

Chambers. Popular Rhymes of Scotland. By Robert Chambers. New ed. Edinburgh, [1892].

Chambers's Journal. "Shetland Marriage." *Chambers's Journal*, Edinburgh, 1860, vol. xii. pp. 383, 384.

Cowie. Shetland: Descriptive and Historical and Topographical Description of that Country. By Robert Cowie, M.D. 3. ed. Aberdeen, 1879.

Dalyell. The Darker Superstitions of Scotland. By John Graham Dalyell. Edinburgh, 1835.

Dennison. "The Play o' de Lathie Odivere." By W. Traill Dennison. Published in the *Scottish Antiquary*, v. viii. pp. 53-58.

Dennison. "Orkney Folklore. Sea Myths." A series of papers by W. Traill Dennison, published in the *Scottish Antiquary*, vol. v. pp. 68-71, 130-33, 167-71; vi. 115-121; vii. 18-24, 81, 112-120, 171-177.

Douglas. Scottish Fairy and Folk Tales. Selected and Edited with an Introduction by Sir George Douglas. London, n.d.

Edmondston, Glossary. An Etymological Glossary of the Shetland and Orkney Dialect. . . . By Thomas Edmondston. Edinburgh, 1866.

Edmondston, Shetland. A view of the ancient and present state of the Zetland Islands; including their Civil, Political, and Natural History, Antiquities, &c. By Arthur Edmondston, M.D. 2 v. Edinburgh, 1809.

Edmondston, Sketches. Sketches and Tales of the Shetland Islands. By Eliza Edmondston. Edinburgh, 1856.

Edmondston and Saxby. The Home of a Naturalist. By Rev. Biot Edmondston and his sister, Jessie M. E. Saxby. London, 1888.

Emerson. Poetical Descriptions of Orkney, M.DC.LII.: The Character of Orkney. By J. Emerson. Printed, Edinburgh, 1835. [A scurrilous work, but containing some items of Folklore.]

Fea. Present State of the Orkney Islands considered. By James Fea. Printed at Holyroodhouse, 1775.

Fea. The Present State of the Orkney Islands considered. By James Fea. Edinburgh, 1884.

Fergusson. Rambles in the Far North. By R. Menzies Fergusson. 2. ed. Paisley, 1884.

Fotheringham. "Orkney Charms." By "F." [W. H. Fotheringham.] In Notes and Queries, 1 ser. vol. x. pp. 220, 221. (In 1848 Mr. Fotheringham communicated these charms to the Society of Antiquaries of Scotland (*MS. Communications*, vol. viii., 1842-52), with the statement that they were found among the family papers of the Traills of Westray.)

Fraser's Mag. "Manners, traditions, and superstitions of the Shetlanders." [A summary of the information on these points in Hibbert, Brand, Old and New Stat. Accts., Witch Trials, etc.] Frazer's Magazine, 1846, vol. xxxiv. pp. 147-158, 323-339, 480-497.

Principal Works Referred to.

Gorrie. Summers and Winters in the Orkneys. By Daniel Gorrie. 2. ed. London [1869].

Goudie. The Diary of the Rev. John Mill, Minister of Dunrossness, . . . Shetland, 1740-1803; with selections from local records and original documents relating to the district. Edited by Gilbert Goudie, F.S.A. Scot. Edinburgh, 1889. [Scottish History Society Publications.]

Hibbert. A description of the Shetland Islands, comprising an account of their Geology, Scenery, Antiquities, and Superstitions. By Samuel Hibbert. Edinburgh, 1822.

Laurenson, Pro. Soc. Ant. Scot. "On certain Beliefs and Phrases of Shetland Fishermen." By Arthur Laurenson. In *Proceedings, Society of Antiquaries of Scotland*, 1874, v. x. pp. 711-716.

Low. A Tour through the Islands of Orkney and Schetland, containing Hints relative to their Ancient, Modern, and Natural History. Collected in 1774. By Rev. George Low. Kirkwall, 1879.

Low, Fauna. Fauna Orcadensis. By Rev. George Low. Edited by W. E. Leach, M.D. Edinburgh, 1813.

Macbeath. The Orkneys in Early Celtic Times. By J. M. Macbeath. Kirkwall, 1892.

Mackenzie. Gaelic Incantations, Charms and Blessings of the Hebrides. By William Mackenzie. Inverness, 1895.

Maitland Club Miscellany. "Acts and Statutes of the Lawting, Sheriff, and Justice Courts within Orkney and Zetland, 1602-1644," in *Maitland Club Miscellany*, v. ii.

Munch. Geographical elucidations of the Scottish and Irish local names occurring in the Sagas. I. The Orkneys. By P. A. Munch. Mémoires de la Société Royale des Antiquaires du Nord, 1845-49, pp. 208-265.

New Stat. Acct. The New Statistical Account of Scotland. 15 vols. Edinburgh, 1845. (The Accounts of Orkney and Shetland form v. xv., each with separate pagination.)

Old Stat Acct. Statistical Account of Scotland. 21 v. Edinburgh, 1791-99.

Reid. Art Rambles in Shetland. By John T. Reid, Edinburgh, 1869.

Rogers. Social Life in Scotland from Early to Recent Times. By Rev. Charles Rogers, LL.D. 3 v. Edinburgh, 1886.

Saxby. The Birds of Shetland. By Henry L. Saxby. Edinburgh, 1874.

Scott. The Pirate. By Sir Walter Scott. Edinburgh, 1891.

Sibbald. The Description of the Isles of Orknay and Zetland. By Sir Robert Sibbald. Edinburgh, 1711.

Sinclar. Satan's Invisible World Discovered. By George Sinclar. Reprint of ed. of 1685. Edinburgh, 1871.

Stewart. Shetland Fireside Tales; or the Hermit of Trosswickness. By G. S. L. [*i.e.* George Stewart, Leith]. Edinburgh, 1877.

Teignmouth. Sketches of the Coasts and Islands of Scotland. By Lord Teignmouth. 2 v. London, 1836.

Thomas, Pro. Soc. Ant. Soc. "A Shetland Ballad." By Capt. F. W. L. Thomas. *Proceedings of the Society of Antiquaries of Scotland,* 1851, v. i. pp. 86-89.

Tudor. The Orkneys and Shetland; their past and present state. By John R. Tudor. London, 1883.

Wallace. An account of the Islands of Orkney. By James Wallace. 1st. ed. London, 1700.

ERRATA.

Pp. 1-80, *passim* for "Edmonston" read "Edmondston."
P. 55, line 3, for "Sinclair" read "Sinclar."
P. 65, line 12, for "bame" read "becam."
P. 159, line 29, for "49 n" read "493."
P. 195, line 22, for "Sandstiney, Aithstiney" read "Sandsting, Aithsting."

PART I.

SUPERSTITIOUS BELIEFS AND PRACTICES.

(a) *SUPERSTITIONS CONNECTED WITH INORGANIC NATURAL OBJECTS.*

HOLY PLACES.

Unst. *Swinaness* is considered too sacred to "put spede intil," for there the sea-kings were wont to contend, and many bloody battles were fought there. A man chanced to delve a small bit of verdant turf in Swinaness, wherein he sowed corn in hopes of reaping a rich harvest; but when the corn grew up it was found that the stalks were filled with blood (cf. I. *h* and II. *a*), and the ears dropped salt tears in the place of tender dew.—EDMONSTON and SAXBY, p. 224.

Unst. *Field of the Dead.*—There is a piece of ground at Burrafiord (and another near Norwick) known by that name, which means "field of the dead." The ground is uncultivated, and the tradition is that no one must put spade in it, or misfortune will certainly befall that individual. Once a woman dared the old belief, and dug up a portion of the death-rig. Shortly afterwards her best cow died. Nothing daunted, the rash dame delved next year, and actually sowed corn on the spot. "Then her husband died, and after that she let the rig alane."

The supposition is that the death-rigs are battlefields.

EDMONSTON and SAXBY, p. 224.

2   *Superstitious Beliefs and Practices.*

Hills. For hills as residence of fairies *see* I. *d;* see also I. *d,* "Wilkie's Knolls."

STONES.

Orkney, Stennis. *The Stone of Odin.*—A young man had seduced a girl under promise of marriage, and she proving with child, was deserted by him : The young man was called before the session; the elders were particularly severe. Being asked by the minister the cause of so much rigour, they answered, You do not know what a bad man this is; he has broke the promise of Odin. Being further asked what they meant by the promise of Odin, they put him in mind of the stone at Stenhouse, with the round hole in it; and added, that it was customary, when promises were made, for the contracting parties to join hands through this hole, and the promises so made were called the promises of Odin.—PRINCIPAL GORDON of the Scots College at Paris in *Archæologia Scotica,* vol. i. p. 263.

[*See also* II. *b,* "Weddings."]

It was said that a child passed through the hole when young would never shake with palsy in old age. Up to the time of its destruction, it was customary to leave some offering on visiting the stone, such as a piece of bread, or cheese, or a rag, or even a stone.—CAPT. F. W. L. THOMAS in *Archæologia,* vol. xxxiv. p. 101.

The Odin stone, long the favourite trysting-place in summer twilights of Orkney lovers, was demolished in 1814 by a sacrilegious farmer, who used its material to assist him in the erection of a cowhouse. This misguided man was a *Ferry-Louper* (the name formerly given to strangers from the south), and his wanton destruction of the consecrated stone stirred so strongly the resentment of the peasantry in the district that various unsuccessful attempts were made to burn his house and holdings about his ears.

GORRIE, p. 143.

North Ronaldsay. *Monolith.*—Here ... a monumental stone stands in the middle of a plain, ten feet high and four broad. ... Around it, on the first day of the New Year, the inhabitants sometimes assemble for their amusement, and indulge for a while in the song and the dance.

BARRY, p. 60.

Birsay. "*Druidical*" *Stone.*—[In the parish of Birsay there is a "Druidical Stone"] with a rather strange and tragic history attached to it. The legend runs that every Hogmanay night as the clock strikes the hour of twelve, this stone begins to walk or move towards Birsay Loch. When the edge of the loch is reached it quietly dips its head into the rippling waters. Then, to remain firm and immovable until the next twelve months pass away, it as silently returns to its post. It was never considered safe for any one to remain out of doors at midnight, and watch its movements upon Hogmanay. Many stories are current of curious persons who dared to watch the stone's proceedings, and who the next morning were found lying corpses by its side. The latest story of the kind is that of a young gentleman from Glasgow, who formed the resolution to remain up all night, and find out for himself the truth or falsehood about this wonderful stone. One Hogmanay ... the daring youth began his watch. As time wore on and the dread hour of midnight approached, he began to feel some little terror in his heart, and an eerie feeling crept slowly over his limbs. At midnight he discovered that, in his pacing to and fro, he had come between the stone and the loch, and as he looked towards the former he fancied that he saw it move. From that moment he lost all consciousness, and his friends found him in the grey dawn lying in a faint. By degrees he came to himself, but he could not satisfy enquirers whether the stone had really moved and knocked him down on its way, or whether his imagination had conjured up the assault.

There is another tale, of a more tragic nature, related of this walking stone. One stormy December day a vessel was shipwrecked upon the shore of Birsay, and all hands save one were lost. The rescued sailor happened to find refuge in a cottage close by this stone; and hearing the story of its yearly march, he resolved to see for himself all that human eyes might be able to discover. In spite of all remonstrances he sallied forth on the last night of the old year; and, to make assurance doubly sure, he seated himself on the very pinnacle of the stone. There he awaited the events of the night. What these were no mortal man can tell; for the first morning of the new year dawned upon the corpse of the gallant sailor lad, and local report has it that the walking stone rolled over him as it proceeded to the loch.—FERGUSSON, pp. 54, 55.

Westray. *Noup-head Rock.*—At the Noup-head in Westra is a rock surrounded with the Sea, call'd Less, which the inhabitants of that Isle say, has this strange propertie—that if a man go upon it, having any Iron upon him (If it were an Iron Nail in his shoe) the Sea will instantly swell in such a tempestous way, that no boat can come near to take him off, and that the Sea will not be settled till the peece of Iron be flung into it. I being there to make an experiment of it, offered a shilling to a poor Fellow to go upon the Rock with a peece of Iron, but he would not do it upon any terms.—WALLACE, 1st ed., pp. 27, 28; 2nd ed. p. 60. [The second edition omits the words "If it were an Iron Nail in his shoe."]

For other legends as to Stones, *v.* III. *d*, "PLACE LEGENDS."

HOLY WELLS AND LOCHS.

Shetland. *Heljabrün.*—There is a fine spring well near Watlie, called Heljabrün, and the legend of it is this:—A wandering packman (of the Claud Halco class) was murdered and flung into Heljabrün. Its water had always been known to possess healing power, and after becoming seasoned by the unfortunate pedlar's remains, the virtue in the water became even more efficacious. People came from far and near to procure the precious fluid. All who took it away had to throw three stones, or a piece of "white money," into the well, and the water never failed to cure disease.—EDMONSTON and SAXBY, p. 216.

The waters of a copious spring, called Yclaburn or Hiclaburn *(the burn of health)*, although pure from all mixture, are esteemed, in the neighbourhood, to be highly beneficial to health. [In a footnote it is added] A custom formerly prevailed, for persons to throw three stones, as a tribute to the source of these salubrious waters, when they first approach it. A considerable pile has thus been raised. But the reputation of the spring begins to decline, and the superstitious offering is now no longer so religiously paid.
Old Stat. Acct., vol. v. p. 185.

Unst. [Here] is a pure stream that has long been celebrated for its supposed sanative virtues. It was of late years usual to walk to its source, and on an adjoining site of ground to throw three stones. This custom is so old, that a considerable pile has been raised by these offerings; but as the influence of the water god has long been on the wane, the acknowledgment is now much less frequently paid. It was also usual, after the sacrifice to the deity had been made, to drink of the water of the spring, which insured health to the zealous imbiber. Hence the stream acquired the name of Yelaburn or Hielaburn, that is, the Burn of Health.—HIBBERT, p. 409.

Mainland. A mile or two to the north-west of Hillswick, among the hills, is a very small pool named Helga Water, or the Water of Health. . . . The pool of Helga Water also appears to have been formerly visited by the natives with superstitious views, and with perhaps the same mysterious ceremonies as were used from time immemorial in Orkney, such as walking round it in the course of the sun, observing strict silence in their perambulations, taking up water in their hands and casting it on their heads.

HIBBERT, pp. 524, 525.

Westray. *St. Tredwell's Loch*, in Westray, is held by the People as Medicinal, whereupon many diseased and infirm Persons resort to it, some saying that thereby they have got good; As a certain Gentleman's Sister upon the Isle, who was not able to go to this Loch without help, yet returned without it, as likewise a Gentleman in the Countrey who was much distressed, with sore Eyes, went to this Loch and Washing there became sound and whole, tho' he had been at much pains and expence to cure them formerly. With both which Persons, he who was Minister of the place for many Years, was well acquainted, and told us that he saw them both before and after the Cure: The present Minister of *Westra*, told me, that such as are able to walk, use to go so many times about the Loch, as they think will perfect the cure, before they make any use of the Water, and that without speaking to any, for they believe, that if they speak, this will marr the Cure: Also he told that on a certain Morning not long since, he went to this Loch, and found six so making their circuit, whom with some difficulty he obliging [them] to speak, said to him, they came there for their cure. . . . [Brand goes on to speculate on the cures recorded, and is in doubt whether to attribute them to imagination or to the "Aid and assistance of Satan." He further says] Yet I hear, that when they have done all, that is usual for them to do; as going about the Loch, washing their Bodies or any part thereof, leaving something at the Loch, as old Clouts and the like &c. It is but in few, in whom the effect of healing is produced. As for this Loch's appearing like Blood, before any disasture befal the Royal Family, as some do report, we could find no ground, to beleive any such thing.—BRAND, pp. 58, 59.

Stronsay. *Well of Kildinguie.*—[Of a chalybeate] spring called the Well of Kildinguie, Tradition says, that it was held in such high repute when the Orkney Islands belonged to the Crown of Denmark that people of the first rank came from Denmark and Norway to drink the waters. Towards the south-east at about two miles distance, the greatest part of the way consists of a flat sand along the sea-shore; there is a place called Guiyidn, on the rocks of which that species of sea weed called dulse, is to be found in abundance; which weed, is considered by many to be a delicious and wholesome morsel. The drinking of these waters, the moderate exercise of walking over two miles of dry level ground, gathering and eating dulse on the rocks, they being exposed to a wholesome sharp sea breeze, from whatever quarter the wind could blow; this happy combination of circumstances was found such a sovereign remedy for the numberless complaints of those, who in ancient times resorted to this famous watering place, that it gave rise to a proverb which is still retained in this island, viz., "The Well of Kildinguie, and the dulse of Guiyidn, can cure all maladies except black death."—That is can cure all maladies which are not absolutely incurable.
Old Stat. Acct., vol. xv. p. 417.

Toward the east coast, among the rocks, are three mineral springs almost close together, differing in strength, though of the same nature; and such confidence do the people place in these springs (which, together, go under the name of the Well of Kildinguie), and at the same time in that seaweed named Dulse, produced in Guiydin, (perhaps the bay of Odin), as to have given rise to a proverb, "That the Well of Kildinguie and the dulse of Guiydin will cure all maladies but *Black Death*."—BARRY, p. 53.

Flotta. *Wunster Well.*—In the island of Flotta, upon a jutting point called the Rhone, there is a small mineral well, to which medicinal properties are attributed. A bottle of water from this well, which is called "Wunster Well" from an old Episcopal clergyman who resided near by when the Episcopal church was recognised in Scotland, was considered sufficient to cure certain diseases. The bearer of the bottle had not to speak, however, to any person on his way back, else the virtue would be gone.

FERGUSSON, p. 214.

For another well *see* under "BUILDINGS."

BUILDINGS.

Orkney. To many of the old places of worship, especially such as have been dedicated to particular favourite saints, they still pay much veneration, visiting them frequently, when they are seriously melancholy, or in a devout mood, repeating within their ruinous walls prayers, paternosters and forms of words, of which they have little knowledge. When they consider themselves in any imminent danger, they invoke the aid of these saints, and vow to perform services, or present oblations to them, on condition that they interpose successfully in their behalf; and they are generally very punctual in performing these vows.

BARRY, pp. 347-48.

Westray. *St. Tredwell's Chapel.*—These Chappels[1] the people frequent, as for other ends, so for Prayer, they placing a kind of Merit therein when performed in such places, and this they observe more than private Retirements; and if they be under any Sickness, or in any danger, as at Sea, they will vow so to do. And when they go to the Chappels to pay the Vows taken on, they use to lay several Stones,

---

[1] [That is, the numerous chapels, mostly now in ruins, scattered over the islands and belonging to pre-Reformation times.]

one above another, according to the number of Vows which they made; some of which heaps we saw in St. Tredwell's Chappel. And none must go empty handed, but leave behind them something, either a peice of Money, or of Bread, or a Stone, which they judge will be sufficient.

BRAND, p. 59.

[Brand further observes that it is especially during Lent, and more particularly on Easter Sunday, that these vows and devotions are observed. P. 60.]

Such was the veneration entertained by the inhabitants for this ancient Saint, that it was with difficulty that the first Presbyterian minister of the parish could restrain them, of a Sunday morning, from paying their devotions at this ruin, previous to their attendance on public worship in the reformed church. Wonders, in the way of cure of bodily disease, are said to have been wrought by this Saint, whose fame is now passed away, and name almost forgotten.

New Stat. Acct., Orkney, pp. 117, 118.

On the West side of *Papa Westra*, between it and *Westra*, there is a Holm,[1] wherein once there was a little Chappel, . . . in which they say there were seven Sisters buried, who were Nuns, and desired to ly in this Holm, about whose Graves this Chappel was built. About a year ago, there were seen several times at midday, about 20 Men walking on that Holm, among whom there was one higher and greater than the rest, who sometimes stood and looked into the Chappel, this my Informer with a hundred People in the Isle of *Papa* saw, who could attest the same: After which appearance there was a Boat cast away on that Holm with 4 Men in her, who were all lost.—BRAND, p. 51.

Unst. *Cross Kirk.*—Cross Kirk, or St. Cruz, is still accounted a holy place, and occasional pilgrimages are made to it by some of the older inhabitants.

New Stat. Acct., Shetland, p. 40.

---

[1] [Probably the Holm of Aikerness.]

Some of its virtues were believed to extend even to the shell snails which sheltered in its mouldering walls. The poor Creatures were collected, dried, powdered, and prescribed as a remedy for jaundice.—COWIE, p. 258.

[*See also* I. *f*, Jaundice.]

Mr. *Hercules Sinclair*, Minister, ... in his Zeal, against superstition, rased *Cross Kirk*, in this Parish; Because the People superstitiously frequented it: And when demolished, behind the place where the Altar stood, and also beneath the Pulpit, were found several peices of Silver in various shapes, brought thither as offerings by afflicted People, some being in the form of a Head, others of an Arm, others of a Foot, accordingly as the offerers were distressed in these parts of the Body.—BRAND, p. 95.

Weisdale. *Church of " Our Lady."*—There was formerly a church at Weesdale dedicated to "Our Lady." It was much (sometimes still is) frequented by people from every corner of Shetland, who, by casting in an offering of money at the shrine of "Our Lady," believed they would be delivered from any trouble they laboured under. There is a tradition regarding the building of it, still firmly believed by the superstitious of the islanders. Two wealthy ladies, sisters, having encountered a storm off the coast of Shetland, vowed to "Our Lady," that, if she would bring them safe to land, they would erect a church to her on the first spot they reached. They landed at Weesdale, and immediately commenced building the church. And each morning, when the masons came to work, they found as many stones ready quarried as they required during the day. One of the elders of the church, who lately lived in that neighbourhood, used regularly to gather up the offerings, which he put into the poor's box.

New Stat. Acct., Shetland, p. 69.

Wisdale Parish [is] remarkable for the superstitious regard anciently paid by the more ignorant inhabitants to its

Church. Those people who, for a small sum, wanted to clear off their old scores, thought they could do it nowhere better than here, they also thought here their works of penance would be more acceptable. I was well informed that not many years ago there was found on the pulpit of this Church a small pyramid of all the different coins generally current in Shetland, from the largest German silver coin down to a stiver.—LOW, pp. 79, 80.

The Church of Wisdale . . . is much frequented by the Superstitious Country People, who light Candles therein, drop Money in and about it, go on their bare knees round it, and to which in their Straits and Sickness they have their Recourse, yea, some are so silly as to think, that if they be in any distress, tho not at this Church, yet if they turn their faces to it, God will hear them. One of the Justices told us, that tho they have laid out themselves to get these Superstitious Conceits Eradicated, yet they cannot get it altogether effectuated, but still they continue among the People. A Minister also told me, that it was much frequented by Women, who when they desire to Marry, went to this Church making their Vows and saying their Prayers there, so assuring themselves, that God would cause Men come in suit of them ; But this is not now so much in use as formerly.—BRAND, p. 92.

Damsay. Ecclesia est in hac insula dedicata Mariæ Virgini ad quam plerumque Mulieres progrediuntur grandes . . . Mulieres hic steriles sunt, et si gravidae evenerint, nunquam cum vita pariunt.
JO. BEN, *apud* BARRY, p. 443.

Shetland. Nearly allied to witchcraft is a firm belief in the efficacy of alms. When a person is anxious for the accomplishment of any particular event, or considers himself in danger, he vows alms to some person, generally an old woman, who enjoys the reputation of being provided for in that manner; and if his wishes are realised, he scrupulously performs his vow. There are the ruins of an old church in the parish of Weesdale, called *Our Lady's Church*, which is supposed to possess a still greater influence in this respect than any living being. Many are the boats which are said to have arrived safe at land, in consequence of a promise to this effect, where death, without such an intervention, appeared inevitable. Several coins have been found, at different times, concealed in the walls of this Loretto of Zetland.

EDMONDSTON, *Shetland*, vol. ii. p. 75.

Deerness. In aquilonari parte istius parochiae in mari est nativum Saxum ubi homines manibus et genubus quam difficillime ascendunt ad cacumen ; illic est sacellum quod nominatur (the Bairns of Brugh).

Confluunt huc ex diversis insulis, homines, juvenes, pueri, senes, servi, innumerabiles, venti vero, nudis pedibus, ut prius dixi, orantes ascendunt ubi nullus preterquam unus ad sacellum uno tempore venire potest : Illic est fons purus et nitidissimus ; quod quidem mirabile est : Tunc homines, genubus flexis, manibusque conjunctis, diffidentes Deum esse, orant (the Bairns of Brugh) multis incantationibus, projicientes lapides et aquam post tergora, et circa sacellum bis terve gradientes, finita oratione domum redeunt affirmantes se vota habuisse.—JO. BEN, *apud* BARRY, p. 443.

SEA.

For superstitions connected with the sea, *v.* I. *i*, Superstitions generally.

(*b*) *PLANT SUPERSTITIONS.*

For Fairies riding on bulrushes *see* I. *d.*

(*c*) *ANIMAL SUPERSTITIONS.*

Bee.—See I. *e*, Trial of Elspeth Cursetter.

Shetland. *Spider.*—One of the Shetland rimes, similar to Scotch, English and German ones [to the lady bird] appeals to the spider, who is called Willie Buck, as a weather prophesying insect.

K. BLIND in *New Review*, Vol. xi., p. 616.

Curlew.—The Shetlanders regard with horror the very idea of using so uncanny a bird as food.

SAXBY, *Birds*, p. 192.

Fulmar.—They do not like to molest it for fear of ill-luck ensuing.—SAXBY, *Birds*, p. 362.

Shetland. *Gull.*—A boat started one summer morning from the Broch of Colviedell, intending to remain at the haaf-fishing for two days. But the men had scarcely launched their boat, had scarcely stepped the mast, when a white gull came hovering overhead, and as soon as the boat was fairly under way, alighted on the rigging. Folding its wings, it fixed its dark eyes upon the boat with an almost human intelligence in its expression, and as the boat sailed on, the bird sat motionless overhead. Night came down, but still the bird remained watching the men at their work. About midnight a sudden squall came on, which grew into a storm that lasted two nights and a day. The boat dared not attempt reaching the shore for the tideways across her path. The only safety was in remaining out at sea, and during all that time the little boat lay tossing among the billows, with the white bird sitting upon the mast. When the storm abated the boat sought her haven, and not until she reached the beach did the bird take wing. As soon as they landed, one of the men said, " Give the bird the best cut of our ling, for she never left us in our trouble, and likely she has been our preservation; for yesterday, when we were in the heart of the storm, I saw an old woman sitting on the water, a little way from the boat, and *she appeared not good.* But of course she had no power to come nearer us while the bird stayed by us. No doubt *she* was a witch, and the bird was a good spirit."

EDMONSTON and SAXBY, p. 205.

Lark.—Thoughout the whole of Shetland, the skylark is held almost as sacred as the redbreast is with us; therefore it is but seldom that either the birds or their eggs are disturbed. In some parts of the north isles, when the reason of the forbearance is sought, the usual reply is, " Weel, if ye look under a laverock's tongue, ye'll see three spots, and they say that every one is a curse upon him that interferes wi' it."—SAXBY, *Birds*, p. 88.

Lark.—No one in Shetland would eat a lark; there are three black spots on its tongue, and for every lark you eat you get three curses.

Notes and Queries, 6th series, vol. ix. p. 26.

[cf. Kaindl, *Die Huzulen*, p. 104.]

Orkney. The lark some call our *Lady's Hen.*

BRAND, p. 61.

Orkney. Boys will not disturb larks' nests, the bird being still called "Our Lady's Hen."—BUCKLEY, p. 122.

Linnet.—See I. *e*, Trial of Elspeth Cursetter.

Shetland. *Owl.*—The old wives say that a cow will give bloody milk if it is frightened by an owl, and will fall sick and die if touched by it.—SAXBY, *Birds*, p. 51.

Raven.—[It is] the belief that the raven is immediately attracted to a house where a corpse is lying.

SAXBY, *Birds*, p. 128.

Orkney. *Rook.*—Rooks are reckoned ominous if they appear. People expect a famine to follow soon after.

LOW, *Fauna*, p. 49.

For Sparrow *v.* Sparrow-telling.

Wheatear.—This bird, for what reason I cannot say, seems to be proscribed in Orkney. Young and old destroy both nests and birds of it and this not for any other end but the seeming effects of wanton cruelty, as it seems quite a harmless creature.—LOW, *Fauna*, p. 73.

The prejudice against these birds seems to have died out.—BUCKLEY, p. 96.

Shetland. *Wren.*—I was once told this bird was too much like a mouse to lay eggs.—SAXBY, *Birds*, p. 143.

Cat. Cats, rats, and mice avoiding certain localities.— The common mouse [is] common everywhere, except in a few of the lesser islands, which our country sages tell us gravely are privileged, and neither cat nor mouse will live in them, even though brought thither. They add further, the earth of these isles brought thence kills them wherever they are. When an honest gray-headed man told me this, I desired to let me have a little of the earth of his isle to make the experiment, but this he would by no means grant; this would, in his opinion, take away the virtue from the rest.—LOW, *Fauna*, p. 26.

Enhallow. *Cat.*—In the Island of Enhallow it is well-known that a Cat will not live. The experiment hath often been tried by putting these creatures ashore upon this Island, but they always died in Convulsions, in a very short time.—Rats will not live in the Island of Eday and none of them was ever seen there, in the memory of man.

FEA, p. 43.

Vaila. There is a little Isle on the West side of *Waes* called *Vaila*, wherein there is no Cat, neither will any stay tho brought in, as hath been done for trial, but will quickly be gone, they either dying or betaking themselves to Sea, they endeavour to sweem to the next Isle: Yet about 50 Years ago there was one seen upon this Isle, about that time when a Gentleman the Proprietor thereof was Tormented and put to death by the Witches, but never any were seen since, save what were brought in for trial, as now said. The reason of this I could not learn from the Ministers, who gave the information, it is like because of the Air, or the smell of something upon the Isle, tho not perceivable by the Inhabitants, which agreeth not with the Temper and Constitution of these animals.—BRAND, p. 110.

See also under *Mouse*.

Shetland. *Cat Unlucky.*—The cat is more frequently spoken of by different names than anything else. Always regarded as more particularly "unlucky" than any other animal, the fisherman had a special horror of it; but it does not appear why he should have been at such pains to name it in so many various ways.

LAURENSON, *Pro. Soc. Ant. Scot.*, vol. x. p. 715.

See also I. *i*, "SEA."

For Cat *see also* I. *d*, *Elfshot*.

Shetland. There are no Venemous beasts found in *Shetland*, no Asks, no Adders, no Frogs, no Snails, no Rats, if these be brought there by Ships, they will not live over a year or two.—SIBBALD, p. 21.

Great Havery. *Mouse, rat.*—A small uninhabited isle, concerning which there is an idle tradition that no mouse or rat will live in it, and that its ground is of such virtue as to kill vermin though removed for the purpose to any other place.—HIBBERT, p. 456.

Havery. Here doth no Mouse nor Rat live, yea its Mold or Ground, hath such a vertue, that if it be carried to places where Mice and Rats abound, it will presently kill them, which hath often times been proved.—SIBBALD, p. 57.

Eynhallow. Rats and mice it is asserted will not live there.—MUNCH, p. 243.

Havera, Hascosea, Uya. [These] three isles are supposed to possess some magic charm about their soil which prevents their ever being infested with mice.—TUDOR, p. 172.

Animals.

North Ronaldsay. Nec ranae, glires, nec bufones hic colunt; et si navis hic adduxerit, glires cito pereunt quasi veneno.—Jo. BEN, ap. BARRY, p. 437.

Rat.—Sometimes, when the Ships are lying nigh Land, the Rats will come ashore, which, when any of the *Hollanders* or others see, they look upon it as Fatal to the Ship out of which they come, pretending that her end some way or other will shortly approach; And likewise it is observed that these Rats will not live above 3 or 4 years in that Land to which they come. Some of our Seamen tell us of the like as to their Ships; It is talkt also that these Creatures will leave Houses before any dismal accident befal them. What ground there is either for the one or the other I know not, but if true it will be hard, I suppose, to give the reason thereof.

BRAND, pp. 111, 112.

See also under *Cat.*

Burra and Hascusay. *Mouse.*—In the Isles of Burra and Haskashy no Mice are to be found, yea if they take some dust or Earth out of these Isles to other places where they are, they will forsake such places, where the dust is laid. It may be for the like reason, why no Cats can or will live in Vaila.—BRAND, p. 111.

See also under *Cat.*

[Cf. *Proc. Royal Irish Ac.*, iii. 631; Grimm, *Aberglaube*, No. 367; *Globus*, xxvii. 104. There is some ground for supposing that these beliefs as to cats, rats, mice avoiding certain localities is a fact of natural history, not of folklore. There is, however, no reason to suppose that all the statements in the text are strictly true; the substratum of fact is overlaid with fancy.]

Orkney. *Lamb.*—When the first lamb seen for the season is white, the omen is fortunate, and the appearance of a black lamb is unlucky.—*New Stat. Acct.*, Orkney, p. 143.

Shetland. *Lamb.*—Early-dropped lambs are "no canny," and ominous of evil.—*Antiquarian Mag.*, p. 136.

Foula. *Sheep.*—Here as in Fair Isle and perhaps elsewhere in Shetland, an objection is felt to selling the young female sheep, which is supposed to be unlucky as diminishing the stock. They do not object to sell the male.—J. KERR, in *Good Words*, 1866, p. 545.

St. Andrews. *Eel.*—[Of a small Loch in the parish of St. Andrews Low says it is] inhabited by Eels only, but these are altogether despised by the country people, who never eat any of them, owing to a ridiculous notion they have of their being bred from the tail hairs of a Stalion; and their resemblance to the Serpentine race.
LOW, p. 58.
See also I.*f.* [Cf. *Globus*, iv. 333.]

Damsay, *Frog, toad.*—[This island] is believed to refuse to breed or support frogs, toads, or any other kind of disgusting or noxious animal.—BARRY, p. 67.

Nunquam ranæ, bufones, nec alia terrestria mala hic sunt.—JO. BEN, *apud* BARRY, p. 443.

For snail *see* under I. *a*, "BUILDINGS"; I.*f, Jaundice.*

Shetland. *Turbot.*—The turbot of commerce, proper, is seldom captured on our coasts. Although I have been a fisherman for many years, I have never seen one caught, while the other (halibut) is very plentiful. Now, I have never yet heard any explanation of the derivation of Holy Buttje, or the holy fluke; and the question is, what was it holy to? Was it hallowed or consecrated to some deity? And next, what deity was it likely to be? ... I have very strong presumptive proof that the fish was held sacred to some one, or some thing, from the superstitions attaching to its capture.... An air of mystery always surrounded its capture, that distinguished it from that of other fish. . . . No sooner did the man at the line feel a turbot (halibut)—and his presence at the bottom of the sea was easily recognised by his manœuvres—than the event was the signal for silence, and signs took the place of words. The utmost freedom allowed on such occasions—and that only when any doubt hung over it—was to ask the question only in an undertone: "Is it a fish, tinks du? or is du i' da grund?"—meaning: "Do you think you feel a fish? or has the line got foul of the bottom"? If the former was affirmed, it was only by a nod of the head, and then a silent activity took possession of the crew, over whom a spell seemed to hang; and woe betide the greenhorn that spake *or uttered the name of the fish!* Should such a calamity happen, as it sometimes did with the uninitiated, and should the turbot (halibut) be lost after the offence, the fisherman in question was solely blamed for the loss, and for a time his life was made miserable by the rest.

I have learned another fact in regard to the turbot—namely, that the "blugga-banes" the (breast-bones) of the turbot were always preserved in some secret chink in the wall of a fisherman's cottage, in order to insure luck. . . .

Another fact I may mention is: the "kinn-fish," that is, the cheek-flesh, of the turbot is never eaten, but always cut out raw. . . . It is a peculiarity, and never observed in the case of other fish.—KARL BLIND (from information supplied by Robert Sinclair), *Gentleman's Magazine*, 1882, pp. 470, 471.

Unst. *Bones.*—It is lucky to catch a turbot, and luck will follow the fishermen who do so if they attend to what a turbot once said:

"Wash me clean and boil me weel,
Pick me banes, *but dinna burn them.*"

EDMONSTON and SAXBY, pp. 227, 228.

Dunrossness. *Sponges.*—Sponges are found upon the shore in great plenty, shaped like a man's hand, and called by the people Trowie Gloves.

Old Stat. Acct., vol. vii. p. 396.

See also I.e, *Witch Metamorphosis, Luggie, Trials, passim*.

For Festival Dishes *see* " FESTIVAL CUSTOMS, YULE."

(d) GOBLINDOM.

Shetland. *Brownies, Trows, Fairies.*—Not above 40 or 50 Years ago, almost every Family had a *Brouny* or evil Spirit so called, which served them, to whom they gave a Sacrifice for his Service; as when they Churned their Milk, they took a part thereof and sprinkled every corner of the House with it for Brounies use, likewise when they Brewed, they had a stone which they called *Brounies Stone*, wherein there was a little hole, into which they poured some Wort for a Sacrifice to Brouny. My Informer a Minister in the Country told me, that he had conversed with an old Man, who when young used to Brew, and sometimes read upon his Bible, to whom an old Woman in the House said, that Brouny was displeased with that Book he read upon, which if he continued to do, they would get no more service of Brouny; But he being better instructed from that Book, which was Brounies Eye-sore and the object of his wrath, when he Brewed, he would not suffer any Sacrifice to be given to Brouny, whereupon the 1*st*. and 2*d*. Brewings were spilt [? spoilt] and for no use, though the Wort wrought well, yet in a little time it left off working and grew cold; but the 3*d*. Browst or Brewing he had Ale very good, though he would not give any Sacrifice to Brouny; with whom afterwards they were no more troubled. I had also from the same Informer, that a Lady in *Unst* now deceased told him, that when she first took up House, she refused to give a Sacrifice to Brouny upon which the 1*st*. and 2*d*.

Brewings misgave likewise, but the 3*d.* was good; and Brouny not being regarded nor rewarded, as formerly he had been, abandoned his wonted service. They also had Stacks of Corn, which they called *Brounies Stacks*, which tho they were not bound with straw-ropes, or any way fenced, as other Stacks used to be, yet the greatest storm of Wind was not able to blow any Straw off them.

BRAND, pp. 112, 113.

See also Luridan below.

Shetland. *Fairy Tunes.*—Some tunes are supposed to have been taught to Shetlanders by Trows, and are known as *Ferry tüns*. One sweet, simple, fanciful *reel* was learned by a man one night when he was passing over a hill in Unst. He heard the Trows playing inside the hill, and he listened until he had mastered their melody.... Of another tune Nurse says it was learned thus:—"An old man, sitting out of doors one summer evening, saw a party of Trows coming lightly over the marshy ground close by. As they skipped along they sang, 'Hupp horse handocks and we'll ride on Bulmints.' The old man instantly called out, 'I'll ride with you.' Thereupon they carried him off and kept him for a twelvemonth, and then they put him back on his own roof, but he never told what he seen or heard while visiting Trowland. Evidently there was an *awe band* upon him." But the tune which the Trows sang, when he desired to join their sport, was remembered and taught to others, and is now known as one of the Ferry reels. Another tune is called "Be nort da deks o' Voe," because it was heard near that place.

EDMONSTON and SAXBY, pp. 201, 202.

There was a Trow called Broonie, who was supposed to be the King of Trowland. He showed himself very often; and it was remarked that if he had been seen in a corn-yard all was sure to be right there, but if the visitant was an ordinary Trow, mischief ensued. Folks were glad when

Broonie paid them a visit, and they were careful not to go near any of the corn which he had been guarding, as it was observed that he objected to being overlooked, and resented such interference by *laying the screws in herda* (*i.e.* scattering the cornstacks). Broonie seemed to have taken a whole neighbourhood under his protection, and was seen gliding from yard to yard in the cold evenings, casting his spells upon the crop. The people felt sorry for Broonie, exposed to the chill night air, so they made a cloak and hood for him, and laid it in a yard which he frequented. Broonie took the well-intentioned gift as an offence, for he was never seen again.

EDMONSTON and SAXBY, pp. 202, 203.

Witches and fairies and their histories, are still very frequent in Schetland, but Brownies seem, within this century, to lose ground.—LOW, p. 82.

Shetland. A girl who was wont to run to the fairy knowes, and call to the Trows to come and fetch her to see their wonderful home, did this so frequently, that at last the irritated Trows breathed upon her, and she became paralysed in the limbs, and remained so all her life.

EDMONSTON and SAXBY, p. 202.

Any woman who has been fortunate enough to see a Trow affirm that he always appeared to walk—or rather skip—backwards. He seemed to have no difficulty in doing so but got over the ground as quickly as if he had been moving along like an ordinary mortal.

EDMONSTON and SAXBY, p. 203.

Unst. There was a girl, whose mother had been taken by the Trows at the girl's birth, who grew up to be a lovely creature, with golden hair. Such hair had never been seen in Unst, so long, soft shining. It fell in golden waves about her, and such an unusual mode of wearing it created much wonder. No maiden—not even a child—ever permitted her hair to fall as it pleased except this girl, and folks did say that whenever she tried to bind it to her head the bright locks refused to obey her fingers, and slowly untwined themselves until they became natural ringlets again. The girl was a sweet singer—and singing is a fairy gift—and she would wander about, lilting merrily to herself, while neighbours wondered, and young men lost their hearts. It was believed that the girl was under the special care of the Trows, for everything seemed to be smooth before her, and her golden hair was called "the blessing o' them that loves her." But it happened that a witch began to covet the maiden's lovely locks, and one day, when the girl lay down among some hay and fell asleep, the witch cut off all her beautiful hair. The poor young thing returned to her home shorn of her glory, and after that she pined away. All the song had died from her lips, all the smile had gone from her young face. But when she lay dead, in her teens, folks said that her golden hair began to grow again, and had grown to its former length and beauty ere the coffin-lid was closed upon her. The witch did not triumph, for the Trows, who had loved and watched over the motherless girl, took possession of the malignant old hag and punished her as she deserved. She was compelled to wander about their haunts and to live in the most strange manner. She was haunted day and night by evil creatures. Whenever she tried to sleep the Trows would come and make such queer noises that she could not rest. She continued in that state till extreme old age, when she was spirited away altogether.

EDMONSTON and SAXBY, pp. 203, 204.

Unst. There was a woman called Katherine Fordyce and she died at the birth of her first child—at least folks thought she died. A neighbour's wife dreamt shortly after Katherine's death that she came to her and said "I have taken the milk of your cow that you could not get, but it shall be made up to you; you shall have more than that if you will give me what you will know about soon." The good wife would not promise, having no idea what Katherine meant, but shortly afterwards she understood it was a child of her own to which Katherine referred. The child came and the mother named it Katherine Fordyce; and after it was christened this Trowbound Katherine appeared to the mother again and told her all should prosper in her family while that child remained in it. She told her also that she was quite comfortable among the Trows but could not get out unless somebody chanced to see her and had presence of mind enough to call on God's name at the moment. She said her friends had failed to sain her (guard by spells) at the time of her child's birth, and that was how she fell into the power of the Trows.

Prosperity came like a high tide upon the good wife's household until the child Katherine married. On the girl's wedding night a fearful storm came on; "the like had no' been minded in the time o' anybody alive." The Broch was overflowed by great seas that rolled over the Skerries as if they had been beach stones. The bride's father lost a number of his best sheep, for they were lifted by the waves and carried away and "some folk did say that old men with long white beards were seen stretching their pale hands out of the surf and taking hold of the creatures." From that day the good wife's fortunes changed for the worse. A man named John Nisbet saw that same Katherine Fordyce once. He was walking up a daal near her old home, when it seemed as if a hole opened in the side of this daal. He looked in and saw Katherine sitting in a "queer-shaped armchair and she was nursing a baby." There was a bar of iron stretched in front to keep her a prisoner. She was dressed in a brown poplin gown —which folk knew by John's description to be her wedding-dress. He thought she said, "O Johnnie! what's sent de *here?*" And he answered, "And what keeps you *here?*"

And she said, "Well; I am well and happy but I can't get out, for I have eaten their food!" John Nisbet unfortunately did not know or forgot to say "Güde be aboot wis," and Katherine was unable to give him a hint and in a moment the whole scene disappeared.

EDMONSTON and SAXBY, p. 207.

Once a girl in a peat hill saw a little grey woman going wandering as if in search of something and making a noise like scolding, only she used a "hidden tongue." All day she was seen going about the peat banks and the girls and boys employed there got frightened a little, feeling sure " she was no güde." At last about sunset, one resolved to speak to the woman, but it happened that the sun went down as the girl got near enough to address the Trow-wife. Then something drew the girl's attention another way for one moment and when she looked again, the creature had disappeared. "It is well known, you see, that if the sun rises while a Trow is above the grass, he or she has not the power to return home, and is day bound, and must stay on the earth in sight of man till sunset."

One Saturday night a boy was sleeping on a shakedown near the fireplace, as some unexpected guests had turned him out of his usual place of repose. Now the Trows require that every hearth shall be swept clean on Saturday night, that no one shall be found near it and above all that plenty of clean water shall be found in the house. Unfortunately all these things had been neglected, so that when the Trows came they were naturally much enraged and made such a noise that the boy awoke. What should he see but two Trow-wives seating themselves not far from where he lay. One carried a baby, the loveliest little creature that ever was seen, only that it had three eyes instead of two—the extra one being in the middle of the forehead. The Trow who was not baby-encumbered sought for clean water but alas! found none, and revenged herself by taking the first liquor she came across, which chanced to be a keg of *Swatts* (*Swatts* is the water that covers sowens, and is used to thin the sowens, or as a drink.) Pouring some of the *Swatts* into a basin, the Trows washed their baby in it and then the baby's clothes, and then poured the mess back into the keg, saying "Tak ye dat for no haein' clean water ae da hoose." They then sat down close by the fire, hanging the baby's clothes on their feet, spread said feet out before the blazing peats and dried the garments in that way.

Now the cute boy who was watching their proceedings knew that if he kept his eyes fixed upon them they could not go away. Accordingly he kept staring and listening to their conversation in hopes of hearing something worth remembering. But the Trow-wives began to fidget, being desirous of departing before sunrise, and at last one of them stuck the tongs in the fire and made them red-hot. As soon as the tongs became glowing she seized them, and approaching the boy "pointed a blade at each ee," grinning at him in the most hideous manner, while she brought the hot tongs in alarming proximity to the wakeful urchin's face. Of course he blinked and screamed and the Trows, taking advantage of the moment when his eyes were closed, fled.

Next morning when the folk of the house went to take sowens from the keg for breakfast, there was nothing left but dirty water.—EDMONSTON and SAXBY, p. 209.

Marie Kirstan was fetched to a Trow's wife and when she was there she saw them rolling up something to resemble a cow. She contrived to throw her bunch of keys into the heap without the Trows seeing her do so. When she got home she found her own cow dead as her husband had omitted to "sain the byre." She told him to open the beast and he would find her keys there; accordingly he did so, which proved that the cow had been changed. When the Trows take anything they always leave some resemblance of the stolen property in its place.

On another occasion when Kirstan was among the Trows, she had to dress a baby and one of the grey men brought a box of curious ointment with which the child was to be anointed. While doing so Kirstan chanced to put up her hand to her eye and left some of the Trow's ointment on it. From that time her sight became so keen that she could see a boat on the ocean twenty miles away and could tell the position and features of every man in it. But she had "taken the virtue from their ointment." So one day a Trowman met her on the hill, and says he "Ye travel light and brisk for sae auld a wife." Never suspecting who he was, Kirstan answered "It's my güde sight that helps me alang." "And which eye do you see best upon, güde wife?" asked the Trow. Kirstan told him readily enough and he instantly put his little finger to the eye she had indicated and she was blind on it ever after. Marie Kirstan said that whenever she was "fetched" the Trows pressed her to eat but she would not touch their food. They even marked a cross upon the butter they set before her, thinking to beguile her in that way, but nothing would tempt her to partake, knowing that if she did so, she would be in their power, and they would be able to keep her as long as they liked. At another time when she was required professionally, the Trow who fetched her, took her in his hands and muttered "Safe there, safe back," and Kirstan found herself over the sea in another island. When matters were satisfactorily concluded in the Trow's domestic circle he told her to follow him and he brought her back the same way. Her husband never knew that she had been farther than her own kailyard until he discovered that she was cold and weary and that her clothes were damp from the sea-spray. "Kirstan!" he exclaimed, "Güde be aboot de! Whars do been?" Then her tongue was loosened and she told her adventure.—EDMONSTON and SAXBY, p. 211.

One fine morning very early a young fisherman got up to see how the sun rose, for by that he could tell if it was to be a day for the haaf, and he saw two grey-clad boys going along the road below the house. He thought they were beach boys and that they were off to their work early; but when they came benorth the house they left the road and went up to where a cow was lying on the grass. They walked up to the cow's face, then turned down again running, and the cow ran, following as far as her tether would allow. A neighbour coming to his door, also to see how the sun rose, saw the same boys and the cow and it appeared to him that all three ran over the cliffs. And that same day the cow died, so it was evident the Trows took the real cow and it was but a semblance of her that was left to die.

EDMONSTON and SAXBY, p. 213.

Two married brothers were living in one house, and the wife of one was expecting to become a mother. Her brother-in-law, being informed of what was going on, took up a fishing rod and set off to the Craigs (crag-fishing) to be out of the way. He had to pass a plantiecrü, the favourite haunt of many Trows, and when he got there he saw a number of them going as if towards his house. Jaimie instantly turned back, for he knew that they had power at such times, and the *saining* might be neglected. Hurrying home he went and opened his trunk, took out a Bible, laid it near the door, and left the key in the lock. Making sure that no door or box was locked in the house (for that angers the Trows and they have power when a key is turned), and exhorting the güde wives assembled not to allow their patient to go past the fireplace, Jaimie walked off, intending to visit a neighbour instead of venturing near the plantiecrü again. But by that time the Trows had got near and found out that he had guarded the way to their coveted treasure, so they took all power from him as soon as he got a stone's throw from his own door. At that place he had to cross a stile and when he had got one leg over the stile, he found he could get no farther. There he sat without power to move; and he sat for hours astride the wall. By-and-by one of the güde wives came out, and seeing Jaimie sitting like that, she cried "Jaimie, güde be aboot de! What's do sitting yonder for a' this time?" As soon as she said "Güde be aboot de" the power to move came back and Jaimie came home to share in the blythe feast. But that very night a child of his took a crying. It cried and cried for exactly eight days, then it lay as if sleeping for eight days, and all folk said that it appeared to be another child. Then Jaimie knew it was a changeling, so he set the cradle outside the house-door, beyond the shadow of the lintel, and the changeling was no more. There was just an image left lifeless in the cradle.

EDMONSTON and SAXBY, p. 213.

One night a family having gone to bed, heard a noise in their but-end-o'-the-hoose, and the woman peeped through a chink and saw a number of Trows at the fire nursing a sick one. She heard them say that their invalid was afflicted with jaundice and they were pouring water on her out of a small wooden bowl (known in Shetland by the name of cap). As they poured the water they said, "This is the way to cure it." The woman instantly fixed her eyes upon the cap and called out "Güde be aboot ye," and the Trows instantly fled, leaving the cap, which was kept in that family and lent to people suffering from jaundice.

Once a man (in another island) dreamed that if he went to a certain place among the cliffs he would there find a shell that would cure the jaundice, if he would use it as directed. He went to the place and found the shell, which he supposed to be a knee cap. It was formed of bone, smooth inside. He was told to use it along with the Trow-cap, and his directions for use were as follows:

The patient must go out fasting—speechless—must utter no word—must go to a well flowing east. The person who accompanies the patient must carry the cap, inside of which must rest the shell. The cap must be dropped on the water and allowed to fill itself as it gradually sinks. When full it must be lifted out and a little of the water poured into the shell. The patient then takes a sip from the shell; then the region of the heart and the top of the head are sprinkled, and the remaining water in the shell is thrown over the patient's head upon the ground. This is repeated three times. No words must be spoken until the patient and attendant return to the dwelling. Then the person who officiated says, "I hae used the means—Lord put in the blessing," and the patient must reply "Amen."—EDMONSTON and SAXBY, p. 215.

Shetland. There is or was not long ago, in Yell, a little brown jar, known by the name of "Farquhar's pig," which contained a substance resembling lard mixed with tar. This ointment was used for hurts of any kind and was never known to fail in curing those who applied it in faith. The curious thing about this "pig" was that the ointment never became less. It was taken from the Trows in the same way that the cap was captured. Property belonging to the Trows has frequently came into the possession of individuals, and always brings luck with it. Once a woman found a copper pan, which was identified by "them that ken the like" as a Trow's kettle; and while it remained in that woman's house she was very lucky.

Another woman walking through the daale of Mid Wick, found a Trow's spoon. It was silver, beautifully carved and strangely shaped. Overjoyed the finder put her

prize in her pocket, but immediately a strange drowsiness began to oppress her, resting on the wayside she fell fast asleep. When she awoke the spoon was gone.
EDMONSTON and SAXBY, p. 216.

Whenever it was suspected that Trows were in the byre milking the cows, someone "tried to hear them doing it," because that brought luck to the byre; but if the listener attempted to look, woe betide that over-curious mortal.
EDMONSTON and SAXBY, p. 217.

Shetland. When a child was not "thriving," and yet did not have the look that stamps the "Trow-stricken bairn," its mother went the round of her neighbours "to beg nine women's meat" for the ailing babe. Three kinds of eatables were given to her by nine mothers of healthy children, and with that food the little invalid was fed. This cure never failed, unless the child had fallen into the power of the Ferry-folk.
EDMONSTON and SAXBY, pp. 217, 218.

[After a wreck.] Some people saw the six men who had been in the boat at the south end of the island, near a well-known Trow haunt. They looked just as they had been in life, only for the kind of something in their faces that was no' just earthly altogether. And often after that they were seen—always the six of them— walking with their faces aye turned to the sea. Sometimes they appeared in the daytime and sometimes at night, but no one had the courage to speak to them until a sensible woman did so. They were passing near her house and she exclaimed, "Oh! what is this?" Then she called the skipper by his name and he spoke, but his voice was like a clap of thunder and she could not understand him. She said, "Moderate your speech, for I'm no' fit to stand it." Then the man spoke quite naturally, and the first he said was, "What is it that goes before the face of the Almighty?" and she replied,—

> 'Justice and judgment of Thy throne
> Are made the dwelling place;
> Mercy, accompanied with truth,
> Shall go before Thy face.'

After that the man conversed just as if he had been alive and he told her that when their boat came off the mouth of the fiord, Madge Coutts (a witch who disliked them) came into the boat and seated herself on the thwart and they knew by her look that she had 'designed for their lives.' They hoped to get rid of her by striking her with their Luggie-staff (large fish-clip) and actually succeeded in turning her over the gunwale, but in a moment she dived under the boat and got in on the other side in the form of a large black ox. Putting down her horns she struck them into the boat and drew out the *hassen* (board adjoining the keel to which the binders of a boat are attached) and then of course the boat went to pieces. The skipper said he could not rest because of some transaction that was not quite honest between himself and a brother, and he begged the women to set it right that the brother might have his own. She did so and the six men were seen no more. It was remembered that upon the day of the accident Madge Coutts was seen going in at her own chimney in the form of a grey cat, and that immediately afterwards a sulphur-tainted smoke was seen ascending.—EDMONSTON and SAXBY, p. 219.

Shetland. *Da Trow's Bundle.*—It was a common belief that the "trows" were in the habit of surreptitiously carrying off men, women, and children, and leaving in their stead some imbecile or fearfully deformed creature. Sometimes, as in the following case, they left behind an effigy of the abducted person. Occasionally, too, they took a cow or other domestic animal of which they might have need, and left in place of it a lifeless mass of matter. At one time there were several folk in Shetland who did a very lucrative business in supplying charms to prevent and various contrivances to remedy such fell disaster. Now and then it did occur that a lay person took it upon himself to deal summarily with a case, without consulting a professional exorcist.

One winter night an old crofter in the parish of Walls was away from home on a short journey. When he was returning across the hills in the darkness and had got down close to his "hill-grinnd," that is, the gate in the outer dyke of his croft, where the enclosed land borders on the hill-side, he met a gang of "trows" carrying a bundle between them. He felt a thrill of apprehension as he saw the bundle, but he allowed them to pass and hurried on down towards his cottage.

As soon as he had entered his cottage door he saw that his wife was gone, and that the "trows" had left an effigy instead of her, in her accustomed chair. Quick as thought he seized the effigy and flung it into the fire. The fire in the "but-end," or living-room of a Shetland cottage, is usually in the middle of the floor. The smoke, or at least a good deal of it, escapes through a round hole in the roof, which hole is called "da lum."

The effigy at once took fire, rose in the air, flaming, amid a cloud of smoke, and vanished through the "lum." As it disappeared, the wife walked in at the cottage door, safe and sound; and ever afterwards the "Trows" took care to avoid molesting this man or his family.—BURGESS, pp. 102, 103.

Yell. *Da Park at Windhus.*—There was a man in the island of Yell to whom, it seems, the "trows" stood in a relation somewhat similar to that in which they stood to the "güdman o' Taft" in Fetlar. This man had a field near Windhouse. The field was on high ground, and therefore in a situation very much exposed. The season was far advanced, and the weather had begun to get cold and wet. The farmer was afraid that the corn might get "laid," that is, flattened out and ruined, by the high winds and heavy rains, and one night he earnestly wished aloud that the field was "in a baand" (cut down), even if it cost him the best ox in his possession. In this case it seems that nobody either saw or heard the "trows" at work, but in the morning the field was "shoarn," and the ox was dead.

BURGESS, p. 100.

Fetlar. *Da Ferrie's Bress Pan.*—the "trows" had been heard on several occasions milking the cows in the byre at Taft. But some among "Da Güd Folk" evidently did not think it right that the folk of Taft should be defrauded of their milk. One afternoon the "güdman" o' Taft was at a place called Urie with butter. He was riding upon a red horse, and leading behind him a grey one laden with the butter. As he was passing a hill called Stakkaberg he heard a voice saying:

> "Du' at rides da ridd an rins da grey
> Geng haem, an inta da byre, an say:
> Varna, vivla, tail a tivla
> Is faain i da fire an brunt her."

When Taft got home he went to the byre and carefully repeated the words he had heard. As soon as he had done so the "trow" that had been operating on the cows, flung down a little, curiously-shaped brass pan on the "brig-staens" and said:

"O care an dül! dat's my bairn at's faain i da fire an brunt her." The "hill-lady" apparently went home at once, and the "trows" were never again heard milking the cows in the byre of Taft. The "güdman" took the little brass pan into the house and kept it for good luck. Every night it was carefully hung up on a nail with a piece of flesh or of some sort of food inside of it. It remained in the family for a long time. But one night it was somehow neglected. Next morning it had vanished, and it was never seen again.—BURGESS, pp. 96, 97.

Foula. [A dissenting clergyman] when walking across the island, observed a group of islanders dancing about, and throwing brands of fire at something. On reaching the spot, he heard them repeating an old Norse incantation; saw a young quey in their midst, at which they were throwing the brands of burning peat, and was told that "the *trows* had taen the quey to the hills, and that they were driving the trows away wi' the burning peats, to get the cow back."—REID, p. 33.

A belief in the existence of *Brownie*, the tutelar saint of husbandry, is beginning to be exploded; but the fairies or trows have still a "local habitation and a name." They occupy small stony hillocks or *knows*, and whenever they make an excursion abroad, are seen, mounted on bulrushes, riding in the air. If a person should happen to meet them, without having a bible in his pocket, he is directed to draw a circle round him on the ground, and in God's name forbid their nearer approach, after which they commonly disappear. They are said to be very mischievous, not only shooting cattle with their arrows, but even carrying human beings with them to the hills. Child-bed women are sometimes taken to nurse a prince; and although the appearance of the body remain at home, yet the immaterial part is removed. Such persons are observed to be very pale and absent; and it is generally some old woman who enjoys the faculty of bringing body and soul together.

EDMONDSTON, *Shetland*, v. ii. pp. 75, 76.

Orkney. Evil spirits also called fairies are frequently seen in several of the Isles dancing and making merry, and sometimes seen in armour.—BRAND, p. 63.

So firmly is the belief of Fairies implanted among the country people that it will be a very difficult matter to persuade them from it. A right shrewd farmer told me he observed on a know called Burying,[1] near his house in Harray, on a Christmas day, a large company dancing and frolicking, but upon his walking up they all disappeared.

LOW, p. xlii.

Fetlar and Yell. In Fetlar and Yell there are several ruins of water-mills in very remote situations, when mills could have been built much nearer; and there are various legends of their having been deserted on account of fairies disturbing them; of an old man being found dead in one; of an old woman being torn to pieces by spirits Wenyadapla in Gyodinali, in Fetlar,—a truly lonely spot.

KARL BLIND, *Gentleman's Mag.*, 1882, p. 369.

Shetland. A medical friend informed me, that a few years ago he was requested to visit a young woman, who was said to be dangerously ill. He accordingly went, and found her ill of a fever, caught in consequence of having accidentally fallen asleep in the middle of the day[2] on the top of a little hill. The patient died, and her father, to the last moment of her life, obstinately persisted in declaring that the fairies had taken possession of his daughter, and left an inanimate mass in her stead. Every effort to convince him of his mistake was ineffectual; and he even smiled at the folly of those who could themselves believe, and endeavour to persuade him of the truth of a contrary opinion. In cases where a person had been paralytically affected, and lost the use of an arm or a limb, the people believe that the fairies have taken away the sound member, and left a log in its place. They have even seared the affected limb with a hot iron, and, from the want of sensation in the part, have triumphantly boasted of the correctness of their opinion.

[1] [" Burying." This mound is known as the " Broch of Burrian. Its exploration has yielded a rich collection of antiquities which are now in the National Museum in Edinburgh.]

[2] Noon and midnight are the periods of the day when the people consider themselves most liable to be seized upon by the fairies.

A belief in the existence of these supposed beings, acquires confirmation among the credulous, by the statements of those who are said to be the objects either of their attention or their malignity. They believe in it themselves, and every dream or reverie of the imagination is related as an actual occurrence. Some persons have the reputation of having resided many years among the fairies, pretend to be familiar with their habits; and even assert that they can recognise individuals among them at a distance.—EDMONDSTON, *Shetland*, v. ii. pp. 76-78.

Stronsay. Maxime etiam fidunt napeis (the ferries), et dicunt homines subito morientes vitam postea cum illis degere, quanquam ego non credo.

JO. BEN *apud* BARRY, p. 439.

Shapinsay. Schapinshaw dicta (the Shipping Isle) populi colentes hanc insulam maxime sunt ignari, colunt napeis et alia nefaria.—JO. BEN *apud* BARRY, p. 440.

For Fairies *see also* " FESTIVAL CUSTOMS, YULE."

Stroma. *Elf Shot.*—On the west side of the island they find several of those small flint weapons commonly called Elfshot (*Sagittæ Lamiarum, patris sermone,* Elfarrow heads) or arrow-heads; they showed me several, but could not be prevailed to part with them, as they imagine as long as they possess one of these, the fairies can have no power over their cattle or persons.—LOW, p. 17.

Orkney. A similar notion prevails very much in several places thro' Orkney as well as Hoy, which is the belief of fairies, and their power of killing their cattle, which they are said to perform with those flint weapons called commonly Elfshots or Elfarrows, of which as many stories are told, and as firmly believed, as could be picked up in all Scotland. They use great pains in recovering beasts struck with the elfshot. An old woman skilled in these matters is called who pretends to find the hole still open

by which the arrow entered, and which is not in this case to be found (for it must be remarked that it is only when it falls short that the arrow is picked up). She then washes the part with mighty ceremony and expects a cure.
Low, pp. 7, 8.

I have met with several of them here, and many a dismal tale of the effects of them, and their pretended uses ... An honest gentleman (in other things, little given to scruples), affirmed he heard one of them rattle after him on his stairs, which he picked up!—Low, *Intro.* p. xlii.

Many of them [*i.e.* "Elf-shot"] have been for ages safely guarded and kept inviolate, from a deeply-rooted conviction that, if parted with or lost, "good luck" would no longer be the heritage of those through whom the heirloom had changed hands.

It is not yet two decades since a friend got for me a fine specimen of a "fairy dart," from a young woman who received it from her grandmother with the strict injunction, "that she was not to part with it; that, if she did, the fairies would take herself, and her luck would be gone for life."

Some years ago I learned incidentally an instance which occurred towards the end of last century, where one of these arrowheads was believed by its owner to have been the handiwork of the "elfs," or "fairies." It was owned by an Orcadian who wore it night and day for the greater portion of a long life. The old man resided in what would then have been considered an isolated district of the group. It had come to him as a heirloom, and he had worn it from youth to extreme old age, suspended by a cord round the neck, superstitiously as a charm. On no account would he part with the heirloom, affirming that, if he died, the "fairies" would come and take him bodily away, so that he would never be seen or heard of again. When he believed himself dying, he left strict injunctions that his heirloom should be buried with him, he leaving no descendants.—MACBEATH, pp. 23, 24.

Dunrossness. A notion is prevalent in the parish [of Dunrossness], that when a cow is suddenly taken ill, she is elf-shot—that is, that a kind of spirits called "trows," different in their nature from fairies, have discharged a stone arrow at her, and wounded her with it. Though no wound can be seen externally, there are different persons, both males and females, who pretend to feel it in the flesh, and to cure it by repeating certain words over the cow. They also fold a sewing-needle in a leaf taken from a particular part of a psalm-book, and secure it in the hair of the cow, which is considered, not only as an infallible cure, but which also serves as a charm against future attacks.—*New Stat. Acct.*, Shetland, p. 141.

Shetland. When a cow has calved, it is the practice with some, as soon after as possible, to set a cat on her neck and draw it by the tail to the hinder part of the cow; and then to set it on the middle of the cow's back, and draw it down the one side and pull it up the other, tail foremost, that the cow may be preserved while in a weak state from being carried away by the "trows." This is enclosing the cow, as it were, in a magic circle.

As the trows are said to have a particular relish for what is good, both in meat and drink; so when a cow or sheep happens to turn sick or die, it is firmly believed that they have been shot by an elfin-arrow, and that the real animal has been taken away and something of a trowie breed substituted in its place. And some who have been admitted into the interior of a trow's dwelling, assert that they have beheld their own cow led in to be slaughtered, while, at the same time, their friends on the surface of the earth saw her fall by an unseen hand or tumble over a precipice. Sometimes, also, the trows require a nurse of their children, for it would appear they too have a time to be born and a time to die, and therefore females newly confined must needs be watched very narrowly, lest they be carried off to perform the office of wet-nurse to some trowling of gentle blood, who has either lost its mother, or whose station among her own race exempts her from the drudgery of nursing her own offspring.

There is one place in the parish, called "Trolhouland," a name which indicates the superstitious notions with which it is associated: it signifies "the high land of the trows." The internal recesses of knolls are considered the favourite residences of the trows, and they are seldom passed without fear and dread by the inhabitants of the upper world. And when, after nightfall, there may be a necessity for passing that way, a live coal is carried to ward off their attacks.—*New Stat. Acct.*, Shetland, p. 142.

Papa Stour. At certain times a cow will grow sick. The idea is often entertained that she has been shot by the Trows. A highly valued cure under these circumstances, is to take a cat, hold it by the tail, and scratch the cow from the tail to the head with the cat's claws.

REID, p. 24.

Shetland. *Da Trow-shot Coo.*—A good many years ago a crofter in the parish of Dunrossness had a cow that suddenly turned ill and seemed about to die. He at once sent for an old woman who was celebrated as a "trowist," and who was consequently the "V.S." usually called in on such occasions. The old woman came, and the crofter took a "collie" and went with her into the byre. Two or three members of the family accompanied them. The crofter held the "collie" while the old woman carefully examined the extensive surface of the cow. At last she discovered a small dimple in its skin just opposite its heart. She then bade all the persons present come and feel the dimple so that they should be satisfied that it was there. This concluded her examination.

"My bairn," she said, turning to the man, "da trows is shot her. Haes du a Bible i da hoose at du cud bring me?" The crofter sent his son into the cottage for the Bible. The old woman took it and slowly turned over several of its leaves. Suddenly she tore one out.

"I sall tak a verse," she said, "oot o dis leaf, an whatin a verse dat is none knows bit me, for it's a saecret, an dem at wid be weel sud never middle wi' things at dey ken no o'." She tore the efficacious verse off from the leaf and rolled the tiny scrap of paper hard up into a pellet which she pressed into the dimple on the cow. After waiting for a little while she withdrew the pellet, and taking it, the torn leaf, and the mutilated Bible, she went into the cottage where she got her usual remuneration in the form of gifts. Then she went home. In a few days the cow was well again.—BURGESS, pp. 99, 100.

Trows.—The Shetlander still *sains* or blesses himself as he passes near their haunts in order to get rid of the fearful visitants. They are described at the present day as a people of small stature, gaily dressed in habiliments of green.

They have the power of multiplying their species: thus a female of the island of Yell, who some years ago died at the advanced age of one hundred years or more, once met some fairy children, accompanied by a little dog, playing like other boys and girls on the top of a hill. At another time whilst in bed, she had occasion to stretch herself up, when seeing a little boy, with a white nightcap on his head, sitting at the fire, she asked him who he was. "I am Trippa's son," answered he. Upon hearing which the good woman *sained* herself, and Trippa's son immediately vanished.

Several Shetlanders, among whom are warlocks and witches, have enjoyed a communion with the *guid folk* and by a special indulgence have been transported in the air, whenever occasion served, from one island to another. In their visits to Trolhouland [near Bigsetter Voe] or any other knoll of a similar description, they have been allowed to enter the interior of the hill at one side and come out of it at the other; and in this subterranean journey have been dazzled by the splendour exhibited within the recesses through which they have passed. They report that all the interior walls are adorned with gold and silver and that the domestic utensils of the place, peculiar to Fairyland, resemble the strange implements that are sometimes found lying abroad on the hills. Then there are innumerable stories told of Trows who in their rambles have carelessly left behind them utensils of a shape unknown to human contrivance. Sometimes the dairymaid observes a fairy woman in the act of milking the cows in the byre upon which she sains herself when the evil spirit takes so precipitous a flight as to leave behind her a copper pan of a form never before seen.

The Trows of the hills have a relish for the same kind of food that affords a sustenance to the human race and when for some festal occasion they would regale themselves with good beef and mutton, they repair to the Shetlanders' scatholds or town-mails and employ elf arrows to bring down their victims. . . . [They always hit] none of their arrows ever glanced aside. When the Trows are so successful as to shoot one of the best fatlings that is to be met with, they delude the eyes of its owner with the substitution of some vile substance possessing the same form as that of the animal which they have taken away, and with the semblance of its sudden death, as if it were produced either by natural or violent means. It is on this account that the bodies of animals which have perished by accident are condemned as unlawful food. A Shetlander of the present day affirms that he was once taken into a hill by the Trows, when the first object he saw was one of his own cows brought in for the purpose of furnishing a savoury supply for the banquet. So precarious at the same time was the man's individual preservation, that he considers himself as indebted for it to the gracious protection of a fairy lady, under whose special favour he had been admitted to the cave. On returning to his friends whom he had left on the earth's surface, he learned that at the moment when with his own organ of vision he had observed the cow conveyed into the interior of the hill, other earthly eyes had beheld the animal in the act of falling over the rocks. In this instance then the real cow had been abstracted and an illusory image left in its place, lacerated and dead.

A good man in the island of Unst had an earthen pot containing an unguent of infallible power, which he alleged was obtained by him from the hills and, like the widow's cruise, it was never exhausted of its contents.

These sprites are much addicted to music and dancing. A Shetlander, while lying in bed, heard one morning before day-light the noise of a large company of Trows passing his door, accompanied by a piper. Having a musical ear he readily learnt the air that was played, which he would afterwards repeat, calling it by the name of the Fairy Tune. The site where the dances by the *guid folk* are held, is, as in other countries, to be detected by the impressions in the form of rings which their tiny feet make in the grass; and within such unholy precincts it is hazardous for a Christian to enter.

The Trows are addicted to the abstraction of the human species. Although visits for such a purpose are to be particularly dreaded at midnight or noon, yet to child-bed women who may be designated for wet nurses to some fairy infant of quality the latter hour is by far the most formidable. On this account it is still a matter of duty not to leave in so fearful an hour mothers who give suck but to pray that the influence of the demon of noon may be averted. Children also are taken away to the hills in order to be playfellows to the infant offspring of the Trows. When an impression prevails that any child-bed women or infants, pining away with disease or betraying a mental fatuity are beings of a base elfin breed, substituted by the Trows in the place of those whom they may have taken to the hills, no inducement can persuade a family to afford the objects of commiseration entrusted to their care, the attention which the situation demands. Nor on such melancholy occasions are there wanting persons who pretend to the power of entering the caves of the fairies and of restoring the human beings who may be immured in them. A warlock of the parish of Walls is said to have amassed a considerable sum of money by assuming such influence over the demons of the hills.

When the limb of a Shetlander is affected with paralysis, a suspicion often arises that it has been either touched by evil spirits, or that the sound member has been abstracted and an insensible mass of matter substituted in its place. A tailor now living reports that he was employed to work in a farmhouse where there was an idiot, who was supposed to be a being left by the Trows in the place of some individual that had been taken into the hills. One night when the visitor had just retired into his bed, leaving the changeling asleep by the fireside, he was startled by the sound of music; at the same time a large company of fairies entered the room and began to bestir themselves in a festive round. The idiot suddenly jumped up and in joining their gambols showed a familiarity with the movements of the dance that none but a supernatural inhabitant of the hills could be supposed to possess. The observer grew alarmed, *sained* himself, upon hearing which all the elves immediately fled in most admired disorder; but one of the party, a female, more disconcerted than the rest at this inhospitable interruption to their sports, touched the tailor's big toe as she left the room, when he lost the power of ever afterwards moving the joint.—HIBBERT, pp. 444-451.

Da Trow's Dart.—It was a current belief in Shetland that, if a person attacked by "trows" invoked the Divine assistance in a certain set form of speech, the trows would disappear. In some districts the doctrine was extended to include the statement that next time the person visited the spot where he or she had been attacked, he or she would there discover something valuable.

A man in the parish of Walls was one night surrounded by "trows" while going along a lonely hillside. He tried at first, and tried in vain, to frighten them away with savage shouting and gesticulation. Then he recollected what he should have done, and said earnestly:

"Güd be aboot me an aa at I see." As soon as he had uttered the words the "trows" absconded, and he saw nothing more of them. He was about to resume his journey when the popular belief regarding the finding of something valuable occurred to him, and he made a careful observation of the spot where he had been attacked.

Next day he went back to the place and found lying on the ground and half-hidden among the heather, a beautifully-wrought "trowie" dart or arrow. He picked it up and took it home with him. After this the weapon remained for a long time in the possession of his family and was very useful as a talisman against all kinds of evil spirits.—BURGESS, p. 101.

Sea Trows.—They tell us that several such Creatures do appear to Fishers at Sea, particularly such as they call *Sea-Trowes*, great rolling Creatures, tumbling in the Waters, which, if they come among their nets they break them, and sometimes takes them away with them; if the Fishers see them before they come near, they endeavour to keep them off with their Oars or long Staves, and if they can get them beaten therewith, they will endeavour to do it: The Fishers both in Orkney and Zetland are affraid when they see them, which panick fear of their's makes them think and sometimes say that it is the Devil in the shape of such Creatures, whether it be so or not as they apprehend, I cannot determine. However, it seems to be more then probable, that evil Spirits frequent both Sea and Land.—BRAND, p. 115.

Stronsay. Monstri maximi nomine Troicis saepissime coeunt cum mulieribus illic colentibus, quod cum ego illic colui, mulier illic erat formosa maritata colono forti ; ipsa vexabatur spiritu maximo, invito marito, concubantibus in uno thoro, et naturaliter concubuit cum muliere, et videbatur. Mulier tandem macera facta est prae dolore : Hortatus sum ut vacaret precatione eleemosyna et jejunio quod et fecit ; durante anno siccine turbata est. Descriptio istius monstri haec est.

Indutus est algis marinis, toto corpore, similis est pullo equino convoluto pilis, membrum habet simile equino et testiculos magnos.—JO. BEN *apud* BARRY, p. 439.

Orkney. *Luridan.*—Luridan a familiar . . . did for many years inhabit the Island Pomonia, the largest of the Orcades in Scotland, supplying the place of Man-servant and maid-servant with wonderful diligence to these Families whom he did haunt, sweeping their rooms, and washing their dishes and making their fires before any were up in the morning. This Luridan affirmed, That he was the genius Astral, of that Island, that his place or residence in the dayes of Solomon and David was at Jerusalem ; That then he was called by the Jewes Belelah, and after that he remained Long in the Dominion of Wales, instructing their Bards in Brittish Poesy and Prophesies, being called Urthin, Wadd, Elgin : And now said he, I have removed hither, and alas my continuance is but short, for in 70 years I must resigne my place to Balkin, Lord of the Northern Mountains.—" Discourse upon Divils and Spirits " in the 1665 edition of REGINALD SCOT'S *Discoverie of Witchcraft*, bk. ii. cap. iv. (Nicholson's ed., p. 511).

[The "Book of Vanagastus the Norwegian" says that Luridan the spirit of the air "travels at the behest of the Magician to Lapland and Finmark, and Skrickfinian, even unto the frozen ocean. It is his nature to be always at enmity with fire, and he wages continual war with the fiery spirits of the Mountain Hecla."—*Quarterly Review*, 1819-20, vol. xx. p. 367.]

Westray. *Wilkie's Knolls.*—[Of two burial mounds (in one of which an urn was found) near Pier-o-wall, Westray, known as *Wilkie's Knolls*] the Orcadians can give no information who this Wilkie was. But there is a tradition prevalent that all the natives of Westray were in the habit of dedicating to him daily a certain proportion of milk. This milk was poured into a hole in the centre of one of the tumuli. It is also said that if any either refused or neglected to give him this portion of milk, that their clothes or other articles which might be exposed, would be stolen; that they, and their cattle, would be in danger of being inflicted with disease, while their houses would be haunted by him. The natives still seem much afraid for Wilkie's influence, although they no longer dedicate to him oblations of milk. It is still customary for the natives to frighten their children to silence by telling them that "Wilkie's coming."—*M.S. Letter* by J. PATERSON on Orkney Antiquities, dated 1833, in the Library of the Society of Antiquaries of Scotland.

Mysterious Noises.—The common people of this district remain to this day so credulous, as to think that fairies do exist; that an inferior species of witchcraft is still practised, and that houses have been haunted, not only in former ages, but that they are haunted, at least noises are heard, which cannot be accounted for on rational principles, even in our days. An instance of the latter happened only three years ago, in the house of John Spence, boat-carpenter, which house stands within the distance of a quarter of a mile from the manse of Stronsay. In the month of April, 1791, this carpenter had almost completed a boat, which he had on the stocks: He, his wife, his servant, and his children, one night sometime after they were laid in bed, heard a noise resembling what he had been accustomed to make when driving nails into the boat. It continued a long time. He supposed it to be boys, who having come that way at a late hour, were amusing themselves. At last he got up, and went out with an intention to reprove and dismiss them. The noise ceased on his going out of doors to the boat, which stood hard by his house; but he could neither see nor hear anybody. The noise was heard by all the family, not only that night, but many nights after; not nightly, in constant succession, but at irregular intervals. Whilst the boat lay on the stocks, it was still apprehended that the noise proceeded from it, although no marks of strokes could be decerned, even after it had been newly covered over with tar, within and without, when the least touch will make an impression. The mistress of the house and the children were alarmed; at her earnest request, therefore, in order to remove effectually the supposed cause of the noise, the boat when finished, was sent home, which happened to be a place on the other side of the island, from which place the noise could not reach the carpenter's house. Yet lo! and behold! the same noise continued even when there was no boat on the stocks, and that for no less than four months; and as the time elapsed, the noise increased with still louder and quicker strokes, until it came to resemble the strokes of two men hard at work on a smith's anvil. It uttered at last, not only the sounds of much fatigue, when men are employed in such work, but moans of great distress.

All which seemed to this family to proceed sometimes from one quarter, and at other times from another quarter within their house. Some of the neighbours were brought to sleep in the house, in order to discover the delusion or imposition, if any such existed. The same noise, at the usual time of the night, was heard by these neighhours as well as by the family. The master of the house himself began at last to be somewhat alarmed; but, putting his trust in God, he resolved to address this supernatural disturber, and to ask what it meant or what it wanted: Accordingly, in the month of August following, one night after he had lain some time in bed with his wife and children, upon hearing the last mentioned aggravated noise, accompanied with dismal groans, he sat up in his bed, and solemnly conjured it, in the name of the Holy Trinity, to speak, if it had anything to say to him. Inarticulate sounds of a faultering tongue unable to speak, accompanied with dismal groans, were heard.

The noise soon after ceased, and did not return any more to disturb this family. The preceding account the minister frequently heard from the said John Spence, and also from his wife, when separately examined by him on this subject, on which occasions they always appeared grave and serious.—*Old Stat. Acct.*, v. xv. pp. 430-32.

Papa Stour. *Supernatural Creatures.*—The islanders say that about a hundred years ago there was a species of supernatural beings in Papa Stour so numerous and even dangerous, that a person could not go beyond the "town-dyke" after twelve o'clock at noon. At Yule time and at weddings they would collect in such numbers as to check the progress of the strongest men, and sometimes bruise and kill them.—REID, p. 24.

Kirkwall. *Auld Cluttie.*—When the Rev. Mr. Yule was incumbent of Kirkwall Cathedral, he was in the habit of rebuking any person who did not behave well during service. On one occasion he publickly rebuked a girl for smiling during the sermon. Being afterwards interrogated by the minister as to her peculiar behaviour the girl replied that if he had seen what she had he would have laughed too. "What did you see then?" asked Mr. Yule. "I saw auld Cluttie up in the rafters, sitting across a beam, writing down the names of everybody that was asleep during the sermon. His paper was very small and being soon filled up he tore a piece from the tail of his shirt; but even that proved too small. So he endeavoured to stretch it out a little more by pulling it with his hands and teeth; but his strength was too much for the rag, so that it tore, and his head came *dunt* against the rafters above, and in his anxiety he let the whole drop down. That's the cause of my laughter." "Wonderful vision! wonderful vision!" said the divine.

FERGUSSON, p. 224.

(e) *WITCHCRAFT.*

Orkney. The belief in witchcraft still prevails here, as in other parts of the kingdom. The character of Norna, in the *Pirate*, was drawn from a living original in Orkney. The old sibyl is indebted, for the fame which she has acquired, to a visit from the great Novelist, when he arrived at Stromness, where she then dwelt. She has since removed her residence to one of the smaller isles. It has been her custom to sell to the whalers charms of various kinds, as preservatives from the winds, during their arduous voyages. . . . She has given, it is said, at various times, indubitable proofs of supernatural power: on one occasion, having discovered that she had just been robbed of some geese by the crew of a brig, she anticipated its exit from the Sound by speedily crossing the hill, and taking up her position on the brow of a beetling cliff, denounced, by all her gods, the ill-fated bark to destruction. The sea instantly opened and swallowed up its victim. On another occasion, she had received some offence from a young fisherman, and predicted that ere a year had passed away his body should lie lifeless on the beach: the prognostication was fully verified.

TEIGNMOUTH, vol. i. pp. 286, 287.

Shetland. Witchcraft is still believed by the peasantry to exist in Zetland; and some old women live by pretending to be witches, for no one ventures to refuse what they ask. About six years ago [c. 1802] a man entered a prosecution in the sheriff-court at Lerwick, against a woman for witchcraft. He stated that she uniformly assumed the form of a raven, and in that character killed his cattle, and prevented the milk of his cows from yielding butter. The late Mr. Scott, then sheriff-substitute, permitted the case to come into court, and was at great pains to explain the folly and even criminality of such proceedings.—EDMONDSTON, *Shetland*, vol. ii. p. 74.

Orkney. *Formula of old used in Orkney to acquire witchcraft.*—Mr. Dennison wrote it down nearly 50 years ago from the recital of an old Orkney woman—granddaughter of a noted witch. The formula to be gone through to obtain witchcraft (or, as Mr. Dennison says, in plain English, a formula for giving one's self to the Devil) was as follows:—

The person wishing to acquire the witch's knowledge must go to the sea-shore at midnight, must, as he goes, turn three times against the course of the sun, must lie down flat on his back with his head to the south, and on ground between the lines of high and low water. He must grasp a stone in each hand, have a stone at the side of each foot, a stone at his head, a flat stone on his chest, and another over his heart; and must lie with arms and legs stretched out. He will then shut his eyes, and slowly repeat the following Incantation:—

> O, Mester King o' a' that's ill,
> Come fill me wi' the warlock skill,
> An' I sall serve wi' all me will.
> Trow tak' me gin I sinno!
> Trow tak' me gin I winno!
> Trow tak' me whin I cinno!

> Come tak' me noo, an' tak' me a',
> Tak' lights an' liver, pluck an' ga',
> Tak' me, tak' me, noo, I say,
> Fae de how o' de head tae de tip of de tae;
> Tak' a' dat's oot an' in o' me,
> Tak' hide an' hair an' a' tae thee,
> Tak' hert an' harns, flesh, bleud, an' büns,
> Tak' a' atween de seeven stüns
> I de name o' de muckle black Wallawa!

The person must lie quiet for a little time after repeating the Incantation. Then opening his eyes, he should turn on his left side, arise and fling the stones used in the operation into the sea. Each stone must be flung singly; and with the throwing of each a certain malediction was said. Mr. Dennison's informant professed to have forgotten the terms of the malediction, but he rather suspected she considered the imprecations too shocking to repeat.

MACKENZIE, p. 4.

Shetland. *How Women could become Witches.*—When it is full moon and midnight the aspirant after unhallowed power goes alone to the sea-shore and lies down upon the beach *below the flood-tide mark*. She then puts her left hand under the soles of her feet and the right hand on the top of her head and repeats three times, "The muckle maister Deil tak' what's atween dis twa haunds." The devil then appears and clenches the bargain with shaking of hands. When this is done there is no retracting. The woman is his slave, and he gives her power on land and sea.—EDMONSTON and SAXBY, p. 206.

Witch Metamorphosis.—I was told once of a witch who had taught her daughter some "tricks of the trade," and the girl, proud of her knowledge, changed herself into a raven, according to the maternal directions. But in learning how to become a bird, the girl had forgotten to receive the instructions necessary for returning to mortal mould, and would have remained a raven if her mother had not guessed somehow the state of the case. With great difficulty the witch contrived to restore her daughter's personal appearance, but not all her art could bring back the girl's natural voice. Croak she would, and croak she could, and all her descendants after her; and that was how the peculiar sound (called *corbieing* in Shetland) known as "a burr" came.

EDMONSTON and SAXBY, p. 221.

[A] witch, desirous of injuring a neighbour changed herself into a black dog, and made her way into the neighbour's ben-end-o'-the-hoose, where she would certainly have created serious disturbance if an old man in the family had not recognised her by a peculiar formation of the eyelids, which, it seems, she could not discard from her canine appearance. Seizing the tongs, the worthy patriarch brought them down upon the black dog's back with might and main. "Tak' doo yon, Minnie Merran" (the witch's name), he cried, "an bear doo da weight o' dis auld airm as lang as doo leeves."

The dog ran howling and limping out of the house, and when next the witch was seen, she who hitherto had walked upright and with the dignity of a Norna, leant upon a stick, and had a hump upon her back. She said she had fallen from a height, and was afraid her spine was broken; but folk called it "the mark o' auld Jockie's taings."

EDMONSTON and SAXBY, pp. 221, 222.

Da Witch's Fee.—In the parish of Whiteness a man's wife was once lying very ill. Everything had been done to cure her, but she had got no better, and at last her husband thought that he would ask an old woman, who had a name for being able to do curious things with the assistance of the "trows," to come and see her. He went to the witch's cottage and explained his errand.

"Yae, my lamb, I'se come," said the old woman. "Gang du haem; I'se no be lang ahin' dee." The man returned home. As he was going up the "gaet" or footpath to his cottage door he looked behind him, but he could see nothing of the witch. Just as he was about to lift the latch he heard quick footsteps near him, and, turning round, he saw the old crone standing by his side. She laughed and said :

"Lift du da snek, and lat me look at Keetie." They went into the house and the old woman walked up close to the bed in which the sick wife lay and looked at her. Then she turned to the man and said :

"Yae, I can set her ipo fit again, but what haes du ta gie ?'" There happened to be in the house at the time an old silly kind of man who used to wander about, begging among the neighbours.

"I kno no," replied the husband, "excep du taks da auld man at's i' da but-room yundru at da fire."

"Kettie sall be able ta geng furt an mylk da kye afore da ouk is oot," said the old witch, and she went out. Next morning the old wandering man was found dead on the hillside not far from the cottage, and from that time the wife got quickly better.—BURGESS, p. 99.

Tingwall. "*Luggie*" *the Witch.*—About a Mile from Tingwal to the North, there is a Hill called the *Knop of Kebister*, or *Luggie's Know*, nigh to which Hil there is a House called *Kebister*, where a Varlet or Wizard lived, commonly designed *Luggie*, concerning whom it was reported that when the Sea was so Tempestuous, that the Boats durst not go off to the Fishing, he used to go to that Hill or Know, wherein a hole, into which he let down his Lines and took up any Fish he pleased, as a Cod or Ling, &c., which no other could do but himself : Also when Fishing at Sea, he would at his pleasure take up any rosted Fish with his Line, with the Intrals or Guts out of it, and so ready for his use : This was certainly done by the Agency of evil Spirits, with whom he was in Compact and

Covenant. He being convicted of Witchcraft was burnt nigh to *Scalloway.*—BRAND, pp. 110, 111.

Cf. SINCLAIR, pp. 237-8.

TRIALS.

Orkney. *Trial of Katherine Caray, June,* 1616.—An alleged Satanic precept was, to make "a wresting thread, and give it in the name of the Father, Sone, and the Holie Gaist, and say, Bone to bone, synnew to synnew, and flesche to flesche, and bluid to bluid, it wald mak ony wrest of man or beast haill."—DALYELL, p. 118.

In her trial it is mentioned that earth taken from the spot where a man had been slain, was prescribed for a hurt or an ulcer.—*Ibid.,* p. 126.

When she wandered among the hills "at the doun going of the sun, ane great number of fairie men mett her" together with "a maister man."—*Ibid.*, p. 536.

Trial of Thomas Cors, 6 *April,* 1643.—Being full of displeasure with James Paplay, he predictively "brust furth in thes speiches, 'thow art now the highest man that ever thow salt be! Thow ar going to shear thy corne, but it sall never doe yow good! Thow art going to sett hous with thy wyff—ye sall have no joy on of on vther: Yle sall not keip yow and hir, ye sall have such ane meit-will and sall have nothing to eat, but be fain to eat grass vnder the stanes and wair vnder the bankis,'" His neighbours not only confirmed the utterance of these predictions, but that they came to pass.—*Ibid.*, pp. 492-93.

Trial of Marable Couper, 1624.—I. In the first, ye, the said Marable Couper, ar indytit and accusit for airt and pairt of the vseing, comitting, and practising of the divelish and abominable cryme of Superstitioun, Witchcraft, and Sorcerie, in that, at Mid-somer, four yeiris syne or thairby, Dauid Mowat in Bankis in Birsay, haveing mareit Margaret Corstoun, they haid thrie new callowit kyne, quhairof the said Margaret wantit the proffeit; and suspecting yow, scho came to yow and reprovit yow, calling, Banisched witche, quhy had ye tane the proffeit of hir kyne; quha ansuerit hir, that it sould be sevin yeiris or ony witche tuik the proffeit agane from hir kyne. Quhairvpoun followit that the nixt yeir, the said Dauid and Margaret had thrie kyne, quhairof the ane deit in callowing, and the calff tane out of hir wombe; the nixt callowit ane calff, and never gave milk; and the thrid thir four yeiris past never tuik bull: And at the Candlemes efter, the said Margaret meiting with yow at your awin dore, and efter many wordis and flytting, the said Margaret haueing strucken yow ffor the lose that scho had of hir kyne, ye said to hir, that by the lose of hir kyne scho sould want worth the best horse that was in Birsay: And at the Beltane thairefter, scho had ane kow that deit, and tua young beastis. Quhilk ye did not onlie be your witchcraft and divelrie, bot gave yourselff furth to haue skill to do thingis.

II. Immediatlie efter the tyme forsaid, the said Dauid Mowat, haueing met yow cuming to your hous with ane stoup of aill, quhairof ye causit him to drink; and that same night efter, he contractit seiknes, and fyftene dayis thair efter ye came to visite him, quha said, ye wald lay your lyff for him, and that he wald ly yit ane moneth seik or he war heall; quha continwit seik, according to your speiche, and never slipit, and at the sext oulkis end he became heall, be your witchcraft and divelrie.

III. In harvest four yeiris syne or thairby, quhen the said Dauid first gaid to his barne with his new corne, ye cam to his hous, and quhen he gaed to the kill ye came agane, and quhen the said Margaret was grinding ane lock of beir on the quernis, ye came to the hous and said ye was come to get your kiltreis that he had borrowit; and he, haveing borrowit nane, was werrie angrie, and said he was euer cumerit with yow, and thoucht to have dung yow; and quhen he saw yow, he had no power to ding yow; bot reprowit yow, flet with yow, and bad yow away; quha gaid away: Bot efter, beith the said Margaret and hir servand could not gar the quernis gang about, and the thing that was ground was lyk dirt; and going to the mylne with the rest, it was lyk dirt as the vther: And James Spens your gud brother, being servant with them, and thay geving yow the wyte, he cam to yow and reprovit yow, and incontinentlie the rest of the meill was asse gud and fair as could be possible, be your witchcraft and divelrie.

IV. Vpoun Monday befor Fastingis evin thairefter, ye came to the said Dauid his hous, and efter mony wordis and flytting, he gaue yow ane cuff, and pat yow to the dore, and ye suore that he sould repent that straik; and four dayis efter he haueing put sex meillis of aittis vpoun his kill to dry, the kill tuik fyre and brunt, and the cornes that he got saiff he tuik to Alexander Ingsayis kill, quhilk lykwayis tuik fyre and brunt, be your witchcraft and divelrie.

V. At Alhallowmes thrie yeiris syne, the said Margaret Corstoun haueing contractit seiknes dwyned be space of foure monethis, and could get no mendis at hame, nor quhen scho wes brocht to the toun of Kirkwall; and sua returning hame againe, and going to Alexander Philipis hous by your hous, ye was standing at your dore, and the said Margaret ending in wordis and flytting with yow, called yow ane banished witche, and said giff scho deid, scho sould lay hir dead vpoun yow; and ye said to hir, scho micht haue reprowit yow quyetlie giff scho had ony thing to say to yow; and ye tuik hir in to your hous, and tuik ane birstane stane and pat it in the fyre, and hate ane drink of ale with it, and gave hir to drink; quhairby as be your witchcraft and divelry, ye cast the seiknes, so be the lyk divelrie and witchcraft scho gat hir health.

VI. [Once] the said Margaret Corstoun cuming to your hous efter Alexander Philipis wyff and ye discordit, and being in your bed, ye layed by the lap of the claithes, and lut hir sie besyd yow, as it haid been ane great bag lyk ane swynes bledder, great at the ane end and small at the vther, quhilk ye said was your guttis that Alexander Philipis wyff had tramped out with hir knees; and that same day Oliuer Garacoat hauing cum to sumond yow to compeir befor the sessioun, ye said to him, how could ye cum, for Alexander Philipis wyff had pussit out your guttis, and butte him sie as it had bene your guttis lying besyde yow, most fearfull to look to, and was nothing bot divelrie.

VII. . . . Vpoun Monday efter Sanct Magnus day, in Boir, Imvjc [1600] and tuentie tua yeiris, Thomas Seatter, in Seatter, haveing enterit his pleuche to the beir seid, and Margaret Bimbister, his seruant, leading the pleuche, the said Margaret luked about and sawe ane cuming vp the burne, and ane blak bruch about hir, quha said to hir maister, I sie ane woman cuming vp the burne, and ane black bruche about hir, and quhen he saw hir, he beseached him to God, and said, it wes Marable Couper; and quhen scho came to the pleuche, scho said hir erand was to lay hir culter, bot scho haid nane with hir, and he bad hir send hir husband or sone, and thet urne sould be done. So ye depairting, gaid to his hous, and ane kow being callowing, ane pair of scheittis stentit about hir that scho sould not be sene, and Elspeth Thomesone, spous to the said Thomas, being besyd hir, or euer scho wist, ye was within the scheittis and luiking ouer her shoulder; quhairat, scho being affrayed, and beseaching hir to God, scho comandit yow away, and ye going furth, enterit in hir byre, and doun betuix tua kyne, and quhen ye was persawit be ane bairne, and the said Elspeth advertised thairoff, scho came furth to yow, and said it was for na gud ye was cum thair; and ye ansuerit hir, ye was cum to advertise hir that hir gudman was wattit on for his lyff, and hir kyne for evill, and that scho wald want hir kyne or hir gudman want his lyff; and schew hir that ye haid brocht ane sort of grass to saue hir kyne; and the said Elspeth being affrayed, gaid to hir gudman, and tald him, quha came hame with hir, and gart yow deliuer the grasse to his wyff, quha draiked it in leaven, and gaue it to tua dogis, quha ran wood, and ane of thame mad the forme of ryding, ane kow, quha, efter he tuiched hir with his feit, scho pisched blud, and schortlie efter raged to dead ; and quhen he was put from the kow, he vsit the lyk to four calffis, quha pisched blud lykwayis, and ceassit not quhilk he was stickit ; and the vther dog lykwayis raged quhill he was libed : And within tuentie four houris efter the said kow was dead, ye came bak agane to Seatter, as it war lamenting for the dead of the kow, and said to the said Elspeth, giff scho wald let yow sie the place quhair the kow deid ye wald tell hir quhidder they war deid or liueing, that had the wyte of the kowis death.

VIII. . . . Ye gaue ane peice bannock to vmquhile Katherine Fulsetter, spous to Jon Crowdan, quha immediatly efter tuik seiknes and dwyned ane lang tyme, and ye cuming to visite her, desyrit almous of hir, and said scho wald be weill, quha gaue yow ane pynt of aill ; and ye, setting the aill besyd yow, ane swyne came and cust it downe : than ye desyrit ane vther pynt of aill, quhilk scho refussit, and ye being angrie, gaid furth at the dore, and said scho sould neuer sell aill again ; quhilk came to pas be your witchcraft and divelrie, for schortlie the said Katherine deid.

IX. The said Elspeth Thomesone came to your hous to seik barme, ye being sitting at the fyre syde, ye gave baith aill and barme to the divell, that was in your hous ; and quhen scho reprowit yow, and said that ye haid baith aill and barme, ye sat downe vpoun your knees, and prayed to God that your soull might newer sie the kingdome of hewen, giff ye haid ayther barme or aill ; bot the said Elspeth going in your seller, quhilk was dungeon mirk, and putting furth hir hand to greap about hir, hir hand chanced in ane barrell of aill with ane hat of barme vpoun it, quhilk scho teasted to be aill ; and the hous growing sumquhat lighter, scho luked about hir, and saw ane halff barrell of new aill standing on ane chest head : And at the Alhallowmes efter, scho reproveand yow for your baning and swearing, and that ye sould have gevin your selff so to the devill, ye said ye haid nothing to do with the devill; bot quhen ye lay in gissing of your sone Robie, your companie came and tuk you away, and that thay fetche yow, and ye ar with thame ewerie mone anse.

X. And generallie, ye, the said Marable Couper, ar indyttit and accusit as ane comoun witche, for airt and pairt vseing, comitting, and practising of the abominable cryme of Superstition, Witchcraft, and Sorcerie, and in going with the divell, quhom ye confest takis yow away ilk mone anes; and, in geving your selff furth to haue sic constand knawledge; thairthrow abuseing the people, and wronging and slaying man and beast, and sua not onlie reput and haldin ane comoun and notorious witche, bot being convict in ane Justice Court of befor, in certane pointis of witchcraft, ye was adjudgit to be banishit the parochin of Birsay of your awin consent, and not to be sene nor found within it, vnder the paine of taking the cryme of witchcraft vpoun yow: And thairfor, and seing ye have maid your continwalle residence in the said parochin sensyne, ye aucht and sould of new agane vndergo the tryall of ane assyse, and be adjudgit and condemnit to the death, for the caussis forsaid, and in example of vtheris to do the lyk; and your guidis and gear to be escheit and inbrocht to his Majesteis vse, conforme to the lawis and daylie practique observit in sic caissis.

Curia Justiciariae vicecomitatus de Orkney, tenta apud Kirkwall, septimo die mensis July, per Dominum Joannem Buchannane, anno Domini 1624.

[She was found guilty of most of the charges before the assize.]

Sentence.

The Judge acceptis the determinatioun of the Assyse, and

ordainis the pannell to be tane be the lockman, hir hands bund, and be caried to the head of the Lon, the place of execution, and thair to be knet to ane staik, wiried to the death, and brunt in asses. Quhilk Donald Kenner, dempster, gave for dome.

Abbotsford Club Miscellany, vol. i. pp. 135-142.

Trial of Katherine Cragie, alias Estquoy, 1640.—Ye, the said Katherein ar indyted and accusit for . . . vsing and practising of Witchcraftis, Sorceries, and Divinatiouns, and in gevin your sel furth to haue sick craft and knowledge, and in companie and societie with the devill, and thairthrow abusand the people. . . .

I. In speciall . . . in comeing to Jonet Cragie, spouse to Robert Robsone, *alias* Costas, hir hous, the said Robert Robsone being deadlie seik, and non that evir cam to visit him expected that he could recover from that sicknesse; ye cam to hir hous befor daylight, and spak to him (who at that time knew nothing that wes done or spoken besyd him for heavie sicknesse) on this maner: "What now, Robbie, ar ye going to die? I grant that I prayed ill for you, and now I sie that prayer hath taken effect": And leiving of farder speaking to him, ye said to the said Jonet Cragie on this maner: "Jonet, if I durst trust in you, I sould know quhat lyeth on your guidman, and holdis him doun at the grund; I suld tell whether it wer ane hill-spirit, a kirk-spirit, or a water-spirit, that so troubles him." The said Jonet Cragie ansuerit yow again, schoe sould nevir reveall any thing vpon yow, if ye helped hir guidman. Whairupon ye replyed to hir, "Well, or the morne at evin I sall witte whether it be a hill-spirit, a kirk-spirit, or a water-spirit, that troubles him." The nixt morne thairefter, [ye] the said Katharein cum to the said Jonet's house befor day, and brocht with yow thrie stones, which ye put on the fyre, wher they continowed all the day till eftir sone sette; and than ye took thame out of the fyre, laying thame vnder the threshold of the doore,

E

where they continowed all night till vpon the morrow timeous befor sun rysing, ye took thame vp frome vnder the said doore threshold, and taking a veshell filled with water, ye put the stones thairin severallie, on after another; of which stones, being thus put into the said water be yow, the said Jonet Cragie hard on of thame chirme and churle into the water, wharvpon ye said to the said Jonet on this maner: "Jonet, it is a kirk-spirit which troubleth Robbie your husband." Thairefter ye gave the vessel with the water to the said Jonet, whairunto ye haid put the thrie stones, and directed her to wasch hir husband thairwith.

II. Item, for putting of vther thrie stones into the fyre, quhair they continowed all the day also, till sunsette, at which tyme ye did tak them out, and layed thame again vnder the threshold of the dure, quhar thay continowed all that night, till vpon the morn tymeouslie, befor sun rysing, ye did again tak vp the said thrie stones from vnder the said doore threshold, and did tak a veshell, as ye did the day before, filled with water, wherein again ye put the thrie stones severallie, on after another, of which forsaid stones, being thus put in the water be you, the said Jonet hard thame again, the secund tyme, chirme and churle into the water; and thairefter gave hir the said vessell with the water, and causit her wasch hir husband with it a secund tyme.

III. Item, ye ar indyted and accusit . . . the thrid tyme, in takin the stones and putting thame vnder the threshold of the doore all that night, and in the vessell with the water vpon the morning therafter, as was done before, and one of the stones chirmed and churled in the water, as twyce before it had done, but wold not geve the said Jonet the vessell with the water to wasch hir husband, as scho haid done befor at your directioun, but ye did wasch him with the water your self.

IV. Item, ye ar indyted and accusit for the devilrie

committit be yow in comeing to the said Jonet Cragie's hous, ye haring tell that scho had revealled these proceidingis of yours vsit upon the said Robert Robbesone hir husband; scho not being at home, and missing her, ye said to on of her children on this maner (as the child reported and as it fell out accordinglie), " Thy mother hes bein tailing tealls of me, but I sall put a buckie in her scheek for that, that all her kinne sall never get out : So it cam to passe that thair grew a great byle vpon the said Jonet's left cheek, which disfigured her face, by drawing her mouth vp to hir right eare, as is manifest: Wharvpon the said Jonet, finding hir self thus tormented, scho sent for yow, and reproved yow, and said to yow that ye had witched hir; ye ansuered hir again, that it was but the Trow that haid gripped her; and vpon the nixt day thairefter, ye cam to the said Jonetis hous befor day, and brought with yow the Trowis gloue, and folded the same about the said Jonet's craige thrie several tymes, and vpol the thrid day the byle brak ; but, as all people may sie, the said Jonet's mouth is not as it was wont to be.

V. Item, ye ar indyted and accusit for . . . comeing to James Traill, he being labouring his land, with a vessel full of water in your hand, which ye offered him, desyring him to ressave it from yow, and to cast the same water amongst his bear-seed, promising to him, if he wold doe that according to your directioun, he sould thairby get a good crope of cornes.

VI. Item, ye ar indyted and accusit . . . for comeing to Issobell Cragie, relict of umquhile George Traill of Wesnesse ; he and the said Issobell being privatlie together, and non with you in the hous of Wesnesse, ye spak to the said Issobell, saying, " Tell me if ye have a mynd to haue Harie Bellendeyne to be your husband, and, if yow please, I will geve yow a grasse which, being vsit at my directioun, it will caus Harie Bellenden never to haue ane other woman but your self."

VII. Item, ye ar indyted and accusit for . . . going to Jonet Sclaitter's hous, William Flais, in Crage, her husband, being lyand seik, and said to her, "Jonet, if ye wold haue your husband ressaue some littill heillth (for he will never recover of that seiknes quhilk he is lying in), ye sall go with me about the Crosse Kirk of Wesbuster, and the Locke of Wesbuster, befor sun rysing," and desyrit hir to keip silence and not to speak a word.

. . . .

The Judge absolvis the pannell.

Abbotsford Club Miscellany, v. i. pp. 164-169.

Second Trial of Katherine Cragie, 1643.—Ye the said Katherine Cragie, *alias* Estayuoy, are indytit and accusit . . .

I. In speciall, in that . . . [in] . . . March 1642 yeiris, James Caithnes in Rowsay, having gone over to Westray for doing sum of his effairis thair, and culd not get home tymeouslie to his hous, for ill weather; in the meantyme, quhill his wyif was thinking long for hir husbandis home-cumming, ye cam to hir, and said to hir, "Give me ane peice of cloath, als much as will be ane pair of handshouse, and your husband sall get fair weather to come home shortlie, before ye get your supper"; and vpoun the morne, the weather becam fair and the said James cam home.

II. Ye ar indytit and accusit that Thomas Corse being lying deadlie seik, and in all menis judgment quha saw him without hop to live langer, and being for the tyme sensles, not knoweing quhat was done or said to him, ye cam to his hous, and said to Margaret Craigie, his wyif, that the said Thomas wold not die of that seiknes; and ye assurit hir thairof, and ye brocht with yow thrie stanes to the hous, quhilkis tymous in the morneing, ye laid in thrie corneris or nookis of the hearth, quher the samen continwit till about day-setting; and then ye did, with your awin handis tak vp the thrie stones from their severall places.

and laid thame behind the dore all night; and tymous in the morneing, ye did tak vp these thrie cold stones, and put thame in ane vessell, with water, when the said Margaret hard on of these stones chirme and churle in the water, but as yit ye told her not quhat spirit trublit hir husband. Efterward ye cam with the water, and washed the said Thomas Corse thairwith, at quhilk tyme he was so sensles that he knew not quhat was done to him : efter as ye haid waschen him the first tyme, ye again took the thrie stanes, and vsit thame the secund and thrid tyme, as at the first, and washed him with the water, as at the first; and quhill ye war wasching him the thrid tyme, he bame somquhat sensible, and knew that ye war wasching him, quhich he perceavit not the two former tymes ye did wash him. And immediatlie the same day, tymeous in the morning, efter as ye haid washen him the thrid tyme, ye desyrit the said Margaret Craigie his wyif to goe about the loch with yow for getting of hir husbandis health; but the said Thomas Corse begining at the same tyme to recover and to becom sensible, hearing your speich to his wyif, stayit hir, that shoe went not with yow.

III. Item, ye ar indytit and accusit . . . in that . . . Thomas Irwing, younger, being verie seik in Quondale, quhairfra he was flitting, he was brocht in to Jonet Sklateris hous in Cogare, heavilie diseasit with a senslesnes, that he knew not quhat was said or done to him; ye cam to the said Jonet Sklateris hous, and knoweing that the said Thomas was lying seik in his hous, ye said that it was the sea trow or spirit that was lying vpoun him, which might weill enuch be flyed away, and efter this, ye went and brocht with yow thrie stones, and laid thame in thrie corneris or nooks of the hearth, from morneing till night, then ye took thame vp in your hand, and laid thame behind the dore all night till tymous in the morneing; at which tyme, ye took vp the thrie cold stones and put thame severallie into a weschell with water, quhair the said Jonet hard on of the stones chirme and churle. Thairefter, ye took the water and washed the said Thomas thairwith; but he was so sensles that he knew not that ye haid washen him. This ye did with the stones and water thrie severall tymes and morningis togither to him, and efter, as ye haid washen him the thrid tym, immediatlie that same night following ye causit him to ryse out of his bed vndir silence and cloud of night, to go with yow to the sea schore, forbidding him to speak at all, be the way, till your returne to the hous of Cogar, and so ye went befoir, and the said Thomas followit yow, and be the way he was sore affrayed and many tymes thocht not to haue gone further with yow; but ye speaking nothing only beakned to him with your hand to goe fordward with yow to the appoyntit place. So ye went with the said Thomas doun beneath the bridge of Savaskaill, at the sea schore, wher ye did tak thrie looffull of water, and did cast the samin ower his head, and afterwardis he returnit with yow to the hous of Cogar, befoir any of the house war risen out of thair beddis; and everie day thairefter he convalescit and becam better of his seiknes.

IV. Item, ye ar indytit and accusit, that . . . ye being in Margaret Craigies hous, the said Margaret haid ane young quoyak calfe, whilk did eat ane beat of lint vnto yow, quhairvpoun, ye being verie angrie, said to the said Margaret, "ye sall nevir milk hir; dogis sall eat hir. Knowe ye not quhat becam of Rowie Flawis kow, quhilk did eat my courtch?" (for it was of treuth, that efter the kow had eattin your curch, shoe nevir did moir good). Efter these your wordis, the calfe becam a beast of thrie yieris auld, went to the hill quhair it died, was nevir found till the doggis haid eattin.

V. Item, ye ar indytit and accusit, That vpoun ane Saturday in winter, . . . when William Flawis in Cogar was lying seik, ye cam to Henrie Yorstounes hous, and lodgit thair all night, and arose tymous in the morneing, being Sunday, a litle befoir the break of day, being verie tempestuous weather with snow and sleit, the said Henrie and Katherin Windwik his spous, and thair children, being all as yet in thair beddis, ye sought ane garter from ane of the bairnes, but they vnwilling to ryse, refusit yow: As ye wer going out of the hous, ye wold haue haid ane of the bairnes to haue steikit the dore efter yow, but the bairnes vnwilling to ryse, desyrit yow to draw to the samen efter yow, quhilk ye wold not doe. Vpoun Monday, in the morneing, the said Katherin Windwik went to Thomas Corse his hous to visit him, thinking that he was eather dead or verie neir, and non that haid sein him the night befor thoght that he culd escap, and quhen shoe cam in to his hous, sieing the said Thomas lying in his bed laughing, and yow sitting in the hous, steppit in by, to goe neir to Thomas Corse, quhair he lay, and in the bygoing, ye spak quyetlie to hir in hir ear on this maner, "quhat sikane morneing, think ye, haid I yesterday?" quha ansuerit yow, "quhy, quhat glangoir war ye doing in that ill weather?" Ye said to hir againe, "I was about the loch with Jonet Sklateris, spous to William Flawis, but it is for no stead, it will never mend hir." These thingis began to be rumorit, and the sessioun being acquantit thairwith, the said vmquhile Henrie Yorstoun was cited, and declarit the samen done by yow, and told to him be his wyif. Afterwardis, ye being lodging in Essen Corse his hous, short efter, ye said "Henrie Yorstoun hes bein making reportis of me, but er ane yeir be at ane end he sall find it"; and so it fell out, that the said Henrie Yorstoun contracted great seiknes, and died within the yeir efter, as ye haid wented your anger againest him, and efter the death of the said Henrie Yorstoun, the said Essen Corse told the said Katherine Windwik your irefull wordis vttered againest hir said vmquhile husband; and this also cumming to the knowledge of the sessioun, and being cited to declair quhat he knew thairin; but er the sessioun day came, the said

Essen, taking with him his sone, ane yong boy to the craiges to draw fish, but the said Essen Corse was takin out with ane swelling sea and drowned, and the chyld escaped: Quhilk was done be your witchcraft and devilrie.

VI. Item, . . . quhen William Flawis in Cogar was lyand seik, ye took Jonet Sklatter, his wyif, and Margaret Irwing, his servant woman, with yow, quhair ye direct the said Jonet to follow yow, and causit the said Margaret Irwing follow the said Jonet, and went about the loch in this ordour, and about the four nookis of the kirk yaird, and none of yow spak ane word all the while, quhair in your progress and regress, ye returnit in that same maner, ye the said Katherin going still befoir. At last, cumming to the hous, ye enterit in the hous first, and steppit into the sellar quhair the said William Flawis was lying seik, and the said Jonet Sklatter and her woman followit yow, and quhen ye and they enterit in the seller, ye than began to speak, and bad the said Margaret lay her hand in William Flawis' hand, quhair he was lying, quhairat the said Margaret began to fear some mischief intendit against hir, and was verie loth to do it; yit, at last, shoe took him by the hand verie slenderlie; this done, ye bad the said Margaret gang but the hous, quhairat the said Margaret became verie fearit, and weipit, and sat doun, and wold onowayis stirr, nor goe first out. Thairfoir, ye went out first your selff; and quhen the lass cam but the hous, ye began to flyt with hir becaus shoe wold not goe first out. After these thingis, vpoun ane vther day, quhen the said Margaret haid come in from hir work, the said Williame being lying seik, shoe fand yow standing vpoun the floore, holding something close betuix your handis, and ye cam to hir, and held the samen to hir left ear, and said to hir, hearest thow that? and the said Margaret hard sumthing chaking werie quyetlie at hir ear, then shoe askit yow quhat it was shoe hard; and ye ansuerit, it was ane stane which was clowen, and water haid enterit in betuix both halfis of it, and it was the water that pized within the stone.

VII. Item, . . . ye being dwelling with Thomas Corse wyf, Margaret Craigie said, if it happint yow to be out of the house in the farthest pairt of the yle, all that shoe wold speak in hir awin house, most secretlie and privatlie, ye at your first home cumming to the hous, ye wold tell her of it: Quhilk revelatioun and foirknowledge ye haid of the devill, your maister.

VIII. Item, . . . quhen ye dwelt with Katherin Windwik, spous to Gilbert Mowat, if it had chanched yow to have bein furth at work, or haid bein in the farthest pairt of the yle, though shoe suld even [do] a thing nevir so secretlie, and it had bein but to heat a drink to her self quyetlie, quhairof shoe thought thair was none that culd have knowledge, yet, quhen ye cam home ye wold tell her of it: Quhilk revelatioun and foirknoweledge ye haid of the devill, your maister.

IX. Item, . . . quhen Magnus Harcas was tormentit with ane intollerable paine in his leg, ye cam to him quhair he was lying, and desyrit to sie his leg, quha let you sie it, and ye strakit your hand tenderlie vpoun it; so it fell out, that immediatlie efter, as ye went furth, the great paine slacknit, and ay becam better: Quhilk was done be your witchcraft and devilrie.

X. Item, . . . when Magnus Craigie in Skaebrek was verie seik, Jonet Ingsger, his wyif, going to Hunclet, to seik sum help for him, and by the way shoe met with yow, and told yow of her husbandis seiknes, and ye said vnto hir that ye haid Ursulla Alexanderis snood, quhilk ye haid keipit since ye put hir in hir winding sheit, and said vnto hir that ye wold give it hir, and cause bind it about hir husbandis waist, and if it war the dead manis sting which trublit him, it wold cuir and heale him. Ye said also that Bessie Spence hes ay ane sore head, it is ay pained, and shoe wold faine have this snood fra yow to wear in hir head, for this snood is good for thame that have sore headis: Quhilk sho ressauit from yow, and band it about hir husbandis waist.

XI. Item, . . . That . . . Katherin Barnie, vpoun ane certain day quhen ye wer out of the hous, did goe to your heavie, quhair it did hing vpon the wall, to sik for ane spindle, and thairin fand, bound in a knott within a clout, thrie grassis, whilk shoe reveilit to Annabell Murray, sumtyme spous to Magnus Corse, quha reveilit againe to hir mother Margaret Craigie, and shoe told Hairie Ingsger hir husband thairof, quha took with him Thomas Craigie in Savaskail (being both elderis), they went and found the thrie grassis bound in a knot and lying in your heavie, and shortefter, the said Annabell Murray contractit ane lingring disease, and nevir recouerit thairof quhill sho died.

XII. Item, . . . quhen Katherin Ethay, spous to John Work in Egilschae, was contractit in marriage and proclaimit in the kirk with him, and befoir they wer mairyit together, ye cam to her and said, quhat now ar ye going to dwell in Egilschae, tak my counsale with yow, and ye be wyse, and ye sall not speid the worse; quhen ye ar going out of Rowsay to your awin hous to Egilschae, remember to tak home with yow the wash cog, and the catt of this hous with yow to your awin house.

[This time she was found guilty, and underwent the usual sentence.]

Abbotsford Club Miscellany, vol. i. pp. 171-180.

[Prefixed to Katherine Craigie's second trial are the following jottings]:

In presens of Mr. George Graham, David Hert, Simbister, and the Chamberlane.

Katherine Craigie deponit that Margaret Ranie *alias* Todlock, heille a kow of John Bellis in Quoysknowis of the baneschaw.

And that Cristane Poock, lait servitour to Henrie

Ingisgar in Papa, and now with Kowie Insgar, can charme the worme and the fauldseiknes; and that scho vsit the said fauldseiknes to ane ox in Havaskaill, and that scho got for doing thairof a pleat of meill and a blood pudding vpoun the heid of the pleat.

Scho confest the going to the watter, and casting the watter ouer Thomas Irwingis heid.

And that scho learned the charme fra vmquhile Elspeth Linay be the vsing of the stones.

And that scho learned a charme for stemming of blood fra hir vmquhile husband.

Abbotsford Club Miscellany, vol. i. p. 171.

Orkney. *Trial of Mareoun Cumlaquoy*, 1643.—Mareoun "was verie anxious to know when David Cumlaquoy wold sow; and after shoe had herd, shoe went and stood just to his face all the tyme he was sowing: and that yeir his seid failed him, that he culd not sow the thrid of his land, albeit, for quantitie, he had as much as ever."

DALYELL, p. 8.

Marion Moir threatened her that she should cause her be burnt if her cow died; but the animal recovered that night: "and her neighbouris ox, struckin with the same diseas as the cow had, presentlie died."—*Ibid.*, p. 109.

She hit a cow thrice "with the skirt of hir coit, and instantly the kow was strukin with a strange seikness."

Ibid., p. 390.

She "cam down to Robert Carstair's hous, be sunrysing with milk to his goodmother, shoe nevir vsing to cum thair befoir nor eftir: and as shoe went furth, shoe turnit hirselff thrie severall tymes round witherways, about the fyre: and that year his bear is blew and rottin; and his aittis gives no meall, bot sic as mak all that eit it, hairt seik: albeit, both war fresh and good, quhen he put thame in the yaird."—*Ibid.*, p. 459.

Trial of Elspeth Cursetter, 1629.—Being refused access to the house of a man in Birsay she "sat doun befoir the dure, and said, 'ill might they all thryve, and ill might they speid': and within 14 dayes thairefter, his best horse fell in that same place quhair scho sat, and brack all his bones, and his thie bone gaid throw his bowells to the vther syd of him."—DALYELL, pp. 33, 34.

She recommended a man to carry the bones of a bird in his clothes to preserve his health: "Get the bones of ane tequhyt, and carry thame in your clothes."—*Ibid.*, p. 150.

Like the fly of Plautus overseeing everything, Elspeth narrating "everie particular disch, and quhat was spoken" at a banquet, declared as her *causa scientiae*, that she was "on the buird in the liknes of a bie."—*Ibid.*, p. 564.

Trial of Jonet Drever and Katherene Bigland.—Curia Capitalis Vicecomitalus de Orknay et Zetland tenta in Kirkwall per honorabiles viros Henricum Stewart de Carlongyie et Magistrum Wilielmum Levingstoun Vicecomites deputatos dicti Vicecomitatus die vij Junij 1615.

The quhilk day Jonet Drever and Katherene Bigland alias Grewik being pannald indytit and accusit for airt part vseing committing and practizeing of the abhominable and divelishe cryme of witchcraft contened in the particular and severall pointis or dittays gevin in aganes thame Compeirit Robert Coltart procuratour fiscall and desyrit persones to be put to the knawledge of ane assyse.

The said persones being receavit sworne and admittit past al togidder furth of court and ryplie advysit inenterit agane fand and delyverit alſ in ane voice for the most part the said Jonet Drever be the mouth of Robert Menteth chancelar To be convict and giltie of the fostering of ane bairne in the hill of Westray to the fary folk callit of hir our guid nichbouris And in haveing carnall deall with hir And haveing conversation with the fary xxvj zeiris bygane In respect of her awin confessioun And sicklyk fand and delyverit for the maist part be the mouth of the said chancelar the said Katherene Bigland To be convict and giltie of witchcraft for standing in the style or the kirkzaird of the croce kirk of Westray with drawin knyffis in her hand quhill Marioun Tailzeour hir mother and vtheris that wes in hir companie cam furth of the said kirk the most part of ane nicht Item convictis and fyles the said Katherene for laying of ane duyning and quotidean seiknes upon William Bigland in Swartmiln hir master Item fylit the said Katherene for practizeing of the said divellische cryme of witchcraft In going furth under clud of nicht about Candelmes last and bringing in to the said William his hous of wattir as apperit And wesching of the said William his back therwith And laying him doun saying he wald get guid rest and lying doun betuix him and the dor having refuissed to ly in any uther place And the said William haveing walknit with fear and crying and feilling a thing lyke a ruche scheip abone him In saying to him be not affrayit for it is the evill spreit that trublit yow that is going away And in taking of the said William upone the morne at nicht efter sun setting under the bankis and wesching of him with salt wattir at that tyme And fyve or six vthir nichtis therefter quhill he receavit healthe be hir unlaufull and divelische airt of witchcraft Item fylit the said Katherene in laying of the seiknes the said William had upone Robert Broun his servand quha continewit therin almost mad tuo dayis quhill schoe cam and graippit his pulses and brow and straikit his hair backwards and saying he wald be weill And casting of the same seiknes immediatlie upon the said William Bigland And the said Katherene being challengit within the said Ile therfor for taking of the said seiknes af the said Robert and casiing the same agane upon the said William In saying if William Bigland livid schoe wald die And thairfoir God forbid he leive Efter quhais deliverance the Judges decernis and ordanes the said Jonet Drever to be tane upon the morne betuix 3 and 4 houris efter nune and scurdgit fra the end of the said toun to the uther And thaireftir to be banisched the cuntre And nevir to returne under the pane of death And siclyke decernis and ordanes the said Katherene Bigland to be tane to the heid of the lone the morne at twa efternune And thair to be bund to a staik and hangit to the death and burnt to asches And dome gevin heirupone.

Maitland Club Miscellany, vol. ii., pp. 167, 168.

Shetland. *Trial of Jonka Dyneis*, 1616.—Being offended with one named Olave, she "fell out in most vyle cursingis and blasphemous exclamatiounis, saying, That within few dayis his bones sould be raiking about the bankis; and sa, within ane short space thairefter he perished be sey, be hir witchcraft and devilrie." Next addressing his mother,— "gat Geelis ane kneel to hir hairt, quhen hir sone Ola dyit! within few dayis she sall get ane othir: and so within fourtein dayis thairefter hir vthir sone Mans perished be sey,"

DALYELL, p. 34.

Being questioned after a vision, "could not give answer, bot stude as if bereft of hir senssis."—*Ibid.*, p. 443.

The husband of Jonka Dyneis being in a fishing boat at Walls, six miles from her residence at Aith, and in peril, she was "fund and sein standing at hir awin hous wall, in ane trans, that same hour he was in danger; and being trappit, she could not give answer, bot stude as bereft of hir senssis: and quhen she was speirit at quhy she wes so movit, she answerit, gif our boit be not tynt, she is in great hazard—and was tryit so to be."—*Ibid.*, p. 474.

Geelis, the overseer of Cultmalyndie's wife, failed to obtain the products of milk, after a quarrel with Jonka Dyneis. Therefore, "the haill wemen of Hildiswick wer desyrit, as the forme wes, to kirne, quha come and kirnet, and wes no butter. The said Jonka being desyrit, and having absentit hirself sundrie tymes, and fleing half a myll frae hir hous; and being followit and fund be the said Geelis, sche fanyeit hir self seik, and wes bluiding at mouth and nois—quha broucht hir back agane, and compellit hir to kirne—at quhilk tyme wes gottin sextein merkis butter, quhair befoir wes gottin bot sevin." Also, having got more butter from one cow than a neighbour obtained from fifteen, he "urged hir to kirne with him, efter mony boisting wordis, quha thaireftir gat his butter."—*Ibid.*, pp. 630-31.

Orkney. *Trial of John Faw, gipsy*, 1612.—He gave the gipsies' vocation as "the geveing of thameselfis furth for sorcerie, givearis of weirdis, declareris of fortownis, and that they can help or hinder the proffeit of the milk of bestiall."

Ibid., p. 235.

Westray, Orkney. *Trial of Jonet Forsyth*, 1629.—Intrat upoun pannell Jonet Forsyth, vagabound, dochter to umquhile William Forsyth in Howrnes within the Isle of Westray for the Witchcraftis underwritten.

In the first ye the said Jonet ar indytit and accusit for airt and pairt of the abominable superstitioun and superstitious abusing and disceveing of the people within the said Isle and for practeising of the wicked and devilish pointis of witchcraft and devilrie done by yow. In maner at the tyme and in the places efterspecefeit. And in giving yourselff furth to have sutch craft and knawledge thairof. Thairthrow abusing the people, viz. for slaeing of four gryss's to Manss Peitersone sumtyme in Kirbuster being dwelling at the said Manss house for the tyme be your witchcraft and devilrie Quhairby Mareoun Flet be eatting of the said gryss's swallit and becam decraipit in bear seid tyme four or fyve yeiris sene and being confronted with the said Mareoun ye could not denny.

Item ye ar indyttit and accusit for devilish and abominable bewitching of Robert Reid in Coat in Gaird in casting seiknes upoun him, he being upoun the sea, in sick sort That the men that wer in the boit with him were forcit to bring him on shore for fear of death And ye being on the shore at his arryvall He challengit yow for his seiknes and threitened yow In thir words : giff he gott not his health againe It sould be wors nor enough with yow Quhairupoun ye washit him with salt watter Quhairby he recoverit and cam to the sea In health upoun the morne.

Item ye ar Indyttit and accusit for the devilish and abominable bewitching of Thomas Port in Gaird In casting seikness upoun him in februar sex yeiris sene or thairby And being challengit ye cam to visit him and curit him being deadlie diseasit and got maill and cornes for youre paines, and cust his seiknes upoun Michaell Reid in Hewsea his meir quhilk deit as the said Thomas grew quholl, And ye being accusit thairupoun be the said Michaell in vore tyme his wyff and ye being chyding togidder ye could not denny and the meir being oppinit thair was nothing in place of his heart bot ane blob of watter.

Item ye are indyttit and accusit for going to the sea about midsomer sex yeirs sene or thairby at full sea quhen the starrs wer in the firmanent and took ane canfull of salt watter and thairby and be your devilisch practeis ye took away the profeit of Johne Herkas ky.

Item ye are Indyttit and accusit for coming to James Rendallis house in Midbie at Festrensevin four yeairis sene or thairby and having sought ane piece of flesh, and getting bot ane littil piece ye were evill contentit and said that ye sould get mair flesh or ye cam againe, quhilk being hard be the said James wyff, quha reprovit yow notwithstanding be your withcraft and devilrie, vpoun the morne bewitchit tua of his ky quhilk took seiknes and deit within aucht dayes and other thrie within ane quarter of ane yeir.

Item ye are Indyttit and accusit for that the same yeir The said James Rendalls wyff, haiving wantit the proffeit of hir butter, ye cam to the hous, and being challengit be hir for it being sitting be the fyre-syd ane beey cam fleing about youre head quhilk ye tuk and desyrit the guidwyff to put under hir kirin and she sould get her proffeit againe, and becaus the said James took the beey and cust it in the fyre ye was angrie and said although he wald not giff you credit otheris wyld giff you credit.

Item, ye are Indyttit an accusit for that ye cuming to the said James' barne about Candlemes thrie yeirsis sene or thairby, desyrit ane lock corne fra Edward Rendall his sone, quha said thair was nane threachin and ye said ye may give me ane lock, and he pleasit out of the cassie under the unthreachin corne, quhilk wes not sene, and becaus he refusitt to geve yow went to the barne yaird and faddomit ane of the best stacks in the yaird about contrair to the sunns cours quhilk the said Edward seing tald his father, and when the said stack was castin the hail cornes laickit the substance and never did him guid be yor sorcerie and witchcraft.

Item, ye ar Indyttit and accusit That thrie yeiris since or thairby ye cuming to William Setter his hous in Halbreck at Festrensevin, and seeking ane piece flesh his wyff refusit yow quhairwith ye was angrie and depairting, be your witchcraft and devilrie he losit ane great number of his sheip, sume by running on the sea and otheris deing upoun shore.

Item, ye ar Indyttit and accusit for cuming to Gilbert Hercas als Westray in Poldrit his hous at the time forsaid and seiking ane piece flesh, said to his wyff giff sho wald giff yow ane piece flesh ye wald giff her ane guid sheip luck as ye haid given to sundreis in the Ile quhom ye had maid up. And sho refusand to geve yow any flesh and saying sho wad tak hir to God's luck ye depairted angrie and the said Gilbertis wyff haveing told it to John Walteris wyff ye returnit and reprovit the said Gilbertis wyff and said that sho sould repent that sho told it, quhairupon he losit Twelff horss and meiris within ane halff yeir efter be your witchcraft and sorcerie.

Item, ye ar Indyttit and accusit for that Marjorie Reid, spous to James Drever in Swartmylne being seik and ye cuming to the hous and she challenging yow for hir seiknes and gevin yow ane look corne ye took the seiknes of hir quhairby she was quholl upoun the morne be yor witchcraft and devilrie.

Item, ye ar Indyttit and accusit thrie or four yeiris since ye cuming to Jonet Sinclairis hous in Clet and seiking amas the said Jonet said sho got litill guid by gevin amas to sick folk as sho and that sho wantit the proffeit of ane meill of malt that she was brewing befoir Yule quha ansrit hir that ye knew quha did it and that sho was ower reddie to geve ane drink of her wort and the said Jonet and her servands haveing forgot that any haid gottin any wort ye said ye knew quha had gottin ane drink of it and called her to memorie that Christane Reid in Clett cam in ane maid errand, seiking woft to ane wob and got ane drink and so took the proffeit off the wort with her and she speiring at yow how ye knew that ye said ye knew it well enough and being speirit quhair ye was then and how ye knew it ye said that ye was lying in your bed above Towquoy and knew it weill enough and being speirit quhair ye gat that knawledge ye confest ye gave ane woman callit Monipenney Three quarteris of lyning for learneing of yow.

Item, ye ar Indytait and accusit for that sex yeiris sene or thairby in vore ye faddomit ane stack of bear of sevin faddome perteining to Michaell Reid and that ye took away the substance of the cornes thairof and gave it to Robert Reid in Coat of Gaird and being challengit be the said Michaell for it ye took twa meillis of it back againe from the said Robert and gave it him and being challengit be the said Robert Reid, ye took the proffeit of the rest of the stak fra the said Michaell quhairin thair was sevin thrave and ane halff quhairoff he got nothing bot shellings and gave it to the said Robert.

Item, ye are Indyttit and accusit for cuming to the said Michaell Reids hous and the said Michaells wyff said to yow quhat Lucifer learned yow that witchcraft ye ansrit her haid sho not bene euill to yow and haid lettin yow abid with your brother it haid bene telling hir xl. £ and the said Michaells wyff said wer not [for] hir guidmanis maister Michaell Balfour he haid bene deid, ye ansrit he sould not sitt upoun your assyss this yeir and upoun the morne thairefter the said Michaell Balfour fell and braik his coller-bone.

. . . .

Curia vicecomitatus et Justiciarie de Orknay et Zetland tenta apud Birssay in aula ibid. per honorabilem virum Magistrum Joannem Dick vicecomitem et Justiciarium deputatum dict. vicecomitatus decimo die mensis novembris 1629.
Curia legitime affirmata.

. . . .

Compeirit Robert Scollay, procuratour ffishall, and producit the dittayes desirit them to be red and the pannell accusit thairupon.

The pannell present dennyit the first point anent the slaeing of the gryss's.

Dennyit the second point anent Robert Reid.

Dennyit the third point anent Robert Port.

Dennyit the fourt point anent the takin of the proffeit of Jon Hercus ky.

Dennyit the haill remanent pointis baith speciall and generall.

The procuratour fishall desyrit the pannell to be put to the knawledge of ane Assyss. The pannell present alleging nothing in the contrair was content to undergo the tryell thairof.

Assyss.
[Eighteen names given.]

. . . .

The witnesses wer admittit and maid faith quhairupon the procuratour fishall askit actis.

Walter Peitersone in Gara bewest depones that Mareoune Flet tald him that she slew the gryss's bot will not say of his conscience that she was the doer of it, and deponed anent Robert Reid that he knew nothing bot as he said to him and the rest that was in the boit.

Michaell Reid in Dyksyd deponed anent Robert Reid *conformis precidenti*.

The said Michaell deponed affirmative anent the takin of the seiknes of Thomas Port and casting the same on his meir and that she was the dead of the meir.

John Hercus in Kirbuster deponed that efter the pannell took the salt watter and gave it to Geills Irving he wantit the proffeit of his ky by it and storit never ane calff of fyftene ky be the space of thrie yeirs.

The said Michaell Reid deponed that he saw hir tak the salt watter and four with him and that sho gaid to Geills Irvingis hous with it bot quhat sho wrought by it he knaws not—[also affirms about the fathoming the "beir stak," the conversation of Jonet with his wife, and the breaking of Michael Balfour's collar-bone.]

James Rendall in Midbie deponed that he knew that she spak the words and be her words he kept the skaith of the death of his beastis and deponed affirmative anent the beey conforme to the dittay. And deponed that she was the instrument of the want of the substance of his cornes. Margaret Marwick, spous to Hercules Grot in Clet, deponed that sho was with the guid wyff of Clet and demandit with hir of the said Jonet Forsyth and that she ansrit conforme to the dittay.

[Found guilty and ordained "to be taine be the lockman and conveyit to the place of execution with her hands bund behind her back and worried at ane staik to the dead and brunt in assis."]

From copy of the M.S. of trial by the late George Petrie, Kirkwall.

Orkney. *Trial of Christian Gow,* 1624.—The minister of Westray's servant applied to Christian Gow to cure his master's horse, who " vsit this charme."

> "Three thinges hath the forspokin,
> Heart, tung, and eye, almost ;
> Thrie thinges sall the mend agane,
> Father, Sone, and Holie Ghost."
>
> DALYELL, p. 27.

" William Mylne being deidlie seik, and the winding scheit laid at his heid to be put on him," Christian Gow, " by ganting and whispering over the said diseased persone, maid him that he instantlie became wholl and weill."

Ibid., p. 124.

Trial of Katherine Grant, 1623.—She went to Henry Janies house " with a stoup in hir hand, with the boddome formest, and sat down ryght fornent the said Henrie, and gantit thryce on him :—and going furth he followit hir ; and being on the brigstane, scho lukit ouer her shoulder, and turned up the quhyt of her eye, quhair by her divilrie, their fell ane great wecht upoun him, that he was forcit to set his back to the wall ; and when he came in, he thoucht the hous ran about with him ; and theirefter lay seik ane lang time."

Ibid., pp. 7, 8.

She directed Christian, the wife of Thomas Smith, she " being deidlie seik," to fill a vessel with sea-water between sunset and dayset, and putting three stones in it, carefully to preserve silence. But, meeting her husband he commanded her to speak, when he was seized immediately with her distemper, and in peril of his life.

Ibid., p. 90.

Being suspected of infecting a child with a disease she was summoned to the house, and on arrival she desired " a cap of water, with ane knyf, and when scho gat it, she movit the knyf in the water, and spat in the cap, and gantit over it, and said,

> The dead upraise,
> To the credell scho gat
> To mend the bairne
> That bitten was,
> In name of the Father, the Sone, and the Haillie Ghaist,

and commandit the water to be cassin out." The child recovered.—*Ibid.*, p. 124.

The mother of a sick child was directed to weigh the child, and taking its weight in barley, to prepare meat for it three successive mornings: then to take the first sup of the meat "and give it to Katherine Sinclairis bairne that was in the hous; quhairvpoun that bairne mendit, and the other bairne grew seik; and quhen the said Katherine heard it, scho was angrie" and threatened the prescriber, "quha bad her set the credell on the other syd of the hous, quher the calff stuid, quhilk the said Katherine did—and sua on the nixt night, the bairne was weill and the calff deit."—*Ibid.*, p. 107.

To cure James Smithe's horse, she demanded "ane pletfull of corne, with an knyff; efter the recept quhairof scho gaid furth of the house, and efter hir divelish consultation reentering, scho bad the said James big on ane fire in his killogie, and schut his horse bak and foir, to the fyre thryse, and tak ane hedder busome and kendle the same, and sweip the hors thairwith, and syne put him out, and he sould be weill."—*Ibid.*, pp. 126, 127.

Visiting a sick man, she laid her hand "thryse on the point quhair his pane was, and thryse to the eard": and giving him a "cogfull of slaik" to be eat raw on a cake, he recovered daily.—*Ibid.*, p. 388.

She was also charged with approaching a house, "knocking thrie severall tymes at the door, and ane houre betuix everie tyme—and scho not getting in, went away murmuring. Thrie days efter the guid-wyff becam mad."

Ibid., p. 390.

She directed that a distempered cow was to be taken backwards into the sea, until washed by nine surges: three handfulls of each were to be laved over her back; when she should be brushed with a bunch of burnt malt straw.

Ibid., p. 393.

Trial of Magnus Greive, 1640.—He was reprehended for "going backward in a harrow to see quhat wyff he suld have, and how many childrien."—*Ibid.*, p. 455.

Trial of William Guide, 1616.—William Guide was charged with practiseing, &c., in that Robert Mowat, youngar, haveing fyit his dochter, Jonet Guide, and he detening the said Jonet fra the said Robertis service, obtenit ane decreit before the bailie for hir fie, and cuming to poynd thairfor, the said William promeisit that he sould deir buy that fie, and sa it fell out that his cornes being als guid as ony of his nychtbouris, he could not get na malt of his beir, for the quhilk the said William, being bayth suspectit and sclanderit, com to the said Robertis barne and tuitcheit baith the cornes freschen and vnfreschen, and baid him mak malt of it, for he said he sould answer that it sould be guid enouch malt, and sa it fell out. . . . For that Sara Stewart, spous to Patrik Boag, haveing caft certane beir quhilk wes givin to him to mak malt of, the beir being sufficient, the malt being returnit fra him, and browen be thame, the aill thairof did stink sa that nane could drink thairof. Thairefter she coft fra Jone Sclatter, in Birsay, ane meill malt, the said William being present, and held vp the malt quhill it wes weyit, and tryit to be sufficient malt. The said Sara reproveing him then for hir first malt went hame to brew the said meill malt quhilk taistit of nathing bot of verie watter, efter the brewing the said Sara and hir husband baith reproveing him for the same, assuiring him that they wald delate him for witchcraft. Immediatelie thairefter he cam to the hous, and that aill that tastit of nathing bot watter of befoir wes sufficient guid aill, and gif thair haid bein ten barrellis thairof it haid bein sauld, or be zeid out of the hous. Item, that haveing aft and dyvers tymes desyreit the len of ane scheret sheilling fra James Hunton in   , quha haveing denyit the same hes continuallie sen syne dwynit in seiknes laid on him be his divelrie and witchcraft. Item, for this yeir on Beltane day last in the morneing, he cuming to William Kirknes' hous, and desyreing ane cashie of hay fra him, quhilk being given to him, immediatlie thairefter that same day ane foill of the said William Kirknessis died, and on the morne ane meir with foill lykwayes dyit, and his haill guidis hes continuallie decayit sen syne be his divelrie and witchcraft. Item, that he and his dochter haveing ane lamb going in Mans Futtspurres corne, and about his hous, cuming in to the said Mans, his stable, his hors strampit vpon the leg of the said lamb and brak it, for the quhilk the said William prayit evill for the said Mans, and that same yeir his four hors and his oxen died, quhilk wes done be his divelrie and witchcraft.

ROGERS, v. iii. pp. 299-300.

Helen Hunter, Inswoman in Brugh, 1643.—[To ascertain whether the properties of milk were abstracted by one deceased or surviving, she directed the owner to milk the cow over an inverted cup, in the pail, when the rise of a bubble on removing the cup indicated a delinquent deceased.]—DALYELL, p. 514.

[Spinning a black rock is alluded to as pernicious to cattle, but no particulars given.]—*Ibid.,* p. 256.

Trial of Jonet Irving, 1616.—The devil while in the form of a woman, on hearing Christ's name uttered ran " out at the holl of the door lyk a black catt."—*Ibid.,* p. 554.

Trial of Helene Isbuster, 1635.—It was charged against

her "that in Paba, the glaid having slaine some fowles, ye commandit him to sit downe on the rigging of the house, quha sat till he died." The charge does not seem to have been proved; but the culprit was convicted of charming mice into a stack, where all were found dead: and she confessed having pronounced some words to expel them from their previous haunt.—*Ibid.*, p. 270.

A man was utterly ruined by nine knots cast on a blue thread, and given to his sister.—*Ibid.*, p. 307.

Shetland. *Trial of Katherine Jonesdochter*, 1616.—It was alleged against her that she "wisheit in her mind" that her husband's infirmities might be transferred to a stranger.
Ibid., p. 6.

She was also accused of being able to transfer disease merely by wishes and grasping the hand of the intended sufferer.—*Ibid.*, p. 106.

She saw the "Trowis ryse out of the kirkyeard of Hildiswick, and Holiecross Kirk of Eschenes, and on the hill called Greinfaill." They came to any house where there was "feasting, or great mirrines and speciallie at Yule."—*Ibid.*, p. 532-33.

[*Cf.* II. *a*, "YULE."]

Orkney. *Trial of James Knarstoun*, 1633.—He came to cure a woman in Dairsay of the "bainschaw" bringing "ane litle pig of oyle, maid of Mekillwort, as he himself allegit." He took such water as was in the house, "and washit hir feit fra hir kneis doun, and hir airmes, nobody being besyd bot ane litle sone of his awin. The watter being in ane daffok, shoe perceavit that their was twa or thrie stones in the watter, quhilk he took and pat about hir kneis, and vsit some few wordis. Efter as he haid washit her feit and airmes, he dryit them, and rubbed of the oyle againe quhilk he had brocht with him, beffor the fyre: and becaus the oyle was not stark enuch, he gat some aquavite to mak it starker the next time." Repetition of this remedy within fifteen days cured the patient.

Ibid., p. 153.

He took "ane stone for the Ebb, another for the Hill, and the thrid for the Kirk-yaird: and thairefter be seithing of thame fyre hott in water, and laying of thame above the lintell of the doore for the space of ane nicht and more: and then taking and puting of thame in ane tub full of cold water, vsing some wordis knowen vnto himselff—thairby to understand be quhat stone that suld mak the bullering and noise, as is maist fairfull to be sein, [be] quhat spirit it is that the person diseasit hes the disease: and so to call thame home againe."—*Ibid.,* pp. 508-9.

For "cuiring of dyvers and sundrie persounes," water was taken at midnight from St. Mary's well at Kirkbuster, and the patient washed between dawn and sunrise, wherein the diviner, probably cast melted lead, " throw the bowle of ane pair of cheiris thrie sundrie tymes, at ilk time saying thir wordis, 'in the name of the Father, Sone, and Holie Ghost.'"—*Ibid.,* p. 511.

The issue of distempers was divined from liquified substances, such as lead or wax congealed in water. Patrick Hobie's daughter being sick, he had promised "to cast her heart-caik of lead quhen shoe suld come to him."

Ibid., p. 511.

While leading peats darkness overspread the sun "and thairwith a monstrous cloak cam fleing and buzing about, and entrit in at his mouth, and he fell to the ground on his face and grew blew—it was als great as ane of the little birds that fleis in the yeird."—*Ibid.,* p. 565.

Trial of Cirstane Leisk, 1643.—After offending and wrangling with Cirstane Leisk, a man immediately "fell deidlie sick that he could not stir him." When brought by menaces "to the hous quhair he lay, and shoe looking on the said Alexander, he presentlie start to his feit, and went to the foot-ball."—*Ibid.,* p. 59.

Trials.

A man sickened while she spread her hand over his back. When this was repeated, the pain ceased "and immediately he became whole."—*Ibid.*, p. 61.

Trial of Oliver Leask, 1616.—On a cow giving a deficiency of milk, grass from the spot whereon the pail stood, was to be thrown among the milk to avert recurrence of the like.—*Ibid.*, p. 126.

Trial of Magnus Linay and Geillis Sclaitter his wife, 1616.—Magnus Linay charged with, &c., inasmuch that his sone being keiping his ky, and suffering thame to go in Robert Grayis corne in Watle, the said Robert finding his ky in his corne, gave his sone ane cuff, quhilk the said Magnus perceaving fleitt with the said Robert thairfoir, and assuirit him that he sould repent that straik, and that same day being about lambmes tua yeiris syne or thairby, the best hors that he had dyit, and his haill bestiall, hors, nalt, and sheip hes dyit, and nathing thryves with him sen syne.—ROGERS, vol. iii. p. 300.

They were accused of having accompanied the Egyptians [Gypsies], and of having "lernit to take the proffeit ot thair nyghtbouris cornis and ky of the saids Egyptians, as the captane of thame declarit."—DALYELL, p. 236.

Trial of Cirstain Marwick, 1643.—While a woman was milking her cow Cirstain "lookit in ower the duir, quhairvpoun the calf died presentlie, and the kow fell seik, that schoe wold nether eat nor yield milk."—*Ibid.*, p. 5.

While Margaret Craigie was recovering, Cirstain Marwick "straikit hir hand ower the said Margaret's breast and that same night" she died.—*Ibid.*, p. 52.

Trial of Katherin Miller, 29 *May*, 1633.—A woman labouring under an extraordinary disease, compelling her to "creip on hands and feit," recovered presently and received as good health as ever, from the hand of Katherin Miller laid on her head.—*Ibid.*, p. 61.

88   Superstitious Beliefs and Practices.

Shetland. *Trial of Marion Peebles,* alias *Pardone, Spous to Swene in Hildiswick.*—In the first, you the said Marion Peebles alias Pardone, is indytit and accusit for the sinful and damnable renouncing of God, your Faith and Baptism, giving and casting of yourself, body and soul in the hands of the Devil, following, exercising, using and practising of the fearfull and damnable craft of Witchcraft, Sorcerie, and Charming, in manner, following, viz.

In the first, you are Indytit and accusit for coming in the month of   Imvjc [1600] and thirty years, to the house of John Banks in Turvisetter, and Janet Robertson his spouse, with a wicked, devilish and malicious intention to cast Witchcraft and Sickness upon them ; and missing the said Janet there, for going to Sursetter, where she then was, and after cursing and scolding her, telling her that she should repent what she had done to your daughter and good-son. And for that immediately with the word, ye, by your devilish art of witchcraft, did cast sickness upon the said Janet, who, immediately upon your departure, fell in an extraordinary and unkindly sickness, and lay eight weeks, taking her shours and pains by fits, at midday and midnight, and so continued most terribly tormented ; her said sickness being castin upon her by your said devilish witchcraft, during the said space, until the said John Banks came to you and threatened you, at which time ye gaif him a gullion of silver, to hold his peace and conceal the same, promising to him that nothing should ail his wife. And thereafter, for that ye sent her ane cheese of the breadth of ane loof, composed by your said devilish art of witchcraft, with ane junke-roll, and desiring her the said Janet to eat the same, when (whereof the said Janet refused to eat), yet immediately she grew well, but two of her kine died, the said sickness being castin upon them by your said wicked and devilish art of Witchcraft.

2. Likeas also, you are indytit and accusit, for that by

your said art of devilish witchcraft, ye did, upon the recovery of the said Janet, cast the same sickness upon Marion Banks, sister to the said John Banks, which troubled her after the same manner, tormenting her for twenty days, until that one Osla in Olsnafirth, coming to you, by direction of the said John Banks, and warned you hereof, whereupon by your said devilish witchcraft, the said sickness was taken off the said Marion and casten upon a young cow of the said John's, which took wodrome, and died within twenty-four hours.

3. Ye the said Marion are indyted for that you being very shroudly suspected, and commonly bruited as a common witch, ye coming along upon some of your said devilish and wicked intentions to umquil Edward Halcro in Overure, quhair he was dichting bear to steep for malt, you being of wicked intention, by your said devilish craft, did unto the said making of malt, and he suspecting you, after he had reproved you for minding you about him, you said to him all would be well touching the said making, as it fell out : so taking upon you and acknowledging by your wordis your power in the said wicked and devilish art of witchcraft. That, after that, he being there scrowing corne, and ye persisting in your said wicked and devilish intentions to undo and provock the said Edwd. you did thereby marr and undo twa whole makings of the said bear, quhilk never did good.

4. The said Marion is indytit and accusit for that in April 1641, the said Edward coming to your houss, after ye had urged him to take meat, he took resolution to go to the war having not intention before, and going with Sueno your husband to the gio heid where they were usit to go down, he being affrayit to go down first, desyrit your husband to go befoir him, quha refusing to go, the said Edward went, whereon he going down and stepping upon a stone which was ever a sure step befoir, ye the said Maron maid the said stone to lows and fall down with him,

whereby his life was in great perill, yet saved to the admiration of all the beholders. And ye being accusit for taking the said occasion and cryme upon you, anserit that it was not for his gud, but for Helen Thomson his spous gud that he was savit.

5. Ye the said Marion are indyttit and accusit for that ye did cast ane terrible and fearful madnes and sicknes upon ane Madda Scuddas-doughter, your awin friend, becaus she wold not byd with you, quhairon she continuit most terriblie tormentit, and throw the torment of the said disease, she was causit many times to run upon her awin sister that keepit her, and divers, so as to have devorit them in her madnes, and so continuit a zeir and half ane zeir, till she, being counsallit, ran upon the said Marion and drew blood of you, within James Halcros Hows, biting twa of your fingers till they bled, whereupon the said Madda Scudda-doughter recoverit of her disease, and came to her ryt sinces.

6. Ye the said Marion Pardoun ar indyttit and accusit for that James Halcro in Hildiswick having a cow that ye alledged had pushed a cow of yours, ye in revenge thereof, maid the said James his cow milk nothing but blood, whereas your awin cow had no harm in her milk; whereupon they suspecting you, shewit the said bloody milk to Marion Kilti your servant, quha desyrit of you the same bloody milk for Goddis caus to shew you, and said she houpit the cow sould be weil; quhilk having gotten, and coming therewith to your hous, and shawing it to you, thereafter the cow grew weil, thairby shewing and proving your said devilish practyce of the art of witchcraft.

7. Ye the said Marion are indytit and accusit for that you having anno 1642 zeirs hyrit ane cow from Androw Smith, younger in Hildiswick, which ye keepit fra the bull, when she wald have taken bull, and the said Andro getting knowledge thereof, causit the same to be brought to the bull and bullit against your will. The next year when she

calved, ye took away her proffeit and milk, so that she milked nothing but water, quhilk stinked and tasted of sharn a long time, till that you comming by the said Andro his hous, he suspecting you, caused you to milk her and look to her, after which doing, immediatlie the said cows milk cam to its own nature.

8. Ye the said Marion ar indyttit and accusit for that ye coming by ane pies of grass quhairin Andro Smith elder in Videfield had six kine tederit, quhairintil ye went, and out of whilk grass, ye and your son, after ye had lousit and taken the kyne, fell in scoulding with and abusit the said Andro, and said to him that he sould not have so many kine to eat grass and milk the next zeir; according to the quhilk wordis, sa it fell out thereafter; for that by your said wicked and devilish art of witchcraft, the said hail kyne died befoir the next half yeir, all fat and gudlike by that same order, as they were lousit by you on tedder, beginning at the first cow, (quhilk was ane black cow, qlk ye lousit, qlk died 20 days before Yule, fat and tydie,) and so furth in succession the rest, by your sd devilish witchcraft.

9. Ye coming to the said Andro Smyth elder, and desyring him len you ane of his hors, to go to Urafirth to lead peatis, qlk he refusit to do, ye out of a wicked and malicious heart said to him that he would repent it; quhereupon ye by your sd wicked and devilish airt of witchcraft, and for outting of your malice, and for keeping of your said devilish promeis, within aught days thereafter did kill ane of his best worke hors, and within half ane zeir thereafter other three of his sd hors; thairby shewing baith in your words and deeds, your wicked and devilish skill concerning the practise of the fursd devilish and abhominable airt of witchcraft.

10. Ye being suspectit to have castin sickness upon the said Andro Smith elder his oy, qrof she lay long benumed and senseless, ye coming tyme foirsd to the hous of Overure, and they challenging and quarrelling you therefor,

ye fell into cursing and swearing and went to the dore, qr ane calf was standing in the dore besyd you, qrupon in your sd wicked and devilish malice, be your sd detestable craft of witchcraft, ye did cast sickness that it presentlie run mad, cracy, and died.

11. Ye the said Marion are indyttit and accusit for coming to Andro Erasmusson's house in Eshaness, qr he having ane cow three days calved befoir, qrupon as ye luikit, ye immediately be airt and devilrie cast sickness that she immediatlie crap togidder, that no lyf was looked for her; till they sent for you, and causit you lay your hand upon her, qrupon scho then immediatlie recoverit, and was weil.

12. Likeas [ye the sd Marion] to cullour and extenuat your sd craft, alledging that ye wantit the profit of your kyne, qlk was not true, but onlie to tak occasion, by your sd wicked and devilish airt of the profit of the said Andro his kyne, came to his hous in July therefter, and efter cursing his wyf, quha shawed you the milk of her kyne, desirit her to caus Usla Sinclar, her servant woman, to go with you to the kerne, qlk she did. Qrby ye touk away with you the profeit of the sd Andro his kyne until the space of throttein dayes; till the sd Andro his wyf went to your hous, and shewit you the milk and butter, and maid publication yrof to the nybours, and immediatlie thereafter gat back her profeit of baith her milk and butter.

[13.] Ye ar indytit and accusit for that ye cam to Thomas in Urabister, and desyrit a quoyach cow of his of four yeir old to hyre, qlk was with calf then, whereof he maid you half a grant, but not the full, until he could advise with his Mrs, the gud wyf of Urafirth, quha would not consent, and becaus ye gat her not, ye outscoldit him and wer verie angrie. And in revenge of his sd refusal, immediatlie yrafter ye cas seeknes upon the sd cow, qlk being at the hill with utheris of his kyne, scho tuik a wodroam or madnes and cam scouring hame frae the rest to the byre dere, brak up the saim and went in, having her head thrawin backward to her back, that four people could not get it back, and thereby dyed throw the sd diseas, cassin on her by your sd airt, working and witchcraft.

14. Lykeas ye not being in your devilish and wicked mynd enough revenget and satisfyct ye be the same your craft, devilrie, and witchcraft, within six weeks yrefter, cast the lyke seiknes upon ane uther cow of the sd Thomas his kyne, whereby scho also died mad and in wodram.

15. Ye the sd Marion are indyttit and accusit for that in anno 1634, at Michelmes, when the cornes were taking in, the sd Thomas in Urabister having aught piere of hors and mairs gaing on the riggs of Olnais firth, ye cam furth with a staff to ding away his hors, qn ye fell and hurt your knee, whereupon ye, to revenge yourself, and to assyth your wicked and malicious heart and mynd, did, by your foirsd airt of witchcraft and devilrie, caus that within aught dayis thereafter his best hors died, and thereafter before Candlemes uther sex hors and mares.

At Scalloway, the 15th March, 1645 zeirs.

We the Moderator and remanent Brethren of the Presbyterie of Zetland, being conveened day and place forsaid and having examined the above wreattin process, doe find and declare the poyntis . . . lawfullie prowin to be witchcraft, and yrfor the pairtie guiltie worthy of death be the law of God and the law of the kingdome, and requyris you judges to put them to the knawledge of ane assyse, and minister justice upon them accordinglie, as ye will be ansrable to God, his Maijestie and Counsel, and to discharge of your deutie heeranent.

NICOL WHYTE, *Moderater.*
W. ROBERT MURRAY, *Clk.*

Fytts. Item, ye the said Marion Peebles alias Pardoun, ar indyttit and accusit for that at Candlemiss or thereby 1643, on ane Sunday, ye coming into the hous of James

Halcro in Hildiswick, where Andro Broun then wis for the time, and falling into contest, and fletting with him about linching ane boat, ye, being enraged, set your venefical malice against him, and cursit him with many wicked and execrable words, and by your damnable and venefical heart wishit and cravit ill may so befall him : whereupon by your develish airt and craft of witchcraft ye bewitched him, and cast sickness upon him immediately that he fell in a deadlie sickness and diseas.—That upon Munday next hereafter, he did contract sa vehement and deadlie diseas and sickness, tormentit thereby fra the croun of his head to the sole of his fute, that there was no lyff expectit of him. Quhairfor his nybers, knawing your detestable brute of witchcraft, and your pouir at your said practising, and that on whomsoever your cursed charm fell, sum notable and extraordinar mischieff and evile followit to yame, they did advys him to send for you, to shaw that there wis na lyff for him, and that they all suspectit you for casting the samin upon him. Quhairupon, after many dinyellis to cum and see him, at last you cam to him, quhen shewing you his diseas and sicknes, togidder with the racking pain thereof, imputit by him and utheris to be your act and doing, Andro thaerfor prayit you to lay your hand upon him, which you wold not do, nor be na intreatti nather of him nor of your nybures moved thereto till that they all that wer in the hous, being wearied of your refusal, went furth grivet, and prayit you for Goddis cause to lay your hand upon him; and then at last, being movit thereto, using your said venefical and damnabil charms and witchcraft, ye did uncover his leg, and pat your finger thereon, and on the ground three severall tymes, to and fra ; qrby immediatlie, by your said airt of witchcraft and charms, he fell, and said his pein and diseas was desolvit frae the crown of his head to the sole of his fute; at qlk tyme he was before her tutch sa heavyly diseased frae top to toe, through all his body, with swelling in his handes, lykwise armis, leges and knees, that he was unable to move or turn himself in the bed ; but after your said tutch, he became able to sit up, and turn himself in the bed, and within twa dayes, was fullie recoverit, and went furth. Quhilk sudden recoverie, togidder with your forme and manner of charming, and cureing of be your said tutch and charmes being spread abrod amang your nybers, and the said cuming to your ears, about 14 days after his recoverie, ye said to your nybbers emgrace on them that had bewitched you, that wald not witch you oer the banks ; quhairupon immediatlie again he fell again in the sd sicknes wors than befoir, and paynet away with sic extremetie of sicknes, that he sent you againe, desyring meat out of your hand ; and after long intreatie, ye wald not cum to him with it, least your witchcraft and charmes again sould cum to lyt, but send wt Swene your husband, ane bannock, after long stryving betwix the sd Swene and you, qlk of you sould give the samin to him ; qlk he having eaten, he again recoverit presentlie thereafter, and the sd sicknes was cassin be you upon ane cow, pertaining also to Andro, qlk then died.

Item, ye the sd Marion ar indyttit and accusit for that, you bearing and deadlie and veneficall malice in your heart agains the sd umquill Edward Halcro in Overure, and incrissing your malice and divelish intentiones of your wicked heart, and taking occasion to renew and bring your wicked intention by your sd wicked airt of witchcraft, to work his ruyine and death,—(being set on edge be a speitch spoken be him to the sd Swene your husband, when he was castin peates to him in Voir last year, as the sd Andro Brown also was castin peatis to him, having callit to your sd husband, and bade him go to you, to desyre you to go to your pobe, the devill, and bid him loose ane knot, that the sd Andro Brown myt be able, being then verie waik, to cast out his bank of peates :)—qrupon ye and the sd Swene being angrie, awaitting your occasion to practise your said abominable airt and craft of witchcraft, to distroy

and put down the sd Edward Halcro, and having covenantit and conversit with the devill to bring the saim to pass, (as ane declaration of umquhill Jvenit Fraser, witch, whom you desyrit the devill to move her to assist you doth prove, qlk she both before and after her conviction did testiffie,) ye be your sd wicked, detestable, abhominable and develish airt of witchcraft, being transformed in the lyknes of an pellack quhaill, (at the [counsel of the said Swene,] and be your consent and wish, the devill changing your spirit, qlk fled in the same quhaill;) and the said Edward being at sey with . . . [other three men], all four in ane fishing boat coming fra the sey at the north bankis of Hildiswick, on ane fair morning, ye did cum under the said boat and overturnit her with ease, and drowned and devourit thame in ye sey, right at the shore, when there wis na danger utherwayis, nor hazard to have cassin them away, it being sik fair widder, as said is. Lykwais when the said umquill Edward wis fund with the said umquill   [1] and you and the said Swino your husband wir sent for, and brought to see thame, and to lay your hands on thame
dayis after said death and away casting, quhaire their bluid was evanished and desolved from every natural cours or caus to shie and run, the said umquill Edward bled at the collir bain or craig bane and the said   in the hand and fingers, gushing out bluid thereat to the great admiration of the beholders and revelation of the judgment of the Almytie. And by which lyk occasionis and miraculous works of God, made manifest in murders, and the murderers, whereby be many frequent occasiones brought to light, and the murderers be the sd proof brought to judgment, convicted and condemned, not onlie in this kingdom, also this countrie, but lykwayis in maist forrin Christiane kingdomis; and be so manie frequent precedentis and practising of and tuitching murderis and murdereris notourlie known, so that the foirsaid murder

[1] The gaps are in the original.

and witchcraft of the saidis persons, with the rest of their companions, through your said husbands deed, art, part, rad and counsall, is manifest and cleir to not onlie through and by the foirsaid precedents of your malice, wicked and malishis practises, by witchcraft, confessionis and declaration of the said umquill Janet Fraser, witch, revealed to her as said is, and quha wis desyrit by him to concur and assist with you to the doing thereof; but lykwayis be the declaration and revelation of the justice and judgmentis of God, through the said issueing of bluid from the bodies, qrby booth you and your said husband ar found takin, and proven in the art of your said witchcraft and murder.

Lykeas ye the said Marion, indyttit and accusit as ane common rank witch, charmer and deceaver, and quaha wer all your dayes, then xl years and more been so report and halden, bearing yourself sa,   Consulting, riving with the devill in his caus, who did change lyknis appearing to you severallie; for that ye being cuming fra Brecknon to Hildiswick, in the month of   last, quhen you wirr to be apprehendit and sent in for the foirsayid crymes to suffer, the devill there in the way, did converse and appear to you, both in your going to and frae Breckon and Hildiswick, in the lyknes of twa corbies, ane on every side of you, clos at your sides, going and happing alongis the way with you to Hildiswick, and stayid where you went, not leaving you three quarters of a mile, till Mr. Robert Ramsay overtuik you, when they came full flyght to the sey, and the   corn land and hills;   he then did challenge you anent the saidis corbies, of the cause of thair so far accompanying you, sa neir and sa far away, it not being the natuir of wyld fuillis to follow sa far, and keep pace sa neir approaching ony man or woman. Ye then did cast a glos upon it, saying they smellit bread on you, quhilk made them, (to quhom ye sayd ye was casting bread) to come,—quhilk wis onlie a lie maid by you, conceeling. At your returne they continuit with you, and conversit *ut supra*, als far back agane as scoir and threttein. As lykways you have not onlie behavid yourself as sayd is, as ane common rank witch, alwayis giving yourself to charmes, and never knowing the trew God, and quhom the truly sentifyed Chryst ar, not sa much as to learne the Lordis Prayer, nor to repeat the samen in all your lyfe time, but ar reprovit from God; has given yourself, boith saul and bodie, to serving the Devill, and bund up in him, that ye will not muster power, nor will cast off the Devill, sa mutch as to follow learning to repeat the Lordis Prayer amangist Goddis ministers and children, but ar, and has been all your dayis ane wicked, devilish, fearful and abhominable curser; quhaver ye ever cursed, ane [and] them ye disendit and wishit evil to, everie evil, seeknes, herme and death followit thereupon, throw your diabolical tongue, witchcraft and cursing. And hes ever behavit yourself as ane common witch and charmer, taker away of your nyber's profeits of their roumes, landes, cornes, grass, butter, kye, sheip, and wul, and a charmer and healer of sum, and caster of sicknesses upon uthers, and everie way living a damnable, wicked and diabolical lyff, contrarie to God and his commandments.[1] Quhilk you cannot deny, and quhairfoir you the said Marion ought and sould undergo the tryal of ane assyse, and being convictit and adjudged thairfoir to the death, and your hail landis, if any be, ye have foirfattit, and your moveabil goods escheat, and inbrought to his Majesty's use, conforme to the lawis and daylie practise of this realme . . .

[21 March, 1644. She was found guilty by the assyse of] the hail poyntis of dittay agains her, boith general and special, except theft of Thomas of Urabister not provin, and anent Edward Halcro's malt, quherein they rest clauseure,

---

[1] "Proven also Mart. Qn thay war waking her, scho speirit qr her husband wis, qn answering her speiring gains her husband, scho assertit he lay tutching her hand, and would not suffer her to confess."
—*Marginal note in the handwriting of the Moderator.*

and, They all in one voice ffylls her of the haill poyntis of dittay producit, and remittis sentens to the Judges, and dome to the dempster.

The Judges adjudges and decerns the pannell to be taken brought hence to the place of execution to the Hill of Berrie, and there wyryt at ane stak, and brunt in ashes, betwix and 2 aftirnoone, qlk Andro of Offir, dempster, gave for dome.—HIBBERT, pp. 593-602.

Orkney. *Trial of Jonet Reid.*—Intrat vpoun pannell, Jonet Reid, for the abhominable superstitioun of vsing and practeising of the Witchcraftis vndirwrittin, viz. :

Ye, the said Jonet Reid, ar indytit and accusit for airt and pairt of the contraveining of the tennour of the act of Parliament, maid be our vmquhile dread sovirane ladie, Marie, be the grace of God, Queen of Scottis, with the adwyse of the Thrie Estates, in the nynth Parliament : That, quhair they being informit of the heavie and abhominable superstitioun vsit be dyverse of the leidges of this realme, be vseing of witchcraft, sorcerie, and necromancie, and credens gevin therto in tymes bygane against the law of God ; and for awoyding and awayputting of all sik superstitioun in tyme cumming, it was statut and ordanit, be the Queenis maiestie and Thrie Estates forsaidis, That na persoun or personis, off quhatsumeuer estat, degrie, or conditioun they be of, tak vpoun hand, in any tyme therefter, to vse any maner of witchcraftis, sorceries, or necromancies, or giue thame selffis furth to haue sik craft or knowledge, thairthrow abuseand the people, vndir the paine of death : And trew it is, and of veritie, that ye, the said Jonet, hes contraveinit the tennour of the said act of Parliament, be vseing and practeising of witchcraftis, sorceries, divinatiounes, and superstitious charmeingis, and in geving zour selff furth to haue sik craft and knowledge, and in companie keiping with the devill, zour maister, at dyverse and sundry places and tymes, and thairthrow abuseand the people, in maner following: And thairfoir, and for vsing and practeising of the said abhominable superstitioun, aught and suld be adjudgit to the death, in example of vtheris to doe the lyk.

I. And in special, ye ar indytit and accusit for airt and pairt of the abhominable superstitioun, in that about aught or nyne yeiris since, William Kirknes in Pow, being bigging his bear stak, ye cam to him, and offered him ane grass, as ye callit it, but to his appearance, nothing but ane litle quantitie of quhyt moss or fogge, and baid him put it in his stack, affirmeing that it suld mak him keip the profeit of his cornis, so that none suld be abill to tak it from him, which, notwithstanding, he refusit to doe, saying that he saw no profit in it; quhairvpoun ye went away discontented.

II. Item, ye ar indytit and accusit, That about the tyme forsaid, ye being ins-woman in the said William Kirkness hous, as he was ryseing in the morneing, he hard yow say to your doghter, wha was onlie with yow in the fyrehous ye being in the meantyme drying corne with ane hott stone one ane flakkit, I am drying this corne to [the] devill; and with that word, he stepped out of the celle where he lay, and saw incontinent the stone and the whole corne ye war drying, flie throw the hous, so that thair culd be nevir ane bit of the stane, or ane pickle of the corne, be sein againe. Quhilk was done be your witchcraft and devilrie, and quhilk ye offerit in ane sacrifice to the devill your maister.

III. Item, ye ar indytit and accusit, That about aught zeiris since or thairby, Robert Sinclair of Nether Gersand, being impotent at that tyme, as he gaue it out himselff, ye gaue Margaret Sinclair, naturall dochter to the said Robert, some liquour like water in ane stoup, and directit hir to put it twa or thrie seuerall tymes in his meat, and he having suppit thairof, within ane night, or at most twa, after, he fand himselfe restorit to his wountit vigour and abilitie; and William Kirknes hearing how the said Robert was restorit, jesting with yow, askit yow how ye haid helped

Robert Sinclair his father in law? ye answerit, If he haid cum to yow befoir he was married, ye suld haue helpit him than alsweill as ye haue done now; quhilk was be your witchcraft and devilrie.

IV.—Item, ye ar indytit and accusit, That,[1] yeiris since or thairby, Robert Sinclair in Gerssand, being efter he haid married his secund wyif, sore trublit in his sleip with apparitiounes of his ffirst wyiff, which wexit him and disquietit him verie much, he was advysit be yow to goe to his first wyfis grave, and to chairge hir to ly still and truble him no moir.

V. Item, ye ar indytit and accusit, That about nine yeiris since or thairby, John Kirknes in Housgar, being heavilie diseasit, ye cam to his hous, and said to his wyif, Your husband hes the beanschaw, and gif ye will I can help him: Quhairvpoun his wyif cam to him, and desyrit him to ryis, and cum to the fyre hous, quhich he did at his wyifis desyr, and ye said to him, Guidman, if ye will, I sall charme yow of the boneshaw: And he consenting, ye gropped all the joyntes of one of his sydes with her [your] hand, and spake certain wordis ower him, and causit Katherin Kirknes, his servant woman for the tyme, repeat everie word efter yow, at your directioun, in presens of his wyif and servant woman.

VI. Item, ye ar indytit and accusit, That,   yeiris since or thairby, ye charmed Elspeth Sinclair, spous to William Kirknes, of the boneshaw (as ye callit it); and that ye vsit besyd wordis, nyne blue stones, quhilk shoe did put in ane vessell with water, twitching her joyntis with each of the severall stones, which ye keipit in your lap, and went fourth with; and efter washed her with the water that was in the wessell in which the stones lay.

VII. Item, ye are indytit and accusit, That,   yeiris since or thairby, ye charmed Henrie Sowie, servitour to Alexander Linklater in Housgar, of the boneshaw; and that ye

[1] Blank in the original.

causit ane sone of the said Alexander repeat the charme after yow; and that ye vsit water and stones, as is aforesaid, whilk was alreddie confest be yow; and the said Henrie, being vnabill to stirr out of his bed for the space of fourtein dayis befoir, recoverit his health, and was abill for his work within twa dayis efter, as ye haid said the charme ower him; whilk was done by your witchcraft and devilrie.

VIII. Item, ye ar indytit and accusit, That,   yeiris since or thairby, that ane of Alexander Linklatteris children in Housgar being leane and ill lyke, ye said that the child haid the hart cake; and that gif ye pleasit ye wold cast the hart cake, and sie what wold become of him; which ye did in this maner: Ze took ane pott with water in it, and laid the tonges athwart the mouth of the pott, and than laid ane codd aboue the tonges, and set the child on it; thairefter ye took ane seif and set [it] on the childis head, and set ane cogge full of water in the seive, and then laid ane woll scheir on the coggis mouth, and then ye took lead and put it in ane iroun lamp, and meltit it, and powrit it throw the boul of the scheir into the water thrie severall tymes devining throw the lead whither the child wold recover or not; and quhen ye haid done all, ye gaue the child ane drink of the said water, and said he wold be weill; [but as yit the child is not].

IX. Item, ye are indyted and accusitt That,   yeiris since or thairby, ye vsit the haill particular charme abouewritten, in all poyntis, with ane child of Robert Sinclairis in Nether Gersand.

X. And generallie, ye are indytit and accusit for airt and pairt of the vsing and practeising of witchcraftis, sorceries, divinatiounes and charmes, as particularlie abouewritten; and in geving your selff furth to haue sik craft and knowledge, thairthrow abuseand the people; and that by your cursingis and imprecatiounes, ye wronge both man and beast. Quhilk evillis ar brocht to pas be the power and working of the devill your maister: And thairfoir ye aught and suld vndirly the law, and be adjudgit to the death thairfoir, in example of vtheris to doe the lyk.

Abbotsford Club Miscellany, vol. I., pp. 181-185.

Trial of Jonet Rendall, 1629.—In the ffirst ye the said Jonet ar Indyttit and accusit for airt and pairt of the abominable supperstitioun and suppersitious abusing and deceiveing of the people and for practeising of the wicked and devilish pointis of witchcraft and sorcerie done by yow in maner at the tymes and in the places efter specifiet and in geving yourselff furth to have sick craft and knowledge thairthrow abuseing the people, To Wit, Twentie yeiris since and mair ye being above the hill of Rendall having soucht charitie and could not have it the devill appeirit to you, Quhom ye called Walliman, claid in quhyt cloathis with ane quhyt head and ane gray beard, And said to you He sould learne yow to win almiss be healling of folk and quhasoever sould geve yow almiss sould be the better ather be land or sea. And these yt gave yow not almiss sould not be heallled and ye haveing trustit in him and entering in pactioun with him, He promeisit to yow that quhasoever sould refus yow almiss and quhatever ye craved to befall thame sould befall thame, and thairefter went away in the air from you, Quhairby ye practeised many and sindrie pointis of witchcraft and devilrie and speciallie the pointis following.

Item ye are Indyttit and accusit for cuming fyve yeiris since or yrby to Manss Work in Windbrek his Wyff and haveing askit almiss of hir and sho refusand ye said sho sould repent it, and within aught dayes efter ane of his ky fell over the craig and deit be your witchcraft and devilrie conforme to the pactioun maid betwix yow and your walliman, and within thrie dayes ye being reprovit be the said Manss wyff ye said that if sho sould geve yow the wyt of it wors sould cum of it and that she sould ather run upoun the Sea or then ane war cast sould befall hir. Quha being quholl then deit within thrie dayes be your witchcraft and devilrie.

Item ye ar Indyttit and accusit for cuming at Candlmes last to Edward Gray in Howakow hous and shakin your blanket as it wer aganes the hous and Patrick Gray his sone having cum furth and seing yow cald his father and fearing your evill went to the barne and geve yow ane look corne and on monday nicht thairefter Tua meiris deit both at once in the stable and that the said Patrick took seiknes the same hour he saw yow and dwyned thrie quarteris of ane yeir and deit, and ye being send foir befoir his death to see him, He being dead befoir and haveing laid his death on you, how shone ye cam in the cors having lyin ane guid space and not having bled any, Immediatlie bled mutch bluid as ane suir token that ye was the author of his death.

Item ye ar Indyttit and accusit for cuming To William Work in Efaday his hous on Hallowevin four yeiris sene or yr by and knocking at his door They wold not let yow in nor geve yow lodgeing Quha depairting murmuring and miscontent his wyff pairtit with child upon the morne.

Item ye are Indyttit and accusit for that in bear seid tyme the last yeire ye cuming to Johne Spence in Uppettoun his hous and the said Johns Wyff being calling ane calff to the grass ye cam in and was angrie that sho sould have called out the calff quhen ye com in and turneing yow twys about on the floor ye went out and Immediatlie the calff being ane yeir old took seiknes and deit be your witchcraft and sorcerie.

Item ye ar Indyttit and accusit for that on Santt Thomas evin four yeiris sene or yr by ye cuming to Williame Scott in Poldrit his hous and knocking thrie severall tymes at the doore and ane hour betwix every tyme and ye not gettin in went away murmuring. Thrie dayes efter the guid wyff becam mad and four beastis deit the same yeir and ane ox fell over the craig and deit of the fall.

Item ye ar Indyttit and accusit for that on Candlmesevin fyve yeiris sene ye cam to Gilbert Sandie in Isbister his hous and saught ane plack of silver in almis fra him for his mearis that they might be weill over the yeir, as ye said David Henrie haid done that day, Quha said to yow that he haid nather silver corne nor meall to spair bot baid his wyff geve yow thrie or four stokis of kaill and bene gane away The said Gilbertis wyff followed yow with the kaill but ye wold not tak thame. And upoun the second day efter his best hors standing on the floor becam wood and felled himself and deit and the thrid night thairefter his best meir deit.

Item ye ar Indyttit and accusit for cuming to the said Gilbertis hous in spring tyme last and the said Gilbertis wyff wald not let yow in, and ye going away took the proffeit of hir milk be your witchcraft and sorcerie.

Item ye ar Indyttit and accusit for yt ye cam to Johne Bewis hous in Waa tua yeiris sene and sought almiss and got nane, and ye said he sould repent it, and about noone his best kow haveing fallen in ane myre and tane out be him his wyff and servands sho wald not stand, and ye cuming thair put thrie earis of bear having first spit on thame, in the kowis mouth and said to them that cam to bear hir home that they neidit not mak yt travell and ane littell quhyll efter the kow being almost dead and not able to draw ane foot to hir, rais with [out] help and gaid home be your witchcraft and devilrie.

Item ye ar Indyttit and accusit for that fyve or sex yeiris sene, ye cam to David Quoynameikill his fathers hous at the making of his yull banket and got almis and yt they wold not sufferre yow to abid all night qlk ye tald to Margaret Alebuster that they refusit yow ludging and said it was guid to wit if ever the guidman of the hous sould mak ane other Yull bankett and within ffyftene days contractit seikness and deit be yor witchcraft and devilrie.

Item ye are Indyttit and accusit for yt thrie yeiris sene or yr by ye cam to David Quoynameikill motheris hous and got na almis and she being feared that evill sould befall hir as did to otheris befoir night—she fellit hirselff upoun the lintell stane of hir byre and deit within thrie dayes and her servand man also be your witchcraft & devilrie.

Item ye ar Indyttit and accusit for cuming to Michaell Firthis hous in Alebuster in Spring tyme last, and getting no almis becaus the milk was suppit, ye said ye might haue keipit milk to me, and they said they knew not of hir cuming, And the next day efter ane calff deit and now quhen he was convoying yow to Birssay He askit yow at the Slap of Birssay if ye knew anything of the death of his calff ye ansrit haid he not bene so cald to yow nane of your calffis sould not have deit this yeir.

Item ye ar Indyttit and accusit that sex yeiris sene or yr by that Johne Rendall in Brek haid tua calffis lying on the grein and ye askit giff both these calffis wer his and said they wer anew for the first year and ane of the calffis deit befoir nicht be your witchcraft and devilrie.

Item ye are Indyttit and accusit for cuming to Johne Turk in Midland his hous about Witsunday last to get almis and haveing gottin ane drink of new aill ye was not content and befoir ye was tua pair buttis from the hous the aill left working and the said Johne haveing sought yow ane day or tua efter brought yow to his hous againe and took [yow] into his seller and ye spitit amongst the aill and said ye sould warrand him got silver for everie drop of it.

Item ye ar Indyttit and accusit for yt aucht yeiris sene ye hanting to Andro Matches hous in Sundiehous, he wantit the proffeit of his milk and having complenit To Sir Johne Buchanan Shreff for the tyme of how ye met the said Andro upoun the morne and said he sould repent yesterdayes work and the same day ane ox Strick of his deit and about thrie quarteris of ane year efter The said Andro haveing cum to Evie to the Session of the Kirk to complene of yow, ye met with him thrie dayes efter and said to him He was alwayes dealling with you and complening yow and

Trials. 107

and yt he sould repent it, And thrie dayes efter the said Andro becam mad and ye being send for, and how shoone ye cam to his hous he becam better and fell on sleip and quhen ye haid gottin meat befoir ye teastit it ye spat thrys over your left shulder and the said Androis wyff fearing ye haid bene doing moir evill strak yow, and ye said let me alone for yor guidman wilbe weill.

Item ye ar Indyttit and accusit for yt four yeiris sene ye cam to Manss Quoynameikills hous and soucht almis and got nane at yt tyme, Bot his mother haveing promeised to geve yow milk qwhen hir kow calved ye cam againe that same day the kow calved and soucht almis bot she wald geve yow nane, And ye said ye put me ay of, geve me yt ye promeised me for now your kow is calved and said she sould have ather mair or less milk or ye cam againe and about aucht days efter the kow deit, be your witchcraft & devilrie.

Item ye ar Indyttit and accusit for yt at alhallowmes bygane ane yeir ye cam to the said Manss and sought ane peice colop quha wald geve you nane and ye said befoir ye cam againe he sould have colopis to geve and within ffourtene dayes efter his best ox deit be yor witchcraft & devilrie.

Item ye ar Indyttit and accusit for yt in winter last ye cam to the sd Manss hous and sought ait meall, and he refusand yow, ye said he sould have mair or less or ye cam againe and fourtene dayes efter his kill with aittis took fyre & brunt be your witchcraft & devilrie.

Item ye ar Indyttit and accusit for yt of your awne confessioun efter ye met your Walliman upoun the hill ye cam to Williame Rendalls hous quha haid ane seik hors and promeised to haill him if he could geve yow tua penneys for everie foot, And haveing gottin the silver ye hailled the hors be praying to your Walliman, Lykeas ye have confest that thair is nather man nor beast sick that is not tane away be the hand of God bot for almis ye ar able to cur it be praying to your Walliman, and yt thair is nane yt geves yow almis bot they will thryve ather be sea or land if ye pray to yor Walliman.

And generallie ye the said Jonet Rendall alias Rigga ar Indyttit and accusit for airt & pairt of the said abominable superstitioun and superstitious abuseing and disceaveing of the people and in useing and practeising of witchcraft and sorcerie and in gevin yor selff furth to have sutche craft and knawledge thairby abusing the people and sua reput & halden. And yr foir and for the pointis of dittay committit be yow In maner above writtin aucht and sould underly the law and be adjudgit to the death for the same and In example of otheris to do the lyk And yor guids and gear esheit & Inbroucht to his majesties use conforme to the act of p'liament and comon law and daylie practeis observit in sick caissis.

CURIA VICECOMITATUS et JUSTICIARIÆ de ORKNEY et ZETLAND tenta apud Birssay in aula ibid., per honorabilem virum magistrum Joannem Dick vicecomitem et Justiciarium deputat dict. vicecomitatus undecimo die mensis Novembris 1629.

Curia legitime affirmata.

The qlk day the sd sheref deput chusit Mr Harie Aitkin in[terim] Clerk, Rob. Scollay in. procuratour fishall, Thomas Young in. Officer.

Compeirit Wm Scollay procuratour fishall and producit the dittayes desyring thame to be red and the pannell accusit yrupoun.

The pannell present confest that Walliman cam to hir first in Nicoll Jockis hous in Halkland and sho maining yt sho was poor and haid nothing. He said to hir yt sho sould leive be almiss and that thair was nather man nor beast seik that wer not deadlie be the hand of God bot she getting almiss and praying to Walliman he wald haill thame, and if she got no almiss he wald be angrie and mak thair beastis die.

Confest the second point of dittay anent Manss Works wyff that sho sd sho sould repent it and yt Walliman gared the kow fall over the craig, and eft. sho was reprovit yt Walliman gared the sd Manss wyff die.

Confest the thrid point that the corne sho got was bot shillingis and yt sho was not content and yt Walliman slew the meiris and the man and as he promeised he was trew to hir.

Confest the fourt point that sho was miscontent that Wm Work wald not geve hir lodging and yt Walliman was angrie at it and gared his wyff pairt with chyld.

Confest the fyft point and yt Walliman gared the calff die.

Confest the sext point that they wold not let hir in and got na almiss and Walliman was angrie at it and gared his wyff run mad and the beast die.

Confest the sevent point yt Gilbert Sandie wald geve hir nothing and yt Walliman wrought conforme to the dittay.

Confest the aucht point and yt Walliman took away the proffeit of the ky.

Confest the nynt point yt sho put bear in the kowis mouth bot dennyis sho spat on it.

Confest the tent point yt sho sd to Mart Alebuster conforme to the dittay, and yt Walliman keipit promeis.

Confest the ellevint point that sho got no almiss fra David Quoynameikills wyff.

Confest the twelff point anent the calffis that sho got na almiss and giff they deit Walliman did it.

Confest the threttin point anent John Turk's aill that it was bot little she got and yr foir Walliman took away the proffeit of it.

Confest the ffourtene point anent Andro Matchis.

Confest the fyftene point anent Manss Quoynameikills

wyff and yt sho sould have ather mair or less milk or she cam againe becaus sho got na almiss.

Denyit the sextene point anent Manss quoynameikills ox.

Denyit the sevintene point.

Confest the hailling of Wm Rendalls horss.

Confest the rest of yt point of dittay.

Dennyit the generall.

The pfishall desyrit that the pannell myt be put to the tryell of ane assyss.

The pannell present could alege nothing in the contrair.

Assisa.

[Fourteen names given.]

That the assyss was laufulie sworne and admittit but objection of the pannell. The pfishall askit actis and protestit for error.

The procuratour fishall producit Manss Inerair, Manss Work, Wm. Work, Jon. Spence, Wm. Scottie, Gilbert Sandie, Jon. Sandie, Manss Wood, David Quoynameikill, Michaell Firth, Jon. Turk, Alexr Matches, Andro Matches, and Manss Quoynameikill in witnesses.

The Assyss passing out of Judgment chusit Hew Halcro chancelar.

Manss Wood and Gilbert Sandie deponed yt they wer send for to bear home the kow bot Jonet Rigga was cuming fra the kow befoir they cam yr.

Michaell Firth in Alebuster deponed yt quhen he was cuming to Birssay with hir out of the slap sho confest to him conforme to the dittay that if he haid geven hir almiss his calff haid not deit.

Andro Matches depones that sho spak these words conforme to his point of dittay and that these thingis befell him.

Manss Quoynameikill depones anent the ox that sho said he sould have colopis anew to geve befoir sho cam againe and yt he sould have ather moir or less ait maill or she cam againe and yt the event followit conforme to hir words and dittay bot will not tak it upoun his conscience yt she did it.

The assyss reenterit and in Judgment all in ane voice be the mouth of the chanr. ffyles the pannell of the haill speciall pointis of dittay conforme to hir confessioun, and in the twelff fourtene and sextene pointis conforme to the probatioun And in the generall that sho was ane disceaver of the people and gave hirselff furth to have knawledge to do evill, and if ever she promeised evill, evill befell, and reput the haldin ane common witch. And remittis sentence to the Judge and dome to the Dempster.

HEW HALCRO.

The Judge acceptis the determinatioun of the assyss and ordaines the pannell to be tane be the lockman and convoyed to the place of executioun with hir hands bund behind hir bak and worriet at ane stoup to the dead and brunt in assis. Qlk Robert Sinclair dempster in Birssay benorth gave for dome.

From a note-book of the late George Petrie, Sheriff Clerk of Orkney, preserved in the library of Society of Antiquaries of Scotland, Edinburgh.

Orkney. *Trial of Elspeth Reoch,* 1616.—Curia Justiciariæ Vicecomitatus de Orknay tenta apud Kirkwall in nova domo prope Palatium de Yeardis ibidem per honorabilem virum Henricum Stewart de Carlougie Justiciarum ac Vicecomitem deputatum dicti Vicecomitatus die duodecimo Martii 1616.

Curia tenta et legitime affirmata.

The quhilk day anent the dittay criminall gevin in and persewit at the instance of Robert Coltart procurator fiscal of the said sheriffdom Aganes Elspeth Reoch dochter to umquhill Donald sumtyme pyper to the Earl Reoch of Cathnes ffor certane poyntis of dittay of witchcraft underwritten That is to say In the first for airt part using committing and practising of the abominable and divilesch cryme of witchcraft in giveing ear and credite to the Illusiounes of the Devell Quhairby scho fenyeit hirselff dumb And illudit and deceaveit his Majesteis subjectis in maner underwritten viz In the first for that sho confest that quhen shoe wes ane young las of tuelf yeiris of age or therby and haid wandereit out of Cathnes quher sho wes borne to Lochquhaber ye cam to Allane McKeldowies wyfe quha wes your ant And haveing remaneit with her be the space of aucht weekes quho duelt with hir husband in a Loch That she upon ane day being out of the loch in the contrey and returning and being at the Loch syd awaiting quhen the boit sould fetch hir in That thair cam tua men to her ane cled in blak and the uther with ane grein tartane plaid about him And that the man with the plaid said to her she wes ane prettie And he wald lerne her to ken and sie ony thing she wald desyre The uther man said she wald nocht keep counsell and foirbaid him He ansuerit he wald warrand hir And she being desyrous to knaw said how could she ken that And he said Tak ane eg and rost it And tak the sweit of it thre Sondayis And with onwashin handis wash her eyes quhairby she sould sie and knaw ony thing she desyrit And to persuade hir he directit her to ane aunttis hous of hir awin quha wes ane widow that haid ane oy that wes with chyld to ane uther wyffis husband onknawen to ony And quhen she cam she sould luik in hir face and tell hir she is with bairne to ane uther wyfes husband And sa within a short space therefter going to hir Aunttis hous how sone she saw the young woman she said she wes with bairne as the man had said to hir And shoe denying said to hir she wald repent it within a short space Thairefter the young woman considering that she knew hir estait desyrit sum cure at hir that she micht part with bairne Quha ansuerit she could give her nane Bot remembering that she wes cum in to Allane McKeldowies hous that day that the tua men came to hir That he haveing speirit at her quhat men thois wer that wer with hir at the Loch syd And quhat they haid said to hir And she denying he foirbaid you to fear For they wer freindis of his quha wald do hir no hurt And that he knew quhat they said to hir So she remembring that Allane had skill she said to the young woman that he wald help hir Quherupoun she and she gaid together to the Loch And spak with him quha refusit to give hir onything to slay the bairne And thairefter within tua yeir she bure her first bairne quhilk wes gottin be ane James Mitchaell at the Kirk of Murthlie upoun Spey within Balveny And being delyverit in hir sisteris hous the blak man cam to her that first came to hir at Lochquhaber And callit him selff ane farie man quha wes sumtyme her kinsman callit Johne Stewart quha wes slane be Mc Ky at the doun going of the soone And therfor nather deid nor leiving bot wald ever go betuix the heaven and the earth quha delt with you tua nychtis and wald never let her sleip persuading hir to let him ly with hir wald give you a guidly fe And to be dum for haveing teacheit her to sie and ken ony thing she desyrit He said that gif she spak gentlemen wald trouble hir and gar hir give reassounes for hir doings Quhairupoun she mycht be challengeit and hurt And upoun the thrid nycht that he com to hir she being asleip and laid his hand upoun hir breist and walkint her And thairefter semeit to ly with her And upoun the morrow she haid no power of hir toung nor could nocht speik quhairthrow hir brother dang hir with ane branks quhill she bled becaus she wald nocht speik and pat ane bow string about hir head to gar her speik And thairefter tuik her three severall tymes Sondayis to the kirk and prayit for hir Fra the quhilk tyme she still continewit dumb going about and deceaveing the people Synding telling and foir shawing thame quhat they had done and quhat they sould do And that be the secund sicht grantit to hir in maner foirsaid She saw Robert Stewart sone naturall to umquhill Patrik sumtyme earl of Orkney with Patrik Traill to quhom she was with bairne and certane utheris with towis about thair craigis in Edmond Callendaris hous at ther efternoones drink befoir the Earl of Caithnes cuming to the cuntrey And that be plucking of the herb callit Merefow quhilk causis the nose bleid He haid taucht hir to tell quhatsover sould be speirit at hir Be sitting on hir rycht knie and pulling and pilling it betwix hir mid finger and thumb And saying of *In nomine patris filii et spiritus sancti* be vertue quherof sche haweit ane bairne to Magnus Sinclair in Sorne at the desyre of his wyf At quhilk tyme on yule day she confest the devell quhilk she callis the farie man lay with hir At quhilk tyme he bade hir leave Orkney and go home to her awin contrey becaus this countrey was Priestgone quhilk he exponit that ther wes our mony Ministeris in it And gif she taryit she wald be hurt And forder for airt part useing hanting and conversing with the Devell at diverse and sindrie tymes and at severall partis &c &c as at mair lenth is contenit in the saidis dittayis The lenth is contenit in the saidis dittayis The said procuratour fiscall being personally present and the said defendar being lykwayis personalie present quha enterit on pannall haveing no lawfull caus quhy she sould nocht pas to the knawlege of ane assyse Quhairupoun the procuratour fiscall desyring the dittay is to be put to the knawledge of ane assyse and the pannall to be accusit therupoun Efter accusatioun the said Elspeth confest the haill poyntis of dittay abone-writtin And therfor the Judg remittit the dittayis to the knawledge of ane assyse quham he ordanit to be callit.

Nomina Assisæ.

[Sixteen names given.]

Quhilk persones of assyse being receavit admittit and sworne but lawfull objectioun of the pannall and removeit out of Judgement nominat and ellectit William Bannatyne of Gairsay chancellar And efter dew deliberatioun haid anent the dittayis produceit and haill poyntis therof And reentering on judgement agane the haill assyse be the mouth of the said chancellar fyllit the said Elspeth of the haill poyntis of dittay abonespecifeit And remittit sentence to the Judge and dome to the Dempster Quhilk deliberatioun the Judge than present acceptit And decernit and ordanit the said Elspeth Reoch to be tane. be the lockmane to the place of executioun betuix and thrie efter none and to be wirryet at ane staik quhill she be deid And therefter to be burnt in assis Quhilk the Dempster gave for dome.—*Maitland Club Miscellany*, pp. 187-191.

Sanday, Orkney. *Trial of Marrione Richart*, 1633.— Examination of the Charges of Witchcraft and Sorcery against Marrione Richart or Layland before the Kirk-Session of Sanday.

The Dittayis giwen in to our Sessioun off Sanday, the 17 day of March, Imvic and threttie and thrie zeiris [1633] wpon Marrione Richart [or] Layland, of Wichcraft.

The quhilk day, annent the tryell of James Fischer, the said Marrione's oy, that quhair the said James Fischer confessit and told, befoir the sessioun, that wpon ane sax or sevin zeir since, that the said James being keiping Magnus Smyth his suyne, and going wpe along ane old house callit the House of Howing Greinay, the quhilk old howse being standing woyd and weast, and the wather being cold and stormie, the said James went in to the said old house to flee from ane cold schowr; and quhen he cam in to the old house, he saw the said Marrioun, his guiddame, siting within the fornameit old howse, accompanied with Cattrein Miller; and deponit that he did sie ane blak man siting betwixt the said Catrein and the said Marrione; and deponit, that the said Catrein cryit fearcelie, Cause take him, for he will tell wpon ws. The said Marrioun ansuerit and said, Let him allone, for he will not be beleiwit. Item, it is deponed be Margrett Smieton, spous to James Fell, that that night that ye wer in the stockis, Catherine Miller said to Marioun Layland, The pleague of God wpon thy oy, for gif yea had done that quhilk I bad ye, he hadd nott beine trowbling ws now.

Lykwayis, the said Marrioun Layland did wasch the feit of James Dauidsones cat into his bait water, becaus he could not get no fisch that zeir, thinking thairby and saying, that the said James in tyme comming wold get more fisch in respect off hir work in wasching off the catis feit into his bait watter; and quhen scho had waschin the cat thairin, did take the water quheirin the cat was waschin, and did cast it after him· quhen he did go to the sea.

Lykewayis, the xxiiij day of March, Magnus Smyth deponit, that the boy presentlie wpone the morning therafter told the said Magnus that he did sie the dewill, and told him the quhilk faschioun. Lykwayes, the same day Dauid Jock and his wyff tryitt and confessit that wpon fyve or sax zeir since, that the said Marrioun cam to the said Dauid Jok his house, and the said Dauid was going to the sea, and was making mone that he had not luck to get fisch that zeir : The said Marrioun ansuerit and said, that that might be eassillie mendit, and callit for the thing that geid about the fyre, quhilk was the cat, and said that scho wold wasch the cat his head and feit into the watter quherin the bait was to be keipit, and said that scho wold take that watter and cast itt about him and wpon him, and into his sea caschie, and into his bait coubbie, and quhen he cam to the sea he schould get fisch.

Farther, it is deponit be Margret and Elspet Sandisones, that the said Elspet vpon fyue or sax zeir since, contrakit ane deadlie disease, in so farre that scho was senceles and myndles for ane long speace; the said Marrione cam to the said Elspetis house, and made ane watter, quhilk scho callis ane remeddie for forspeaking; the said Marrioun tuik watter into ane round coupe, and went out into the byre, and tuik sumthing out off hir pursse, like wnto great salt, and did put it into the watter, and did spit thrie severall tymes into the watter; and scho confesit hir selff quhen scho had done so, scho *aundit in bitt*, quhilk is ane Nourne terme, and to exponit into right languag, is alse mikill as scho did blew hir breath thairin, and sent it in to the woman, with the servant woman off the house, and directit that the woman should be waschin hand and face thairin, and scho should be restorit to hir health againe. This the said Marrioun confesit befoir the sessioun; and it is grantit be the woman that the watter was made wnto, that the said Marrioun said wnto the lass, that iff ewer the lass reueillit it againe scho should never thryue, and so schune after that the lass reueillit the wordis, scho deit.

Quhilk day it is confest be Robert Drewer and his wyff, that threttein zeir since, the said Marrioun and Robert Drewer was duelling both at ane house and ane biging; that thair was ane powr woman that was trauelling of chyld in the said Marriones house, and desyrit ane soupe off milk from the said Marrioun, quhilk in no wayis the said Marrioun wold grant, the powre woman sent in to the said Robertis house and got ane soup off milk from his wyff, and immediatlie thairefter the said Robert his wyff lossit hir proffit of hir haill milk; quhairfor the said Robert Dreweris wyff cam in to the said Marrioun Layland, and did lament for her profeit that scho wantit. The said Marrioun ansuerit the woman and said, Goe thy way to the sea, and tell nyne beares off the sea come in, that is to say, nyne waues off the watter, and let ane off the nyne goe back againe; and the nixt thair thairafter take thrie luiffullis off that watter, and put within thy stowpe, and quhen thou comes heame put it within thy kirne, and thow will get thy profeit agane.

The last day of March.

Compeirit Helin Hamiltoun, spouse to James Keith, and deponit, that scho and hir haill fammillie was straitit with drouth for the space off xx dayis ore ane mounth, that no drink could quench thar dreuth; quhairfor the said Helin and her husband alledgit the said Marrioun for the great thrist that thay had. Wpon ane Sunday the said Marrioun cam to the said Helins house, and had ane muchkin off small-aill with hir into ane chapping can, and offerit it to the said Heline and hir famillie to drink; and the said Helin refusit to drink it, bot the said Marrion wrgit it more and more vpon hir, and said that scho had ane sonsie hand and hir mother befoir hir day, and made euerie ane off them to drink thairoff; and immediatlie thairafter thair thrist was easit, and the heauie wycht that was wpon them was easit during the time of their thrist and dreuth.

The samen day, Williame Fothringhame, benorth, deponit be him, that the said Marrioun cam to his house to get almis, and his wyff not being at leasur to giwe her almis, scho went to the dore, and did say, going to the dore, that scho should losse alse mikill schortlie; and aucht dayis after that his best cow diet.

Quhilk day, deletit by Margret Thomsone spouse to James Rolosay, to James Cok in Lopnes, Nicoll King and Magnus Skea, quhilk are thrie elderis off our sessioun, that the said Marrioun cam to Stronsay, to the said Margretis house, and the said Margret had nyne ky quhilk was not riddin; and scho said to hir, Giwe me almis, and befoir this day fyftein dayis ilk kow in zour aucht sall be riddin; quhilk almis scho gave hir, and befoir that day aught dayis, ilk kow that scho had was riddin.

The 7 day off Appryll 1633.

Quhilk day, annent the dittayis of Wichcraft given in to the sessioun, when Catrein Miller compeirit, Hew Peace and Wrsalay Fea, his spouse, and deponit, that wpon ane sax zeir since, that the said Vrsalay wantit the profeit off hir milk, and the said Wrsalay sent hir servant woman and milkit the said Cattrein Milleris kow, and did put it into her kirne; and immediatlie quhen scho kirnit the milk, scho got ix markis butter, quhair befoir, off alse mikill milk, alse mony dayis milk, alse mony mealtitis off milk, during the time that scho wantit hir profit, did not get bot tua markis butter; and quhen scho had the best, scho got not bot tua markis butter ay and quhill that scho got the milk off her cow; and four and xx houris after the said Wrsalay contrakit ane deadlie disease, quhilk contenint for the space of sax weikis; and at the end off the sax weikis, the said Marrione cam to the said Wrsalay and desyrit ane drink off milk from the kirne, and said iff scho got it scho should get hir health, and scho gave hir ane drink off milk, and scho was presentlie better off hir disease, and losit the profit off hir milk, and wantis it as zitt.

Farther deponit, be Margaret Orrok, laughfull daughter to William Orrock, that the said William had ane horse quhilk was seik; the said Catrein bad the said Margret get thrie sundrie sortis off fillneris, and put them within ane siwe, and sift them ouer the bak of the horse quhilk was seik, and he wold be haill.

The 14 day off Appryll 1633.

Deponit be Barbaray Sinclair, spouse to the said William Orrock, that scho had ane kow that was standing haill in to the byre, and the said Catrein cam in to the said Barbarayis house to puik sum bair, and presentlie the kow fell seik; quhen scho geid away with the corne that scho was knoking, and that word did rys that the cow was seik, the said Catrein cam to the house; and quhen scho cam in and sau the cow, scho was restorit to health agane, and did eat hir meat weill enugh.

The 19 day off Appryll.

Deponit be Margret Browne, spouse to William Flet, that quhair the said Margret discordit with Catreine Miller, the said Margret contrakit ane deadlie diseas; and scho said to the said Margret, "evill might thow put the yeir aff the;" thairafter scho contrakit ane senslesnes quilk continuit for the space of ane halff yeir; and at the halff yeiris end, the said Margret cam to hir, and the said Catrein tuik her by the hand, and immediatlie got hir health, and ay since was weill.

The samen day compeirit Catrein Sowents, and deponit befoir the sessioune, that the said Catrine Miller wrongit hir, in respect that scho faund fault with hir, becaus scho did take keall out off hir maisteris yaird, and hir daughter did tak keall out off the yaird, and did goe heome to Catrine Milleris house with the keall, and told hir mother that the said Kaitrine Souanes fand fault with hir for takeing away of the keall; the said Catrine Miller sent hir daughter bak to the house with the keall, and did cast the keall upon the said Catrine Sowenes breist, being nurisch to John Browne in the tyme, and presentlie scho losit hir milk for the speace of xiiij dayis; and at the isschow off the xiiij dayis, the said Catrine Miller cam to the house quhair the nurisch was, and told the guidwyff off the house that scho had dreamit, that iff scho wold giwe hir daughter almis, the nurisch showld get hir milk againe; and quhen scho got almis, scho get hir milk againe alse weill as it was befoir.

The samen day compeirit Dauid Peace, and deponit, that the said Catrine Miller had ane sone keiping his ky, and becaus that he did put away the boy from the ky, scho said that he should rew it, and immediatlie ane off the ky dieit, and schort after, the rest dieit also.

The 21 day off Appryll.

Deponit be James Fea, bailzie, that the said Catrine Miller had ane sone keiping Johne Broune his ky and guidis, and the boy was put from the guidis ; and scho did curse and pray ewill for the guidis, and therefter the most pairt of them dieit, and the rest that liewit did neuer guid, nor zit yield milk, since the boy ged from them. Farther, it is deponit be Wrsalay Fea, that the said Catrein Miller cam into Hew Peace hir husbandis house, and did pray ewill for Jon Brounes guidis, and said, " God, let his guidis newer thryue better nor hir sone did."

Quhilk day deponit be Jennet Fothringham, spouse to John Peace, younger, that quhair the said Jennet was angrie with hir for comming so earlie ilk moirning to hir guidmotheris house befoir the sone ryseing, presentlie the said Jennet falis in to ane extraordinarie diseas, so that scho might not goe out off hir guidmotheris house in to hir awin house, quhilk was both closse togidder, bot did creip wpon handis and feit quhill scho cam to hir bed ; and the said Catrine cam in to hir and did lay hir hand upon hir head, and did cause give hir ane sowpe off milk, and scho grew also weill and in also guid health as ewer scho was befoir ; and all this was dune within the speace of tua houris.

Farther deponit be Williame Roy, elder, that the said Williame discordit with hir, and scho did strik him upon the back, betuixt the shoulderis, with hir hand, and presentlie the power off his body was takin away, in so farre that he could not no duetie off ane man touardis his wyff, quhair tua nightis befoir he was alse apt and abill for his wyff as ever he was befoir ; and never since the discord was weill as he should be.

Abbotsford Club Miscellany, pp. 150-156.

[In the record of her trial which follows her examination the same charges are produced against her with the addition of the following.]

Attour, ye are indyted and accuised for airt and part of the said abominable superstition, in that ye cam to Stronsay about tua or three yeires since, in simer, and asking almis fra Andro Couper, skipper of ane bark, he said to yow, "Away, wich, carling, devil, a farthing ye noll fa"; quhairvpoun ye departed very offendit, and incontinently he going to sie, the bark being vnder saill, he ran mad, and wold have luppin over burd, an his sone seing him, gat him in his armes, and held; quhervpon the seiknes imediatly left him, and his sone ran mad; and Thomas Patersone seing him tak the madness, and the father to turne weill, ane dog being in the bark, took the dogg and bledded him vpon the soné his shoulders, and therafter keist the said dog mad, quhairby these in the bark wer saifed; quhilk being done, all the doggers at the sch[ore] . . . [*torn in MS.*] landlyeris for feir gaue yow abundantly; quhilk all wes done be your witchcraft and [divelrie]: Quhilk ye cannot deny.

[She was sentenced to be worried at a stake and afterwards burnt to ashes.]

[On the back of the dittay against Marion Richart mention is made of a woman "that took girss and baik a bannok, and give it to the goodman of Papa his grieve, quha deit; and the dog that got the bannok deit. The bannok wes for keiping thair profite."

"Elen Forster can mend baith the heartcake and beanschaw, and put down horss to the goodman of Langskaill."]

Abbotsford Club Miscellany, pp. 161, 163.

Orkney. *Trial of Agnes Scottie*, 1616.—Agnes Scottie was charged "with committing and practiseing the devilishe and abominable cryme of witchcraft in that she, vpoun ane Sonday befoir the sone rysing, about fastings-evin, came to ane wall besyde James Corrigillis hous, and thair wasch[ed] hir face and certane partis of her claythis; and Robert Gadie persaveing hir, quha wes servant to the said James, contractit presentlie ane trembling and shuddering in his flesh, tuik seiknes, and thairefter dyit.

... Item, for that seven yeiris syne or thairby, sche haveing discordit with vmquhill William Tailzeouris sister, quha comin to reprove hir for hir evill speiches aganes hir sister, in quhais face she spat, being on a Sonday,—the said William immediatlie thairefter conceaveit a great fear and trembling in his flesch, contractit seiknes, and dyit on Weddinsday thairefter. Item, for that Nicoll Smyth havein takin ane cottage fra the gudman of Brek, quhilk wes in hir possession, and haveing transportit his cornes thair, she cam about hallowmes, being washing hir claithes, and laid thame on his corne, and nocht on hir awin, and set ane cog full of watter in the said Nicollis way, quha in the cuming by cust ouir the samen, thairefter contractit ane great seiknes. His vmquhill master, callit Mans Matthes, cumand to reprove hir for his manes seiknes, efter she haid tuckit him and given him mony injurious wordis, he conceaveit ane great fear and trembling, contractit seiknes, and within sevin dayis thairefter dyit."—ROGERS, vol. iii. p. 298.

Amidst various suspicious proceedings, wherein washing herself and her clothes were included, she "past the boundis of hir ground, and thair sat doun plaiting hir feit betuix the merchis."—DALYELL, p. 448.

Trial of William Scottie, vagabound, warloche, 1643.— A cow being drawn out of the byre as dead, William Scottie " straikit the kow along the head, and then drew his hand vpoun the cattis head, and shoe fell dead."

Ibid., p. 109.

He put his hand on the sufferer's "sore syd, and after vpone the hearth stone," which cured her in an hour.

Ibid., p. 125.

Coming to William Okilsetters, he "yeid about his hous twys or thrys witherwardis: and again, he being in Patrick Gareochis hous, yeid and cum witherwardis about the William's hous back againe: that same night, befoir day sett, the said William Ockilsetteris wyf fell deadlie seik, and tint hir milk that shoe had in abundance befoir, and continewit seik quhill he laid his hand vpoun hir: and incontinentlie shoe gat hir health, and the young mear foill, that was standing vpoun the hous floore, took seikness, and did byt the stones untill shoe died presentlie."

Ibid., p. 459.

Trial of Isobel Sinclair, 1633.—It was alleged against her, that during seven years, " sex times at the reathes of the year, shoe hath bein controlled with the Phairie; and that be thame, shoe hath the *second sight*: quhairby shoe will know giff thair be any fey bodie in the hous."

Ibid., p. 470.

To preserve cattle she directed people to "fyre ane piece of linying cleath, and sing ane hair of the beast at alhalow even."—*Ibid.*, p. 193.

Trial of John Sinclair, 1633.—"Vnder silence and clud of nycht, Imvic. ten [1610] years," he carried his distempered sister along with him: "he horsed her backward from quhair scho lay, to the Kirk of Hoy, quhair he met the kirk sevin faddome; at quhat tyme ane voyce appeirit saying, 'sevin is ower many for ane syne.' Thairefter, he tuik hir, and layed hir at the north syd of . . . be directioun of the devill: And in the morning, the first thing scho saw, was ane boit with fyve men, quhairof four perischit, and ane was saiff—be the quhilk divellrie the woman becam weill." The wonted test which betrayed so many, denoted that the culprit had accomplished this sacrifice to redeem his sister; for, when accused of the foul fact, "after the dead men wer found, and forcit to lay his handis vpoun thame, they gushit out with bluid and watter at mouth and noise."—*Ibid.*, pp. 179-80.

Trial of Bessie Skebister, 1633.—She was accused of acting thus towards Margaret Mudie, whose cow trespassed among her corn. "Ye sat doun, and taking of your curtch, sheuk your hair lous, and ever since shoe has bein so vehementlie pained, that shoe dwins and becoms wors and wors: and hes nevir bein weill since ye curst hir, or sheuk your hair lous." The jury convicted her of "taking of hir curtch, shaking of hir hair [lous], and Margaret Mudie's diseas."—*Ibid.*, p. 451.

It was also alleged against her that James Sandieson, under a severe distemper, affirmed, "that in his sleip, and oftymes waking he was tormented with yow, Bessie, and vther twa with yow, quhom he knew not, cairying him to the sea, and to the fyre, to Norroway, Yetland, and to the south—that ye had ridden all thes wayes with ane brydle in his mouth."—*Ibid.*, p. 591.

At Sowlis Skerrie, on a certain day, it was alleged against her that "James Chalmers came to yow, and finding yow weiping for the boittis, he said to yow, all is not weill if ye be weiping: ye answerit, ye weipit for the truble they wer in, but not for their death, for they wold come home. It was replyit to yow, be the said James, they culd not be saife vnles they went be north the cuntrey: ye answerit, that ye suld warrand they suld not goe about the cuntrey; but that they suld come home that same way they yeid, quhilk cam to pas as ye spak." Another boat being driven out to sea, and one of the oars cast ashore on the Isle of Wais, "the gudwyff of the Bow, having hir eldest sone vpoun the boat, send on of hir servands to speir at yow giff the boat was weill." She answered, "goe your way home, for they ar all weill, and will be home or they sleep: and so it was that they came home that same nicht."

Ibid., p. 474.

The particular side of a coin dropped into water proved the health of an absent friend. If "the cross of the sexpence be vp, then they are weill; gif not, they are not weill."—*Ibid.*, p. 512.

Hay, Orkney. *Elspet Smith, a witch,* 1672.—With respect to taking away the strength of ale they give the witch the same power, as the curious reader may see by the following extract from an old Session Register of Hay:— "4th August, 1672.—After preaching sedr. the minr. and elders This day compeared Elspet Smith and gave in a complaint upon Mareon Mangie for slandering her as guilty of witchcraft, in saying that the said Elspit Smith complainer, by sending for ane pynt of aill from the said Mereon selling the same, Did thereby take awa the fruit and fusion of ane dusson of pynts or thereby that remained in the vessel &c."—LOW, p. 6 *note*.

Shetland. *Helen Stewart, a witch.*—In Shetland a few years agoe, a Judge having condemned an old Woman and her daughter called Helen Stewart for Witchcraft, sent them to be burn'd. The Maid was so stupid, that she was thought to be possessed. When she had hung some little time on the Gibbet, *a black Pitchy-like ball* foamed out of her mouth: and after the fire was kindled, it grew to the bigness of a Walnut, and then flew up like Squibs into the air, which the Judge yet living attests. It was taken to be a visible sign that the Devil was gone out of her.—From "Relation Anent Major Weir," 1684, in SINCLAIR, p. 231.

Orkney. *Trial of Anie Tailzeour, alias Rwna Rowa,* 1624.—Intrat vpoun pannell, Anie Tailzeour, alias Rwna Rowa, to vnderly the law befor Sir Johnne Buchanane of Scottiscraig, Knyght, justice, and schireff-principal of Orknay, at the instance of Robert Chalmer of Ryssay, procuratiour fischall of the said schireffdome, for certane pointis of Witchcraft, Sorcerie, and Superstitioun, at the least behaueing hir selff to haue sic skill and knawledge, thairthrow abusing the people as followis.

In the first, ye the said Anie Tailzeour ar indyttit and accusit for airt and pairt of the vseing, comitting, and practising of the divelische and abhominable cryme of

Superstitioun, Witchcraft, and Sorcerie, in that aucht or nyne yeiris syne, in fauchland tyme, Williame Burwick in North Ransay, and William Swanisone thair, being in Airsay, ye came and soght ane luik beir fra the said William, and Thomas Burwick, sone to the said William, reprowing your importunitie, ye was angrie, and called him, "gallow bread"! quhilk is, hangit man; and his father being angrie, baid yow "Away, witch, rigand theiff!" quhairat ye being angrie, fleat, and chyded, and past your way. And quhen they yocked the pleuche, the pleuche wald not enter in the ground, neither for the ane nor the other, temper hir quhat scho wald; and thairefter the culter and sock gaid out off the pleuche be your witchcraft and diuelrie.

II. Item, ye ar indyttit and accusit for the said cryme of Witchcraft, in that, vpoun the third day of September, Imvjc and sextene yeiris, ye being wardit be the Sessioun in the Croce Kirk, Thomas Logie, cuming to his awin hous leat ane evin, and meitting ane number of cattis within the dyk of Colzigar, vpoun the brae, among the beir schaues, quhilk vnbesett him, the said Thomas saw your face vpoun ane of [the] cattis; and at the Candlemes thairefter, ye cuming to his hous, and he reproueing yow, alledgand yow to haue bene among the cattis that vnbesett him, ye lughe and skorned it; vpoun the quhilk reprooff, the said Thomas contractit seiknes for the space of tua yeiris, quhill his wyff came to yow, and fleat with yow; and thairefter the said Thomas convalest, and his said wyff immediatlie tuik seiknes, quha yit continwis seik, and not lyk to liue, be your witchcraft and diuelrie.

III. Item, ye ar indyttit and accusit, in that, ane yeir efter, ye cuming to the said Thomas' hous, keipit not the hie gait, but went in through the cornes, and came through his kyne, quha presentlie wanttit thair proffeit for the space of tuentie dayis, and quhen the said Thomas socht yow, and reprowit yow, and boastis to ding yow, that same nycht the proffeit of the kyne was restored, be your witchcraft and diuelrie.

IV. Item, ye ar indyttit and accusit for the forsaid cryme, in that ye, being demandit be Mr Thomas Cok, and Thomas Sinclair, baillie, how ye tuik the proffeit of the kyne and gaue it to vtheris, ye ansuerit, it was to tak thrie hairis of the kowis taill, thrie of her memberis, and thrie of hir papis, and gang thryse woderwardis about the kow, and straik hir in the left syd, and cast the hair in the kirne, and say thryse, "Cum butter, cum," and sua thei sould haue the haill proffeit of that flock, quhair that kow was: Quhilk ye practise be the directioun of the diuell.

V. Item, ye are indyttit and accusit for the cryme forsaid, in that, about mid somer, fyve yeiris syne, James Ego, smyth, his wyff, haueing tane ane loik of your beir, ye said scho sould repent it, and immediatlie ane meir deit to hir worth xx lib.: And becaus scho wald not geue you ane soup milk of ane new callowit kow, ye said so sould scho find it; and presentlie the kow deit: And in winter last, ane foill of the said James, haueing eatten ane schaue of youris, ye prayed God nor the foill burst and beall; quhilk schortlie came to pas, and the foill deit be your witchcraft and deuelrie.

VI. Item, ye ar indyttit and accusit for the cryme forsaid, in that, in Maij Imvjc and auchten, ye being cum to Iver Deirnes hous, ye said that Hew Peace was ane hauey hand vpoun yow, and that he was getting ane quhip for it; and giff he wald not let you alone, he wald get war yit: And the said Hew his wyff being informit thairof, he being diseasit of ane byll, he cam and tuiched the byll, quhairby he was haill within fourtie aucht houris, quhilk, to his opinion, could not have bene in ane quarter of ane yeir, be your witchcraft and diuelrie.

VII. Item, ye ar indyttit and accusit for the said cryme, in that, in November Imvjc and tuentie ane, ye being in Thomas Mure of Quoykankeris hous, ye came to him in the nyght, he being in his bed, and it being ane great storme, and bad him ryse vp and gang about the schoir and he sould find fische; and he being sueir to ryse, ye vrgit him, and said he sould find ane quhaill at the West Bankis, quhilk he did find: Quhilk ye fortald be your witchcraft and divelrie.

VIII. Item, ye ar indyttit and accusit for the said cryme, in that, in haruest thrie yeiris syne, William Spens wyff, haueing refussit you ane schaue of corne, ye tuk the proffeit of his cornes from him and gaue it to his brother, James Spens, be your witchcraft and diuelrie.

IX. Item, ye ar indyttit and accusit for the cryme forsaid, in that, in somer thrie yeiris syne or thairby, vpoun our Lady day in haruest, ye came and soght one loik of beir fra William Namlandis wyff, and scho refussing you, ye cast seiknes vpoun hir, quha lay almost ane half yeir; and quhen, be the persuasioun of his dochter, ye cam to his hous, and gaue hir ane piece of bannock to eat, scho presentlie grew haill, be your witchcraft and diuelrie: Quhilk ye cannot deny.

X. Item, ye ar indyttit and accusit for the said cryme, in that, in May last, Mareoun Paulsone, spous to James Fothringhame in Burnes, in Sanday, haueing tane ane luik meall furth of your pock, ye prayed that scho sould suall that eat your meall; quhairvpoun the said Mareoun swalled, and now is dead, be your witchcraft and diuelrie.

XI. Item, ye ar indyttit and accusit for the cryme forsaid, in that, fyve yeiris syne or thairby, ye being in Johne Flettis hous, and haueing brocht in some of Annie Peace's peatis, and brunt thame, and scho finding fault with yow, ye said scho sould never burne the rest; and sua thair roise ane great storme that same nyght, and the sea came vp and did wasche all the rest of the peattis away, be your witchcraft and diuelrie.

XII. Item, ye ar indyttit and accusit for the said cryme, in that, efter Yule last, ye being in Robert Ising Millaris hous, in Sanday, and ane lass of his keiping ane bairne, haueing ane luik thrid in hir hand, ye soght the said thrid, and the lass refussit, quha presentlie tuik sick ane franisie, that scho almost cuist the bairne thryse in the fyre, giff scho had not bene stayed; and that the franisie continwit quhill ye gatt the thrid, be your witchcraft and diuelrie.

XIII. Item, in that, efter Yule last, ye haueing cum to the said Robertis mylne, and haueing soght ane luik of meall fra thame that was grinding, and lykwayis fra him selff, and ye being refussit, passing away murmuring and speaking to your selff; the said Robert haueing put on the mylne with the same cornes, quhairof thair was ane pairt grund, for all his skill he could not mak the mylne to gang that day, be your witchcraft and diuelrie.

XIV. Item, ye ar indyttit and accusit for the said cryme, in that ye being broght out of Ethay, be Stevin Tailyeour in Papa Wastray, cam to his hous, and efter aucht dayis haueing soght ane peice butter fra the said Stevin's wyff, and scho refussing yow, vpoun the morne efter, the kow wald not suffer ane to milk hir: And ye being challangit and delaitit to the kirk, and straitlie flightered with ane tedder the tyme of the sessioun, quhen the sessioun raise, ye was standing at the end of the kirk louse, nane being to help yow; and the said Stevin's wyff thairefter incontinentlie contractit seiknes, continwit seik quhil ye came and charmed hir, falddomeing the woman, laying ane hand to hir head, and ane other to hir fute corslingis, saying, "Motheris blissing to the head, motheris blissing to the feit, and motheris blissing to the heart," in plaine scorne; for the wyff continwit seik and deit, be your witchcraft and diuelrie.

XV. Item, ye ar indyttit and accusit, in that, in Junij last, ye being tane to John Chalmeris, officer, ye prayed him to let yow gang or else ye sould rune on the sea and drowne you; and giff he wald keip yow that nyght vndelyght, he sould fische weill, and his kow sould milk weill that yeir.

XVI. And generallie, ye, the said Annie Tailzeour, ar indyttit and accusit as ane comoun witche, for airt and pairt, vseing, committing and practeising of the abhominable cryme of Superstitioun, Witchcraft, and Sorcerie, and in geving your selff furth to have sic craft and knawledge, thairthrow abuseing the people, and wroning and staying man and beast, and sua reput and haldin ane comoun and notorious witche; and thairfor, aucht and sould vndergo the knawledge of ane Assyse, and be adiugit and condemnit to the death, for the caussis forsaidis, in example of vtheris to do the lyk; and your guidis and gear escheit and inbroght to his maiesties vse, conforme to the lawis and daylie practique obseruit in sic caissis.

I. Thomas Burwick maid fayth conforme to the points of the dittay. The pannell denyet.

II. Thomas Logie, present, maid fayth conforme to the dittay to his knawledge.

The pannell denyet.

Lyk as the said Thomas this day deponit and declarit, that scho said, giff he wald get hir out, scho sould do quhat scho could to gar his wyff get hir health, and help hir giff scho myght be helpit.

Jerohme Fothringhame, and Ard Dase, with diuerse vtheris, verefeit the same.

Indifferent anent the vnbesetting of the cattis, and fyllis hir anent his seiknes.

III. The said Thomas maid fayth conforme to the dittay. The pannell denyet. Fyllis.

IV. Mr Thomas Cok confest it is trew. The pannell denyet not, but scho said scho was vncouth, and wist not quhat to say. Fyllis.

V. James Ego, present, maid fayth conforme to the dittay. The pannell denyet. Fyllis.

VI. Hew Peace, present, maid fayth conforme to the dittay. The pannell confest scho tuiched the byll. Fyllis.

VII. The nyghtbouris in Sanday buir it to be trew, and Mr Thomas Muster, present, declarit that Thomas Mure suir in their session, and scho said, giff he reveild it he sould repent it, and that he is continwallie seik sensyne. Fyllis.

VIII. William Spons maid fayth conforme to the dittay. Becaus his brother haid tua mells, and he haid bot four schaves being growing in ane rig. For the corne, ryffis *clauso ore*. The pannell denyet.

IX. The pannell denyet. Fyllis.

X. The pannell denyet.

Mr Thomas Cok, present, declarit that the said Mareoun, in his presens and John Richartsones, maid fayth that the said Mareoun deponit conforme to the dittay. Fyllis.

XI. The minister declarit that John Flet suir the dittay in presens of the Sessioun. The pannell denyet. Fyllis.

XII. Robert Millar, present, maid fayth conforme to the dittay. The pannell denyet. Fyllis.

XIII. Robert Millar maid fayth conforme to the dittay. The pannell denyet. Fyllis.

XIV. The pannell denyet. Fyllis.

XV. Mr Thomas Cok declarit that he sure it in the Sessioun. The pannell denyet. Fyllis.

XVI. Fyllis.

> Curia Justiciariæ, vicecomitatus de Orknay et Zetland, tenta apud Kirkwall in templo Sti. Magni ibidem, per honorabilem Dominum Joannen Buchannane de Scottiscraig, Militem, vicecomitem Principalem eiusdem, et Edwardum Sinclair de Essinquoy, eius Deputatum, decimo quinto die mensis Julij 1624.

The quhilk day compeirit Robert Chalmer, procuratour fischall, and desyrit the dittayis to be put to the knawledge of ane Assyse.

The pannell, present, could alledge no reasonabill caus in the contrair.

Assisa.

[Fifteen names given.]
That the Assyse was receavit and suorne the procuratour fischall askit instrumentis.

The Assyse, passing out of judgment, nominate James Fea in chanseler:

And reentering againe, the haill Assyse, all in ane voice, Fyllis hir in the haill pointis off dittay aboue writtin, speciall and generall, except the first pairt of Thomas Logeis dittay anent the cattis; and anent William Spens' dittay anent the corne; quhairanent they ryf *clauso ore*, and remittis sentens to the judge and dome to the dempster. JAMES FEA, Chansseler.

Sentence.

The judge ordanis the pannell to be tane be lockman, hir handis bund behind hir bak, and tane be the lokman to the Lon-head, and wirried at ane staik, and brunt in asses: Quhilk Donald Kenner, dempster, gaue for dome.

Abbotsford Club Miscellany, pp. 143-149.

Stromness, Orkney. *Trial of Kathrine Taylor.—Saturday, July last,* 1708.—After Prayer Sedr., Minister and elders *pro re nata.*

The said day the minister reported that being informed that Kathrine Brown, spouse to William Stensgar in South-side, had been employing one Kathrine Taylor, a cripple beggar woman in Stromness, to come to her house and wash the said William, who had been long sick and afflicted in his bed, that by her Sorcerie and charming he might come to his health, and that the said Kathrine Brown coming to a common Slap on the high way, carrying the water wherewith the said William was allegit to be washed, in a large Stoup, upon the twenty fourth of June last, about one or two hours in the morning, and emptying the said Stoup in the said Slap: wherefore he had appointed to Summon ye said Kathrine Brown and her Husband to this Dyet. The said Kathrine and her Husband being called compeared, and both of them being accused, denyed the charge, and the said Kathrine stiffly denied that she had been at the common Slap above written, whereupon the witnesses being called, compeared.

John More son to William More in Yeldabrec of the age of twenty four years, being admitted and deeply sworn purged of malice and partial counsell, deponed; That he saw Kathrine Brown upon the twenty fourth day of June last more than an hour before sunrising, empty a stoup of water in the above mentioned Slap, and he coming to the said Slap did find a Stone and feal on the said water, or where it was spilled and as he was coming near he saw the said Kathrine gather up her coats, and run away most speedily. And that he suspecting some devilrie did break down a slap in another place of the dike and passed over.

. . . . . .

George Langskail Deponed, That upon the twenty fourth of June he passed thro' the slap forementioned before sunrising and that he saw water in the said slap, and a little while after his passing the same he was overtaken by bodily indisposition [1] tho' he would not blame the said Kathrine Brown therefore.

After several things had passed in the Session we are told That the said Kathrine Brown and her Husband confessed that the said Kathrine Taylor was called and came to their house, and all She did was to say over half a dozen words out of a psalm like a prayer beside the Husband.

The Session appointed Kathrine Taylor to be summoned to answer for using Sorcerie.

[1] The meaning of this is:—They imagined the person who went next thro' the gateway was infected with the disease which had now left the other.

Sess. 2d on the same.

Sept. 5, 1708.—Which day compeared Kathrine Taylor in Stromness being summoned to this dyet as were also William Stensgar and Kathrine Brown before mentioned, and the said Kathrine Taylor being accused of alleged Sorcerie and charms—she confessed that Kathrine Brown came for her when she was in Oliver Taylors house in the Southside and told to her her Husbands condition viz., That he wanted the power of one of his Knees, and enquired her if she could not *tell out the paine* of the said knee. Whereupon the said Kathrine Taylor condescended and went with the said Kathrine Brown to her house, and did *tell out the pain* of his knee. Being asked by what means she did it, She answered, She laid her hand on his bare Knee and spake these words,

"As I was going by the way, I met the Lord Jesus Christ in the likeness of another man, he asked me what tydings I had to tell and I said I had no tydings to tell, but I am full of pains, and I can neither gang nor stand." "Thou shalt go to the holie kirk, and thou shalt gang it round about, and then sit down upon thy knees, and say thy prayers to the Lord, and then thou shalt be as heall as the hour when Christ was born."

She repeated also the twenty third psalm indistinctlie and declared she did or spake no more. She likewise declared she learned this from an old woman when she was a child; and that she has heard from others that a pain or a stitch has been *telled out* in that manner, and that she herself has done it before.—LOW, pp. 201-203.

Shetland. *Trial of Barbara Thomasdochter, alias Stovd,* 1616.—The "selch bone" with which she stirred her milk to divine the product, "being thereafter cast in the fyir, it crackit and affrayit the hous."—DALYELL, p. 384.

She told one who churned in vain, that "the lid of hir kirne wald be weit gif she had the profeit of hir milk, and gif it wes dry she wantit it—she wald gif her sum thing gif she wald heild it, that wald do hir guid : and oppnit hir pwrs and tuik ane bone furth therof, quhilk wes the bone of ane manes finger, great at the ane and small at the vther, of twa insh lang or therby, and bad hir steir hir milk with it and she wald get hir profeit : and quhilk bone wes sumquhat bread, and sum hoillis in it, but not throw." After explaining that it was not a human but "ane selch bone" the charmer was convicted of superstitious practices.

Ibid., p. 264.

A person named Garth, in Yell, having contracted " ane great fever and lyghtnes in his head, that he could get no rest nor sleip in somer 1613 : and Gregorius Thomasone haveing cum to visite him, and informit of the said diseas, he tauld Garth that thair was ane woman in Delting, called Barbara Stovd, quha culd give him ane resting threid." Gregorius repairing to the woman under silence of night, and describing the patient's state, she refused to give him a thread until he should himself apply for it : " quhairof Garth being aduerteisit be the said Gregorius, he come over to hir, and [they] come togither to hir in ane somer morneing, earlie befoir the sone, about Jonesmes 1614 : and at said conference, she tuik ane woll threid, and vsit certane crossis and coniurationes vpoun it. She gave it to hir dochter to be given to the said Garth, to be woone about his head nyne nyghtis, and then to be burnt : quhairby Garth gat rest." Afterwards, because, " at certyne tymes of the moone, he found himself not so weel as he wount to be, he came to hir this somer, and desyrit hir to mak him perfyt haill, quhilk she promeisit to do at hallowmes nixt."

Ibid., pp. 118, 119.

Orkney. *Trial of Jonet Thomesone, alias Grebok,* 1643.— Helen Languor having quarrelled with Jonet Thomesone, she sickened, and the meat prepared for her became full of worms ; but none were seen either in that prepared for her husband or her household. After a donation to the sorceress, she recovered and worms were seen no more.

Ibid., p. 260.

A desperate attack on someone by a bird, from the instigation of the panel is specified in her indictment.

Ibid., p. 271.

Jonet Thomeson testified much displeasure with Andrew Burwick for refusing her some corn, and departed full of wrath. "Quhen the corne was caryit to the grind it lap upoun his wyffis face lyk myttis, and as it war nipit hir face vntill it swallit: and quhen it was maid in meat, he and his wyfe culd not feill the smell of it: and quhen the eattit of it, it went owre lyk preinis, and culd not be quencit for thirst: and the dogis wold not eat of it—and quhen they chaingit the same with their neighbouris, it was fund sufficient, without any evill taist."—*Ibid.,* p. 266.

A man suffered various injuries; his cows lost their milk, or cast their calves, and his daughter fell sick during half-a-year; all through the malevolence of Jonet Thomeson; but on his reproving her, "the las becam whole: and having a mear lyk to die, he gave hir almis to heale hir, and the mear was presentlie maid whole."—*Ibid.,* p. 58.

Being urged "to goe and look vpon" a man who had contracted a desperate malady after her imprecations; on her compliance, along with some other remedies, he returned to his work on the same day. Also, having quarrelled with another, "his mear took seikness and was lyk to die; and shoe cuming to the hous, the bairnis gave hir almis to look vpone the mear, she was immediatlie maid quhole."—*Ibid.,* p. 59.

Trial of Helen Wallas, 1616.—Helen Wallas was indytit for witchcraft chiefly on the following grounds:— "That William Holland and she haveing discordit for ane peice of gras, the said William being keiping his kyne on the said gers sche come to him, and efter mony injurious wordis, raif the curtch aff her heid and pat it vnder hir belt, shuik hir hair about hir [head], and ran to the Ladie Chappell hard by, and went thryse about it vpoun hir bair kneis, prayand cursingis and maledictiounes lycht vpoun for the woman, and cast his left fute shoe over the hous, and gif it fell to the hous[1] he wald speid, and gif fra the hous he wald nocht. . . . Item, in that in beir seidtyme a yeir syne, Peter Hollandis wyfe come to the said Helen, the said Peter being seik, and askit at hir quidder or nocht hir husband wald die or leive. The said Helen commandit hir to tak his left fute shoe and cast it ouir the hous, and said gif the mouth of it fell up he wald leive, and gif doun he wald die. Item, for that hir dochter haveing cum to the gudwyfe the said William, and thairefter come to the said William his hous, and zeid sa about his fyir syde, and did the lyk; and thairefter cuming furth quhair his guidis wes pasturing, said thir wordis to thame following :—(Gleib wind luik in the air of the lift, and never have power to eat meat). Swa it fell out that his beastis dwyneit away daylie be hir divilrie. Item, in doing of the lyk to David Wod in Marsetter, ane yeiris syne or thairby. Item, in that Adame Bewis, in   , being a young man, and owand hir dochter, sche desyrit him to mak tua corssis, and lay in the watter ane for the man and the vther of Wall, and desyrit sum meall and a drink of milk, quhilk being offerit to hir, sche desyrit that the milk and the meall mycht be baikeit togither, quhilk being done, the gudwyfe of Wall gave hir the half thairof, quhilk she caryit to the said Helen, hir mother, and thairefter the kow that gave the milk lost hir milk, and gave onlie bluid, quhill Hallowmes being half a yeir thairefter."

ROGERS, vol. iii. pp. 302, 303.

A cow almost suffocated by falling into the mire, was preserved by three ears of barley spit upon, put into her mouth.—DALYELL, p. 389.

[[1] *I.e.* with the toe pointing towards the house.—G. F. B.]

Trial of Agnes Yulloch or Tulloch, 1616.—Against Agnes Yulloch [or Tulloch] was charged the " abominable cryme of witchcraft, inasmuch that Marjorie Swonay, being chargeit to the toun for sindrie poyntis of witchcraft, sche said to the said Agnes Zullock, gif she come nocht home agane, mak hir to pas that same way, for said she, ' Ye have als guid skill as I.' Item, for that sa lang as James Swoney interteinit hir in his house his cornes and guidis prosperit, bot alsoone as she went out of his hous, he lost baith the profeit of his cornes and guidis be hir divilrie and witchcraft. Item, for that Oliver Faquoy, and Marioun Sclatter, his wyfe, thrie yieris syne or thereby, passing to the hous of Scorne to ane arff, the said Agnes being thair. The guidwyfe of Scorne being seik, the said Marioun Sclatter fand falt for hir being thair. Quha immediatlie tuik seiknes, and thairefter send for the said Agnes, and recoverit hir health be hir divilrie. Item, for that sum evill speiches being betwix Marioun Lincletter, spous to Henrie Growgar in Birsay, and Elspeth Browne, spous to David Mair thair, the said Agnes come to the said Henryes hous, and thair fleat w^t the said Marioun Lincletter, quha immediatlie thairefter contractit seiknes and dyit. The guidwyf of Langskaill, reproveing hir thairof, sche lykwayis fell seik, and lay fourtein dayis, and haveing send for the said Agnes, threattining to dilait hir, the said Agnes tuicheing hir, sche recoverit hir health."

ROGERS, vol. iii. pp. 301, 302.

Stromness. *Bessie Miller*, 1814.—At the village of Stromness, lived, in 1814, an aged dame called Bessie Miller, who helped out her subsistence by telling favourable winds to mariners.

[An account of her is given by Sir W. Scott, who seems to have visited her.]—SCOTT, *The Pirate*, note G.

For Witches *see also* under I. *g*, I. *h*, " SEA."

(f) LEECHCRAFT.

Orkney. [The natives have a] multitude of charms, that are still in practice, for killing sparrows that destroy the early corn; expelling mice and rats that infest houses; for securing the successful brewing of ale, and churning of milk; as well as those that respect women in labour and marriage; and those that are made use of for procuring good luck, curing the diseases of sheep, horses, and black cattle, and driving away toothach, haemorrhagy, consumption, and other distempers.

BARRY, p. 349.

Several other Charms also they have, about their Marriage, when Women in Travel, when their Cow is Calving, when Churning their Milk, or when Brewing, Or when their Children are sick, by taking them to a Smith (without premonishing him) who hath had a Smith to his Father, and a Smith to his Grandfather; and of several such like Charms, we had an account from the Minister, as likeways how these Charms were performed; but of these enough.—BRAND, pp. 62, 63.

Worms as cause of disease.—Some have a way (if they be to cure any akeing or inward pain in any part of the Body) to draw out several little worms out of the part affected (whereof I had occasion to see some) whereby they remove the pain; Others there be also that use charms for the curing the *Heartake* and *Rickets*.

WALLACE, p. 67.

Orkney. There is a Charm likewise they make use of for the Toothach, whereof I had the following instance from an Honest Man worthy of Credit. Some years ago, there was one who used this Charm, for the abating the pain of one living in *Eda*, tormented therewith, and tho' the Action then was at a distance, the Charmer not being present with the Patient, yet according to the most exact calculation of the time when the Charm was performed by the Charmer, there fell a living worm out of the Patient's Mouth when he was at supper.—BRAND, p. 62.

See also " *Wormy Lines* " *below.*

SPELLS.

Orkney. "*Forespoken Water.*"—When a healthy child suddenly becomes sickly, and no one can account for the change, the child is said to have been *forespoken*—or, when a grown up person becomes hypochondriac, or affected with nervous complaints, he is said to be *forespoken*. Some one has perhaps said, "He's a bonny bairn," or "Thou'r lookin' weel tha day;" but they have spoken with an *ill tongue*, or they have neglected to add, "God saif tha bairn," or "safe be thou." For the cure of this malady the following charm is repeated over water, which the patient must drink of, or be washed with:

> "Father, Son, Holy Ghost!
> Bitten sall they be,
> Wha haif bitten thee,
> Care to their near vein,
> Until thou get'st thy health again!
> Mend thou in God's name!"

During the repetition of this charm there is a certain weed put into the water. I have not been able to ascertain what plant this is, but it is called by the country people "forespoken grass." Cattle and horses may also be forespoken, and the same charm is applied towards their cure.—FOTHERINGHAM, p. 221.

In Orkney and Shetland, praise . . . receives the name "Forespoken." If one says to a child "He is a bonnie bairn;" or "Thoo are looking well the day," it is regarded as coming from an "ill-tongue," unless the expression "God save the bairn," or some such blessing is also used. When one was "Forespoken," the cure in Orkney was

"Forespoken Water"—that is water into which something has been dropped, supposed to possess magical powers, and over which an Incantation has been pronounced,—probably a reminiscence of Holy Water. The articles dropped in the water were, as a rule, three pebbles of different colours gathered from the sea shore. The charm was considered most potent when one stone was jet black, another white, and the remaining red, blue, or greenish.

An incantation was then muttered over the water, the reciter commencing by saying the word "Sain," and at the same time making the sign of the cross on the surface of the water. The incantation was as follows:

> "In the name of Him that can cure or kill,
> This water shall cure all earthy ill,
> Shall cure the blood and flesh and bone,
> For ilka ane there is a stone;
> May she fleg all trouble, sickness, pain,
> Cure without and cure within,
> Cure the heart, and horn, and skin."

The patient for whom the "Forespoken Water" was prepared had to drink a part of it; the remainder was sprinkled on his person.—MACKENZIE, pp. 35, 36.

When the Beasts as Oxen, Sheep, Horses, &c., are Sick, they sprinkle them with a Water made up by them, which they call *Fore-spoken Water*; wherewith likeways they sprinkle their Boats, when they succeed and prosper not in their Fishing. And especially on *Hallow-Even*, they use to sein or sign their Boats and put a Cross of Tar upon them, which my Informer hath often seen. Their Houses also some use then to sein.—BRAND, p. 62.

The people of Hoy . . . are very much given to superstition, and an universal belief of witchcraft prevails among them, which by no arguments can be rooted out even from among people otherwise not a little sagacious. They put a great deal of trust in the cure of diseases by spells and enchantments, also they give great power to witches to inflict these by the same means; and this is not confined to themselves, but extended to their goods and cattle, which they imagine witches have power to hurt, or at least to take away their milk, butter, or cheese, &c., by their magical incantations. They are afraid of hurt either in person or goods from an evil eye, and have particular ceremonies to avert the malignity of it, but pretend to make a mighty mystery of their rites. They also fear an evil tongue, and there are not a few instances of poor creatures falling ill thro' mere imagination upon being cursed by an enemy. Nobody must praise a child or anything they set a value on, for if anything evil afterwards befals it, these poor ignorant creatures will be sure to attribute to the tongue that spoke of it, and very probably quarrel on that account. This they call forespeaking, and pretend to cure persons so forespoken by washing them with a water compounded with great ceremony, the recipe of which our female sages, the only administrators, make an impenetrable secret; however these superstitious notions are not confined to Hoy alone, but are spread up and down the whole country, and to be found more or less in every corner of it.—LOW, pp. 6, 7.

See also I. e, "TRIALS," *passim*.

Sanday, Orkney. *Wormy Lines.*—Toothache in Sanday is called *The Worm* from a notion the country people have that this painful affection is caused by a worm in the tooth or jawbone. For the cure of this disease the following charm, called *Wormy Lines*, is written on a slip of paper, which must be sewed into some part of the dress of the person affected, and must be carried about with him as long as the paper lasts:

" Peter sat on a marble stone weeping,
  Christ came past and said, 'What aileth thee, Peter?'
  'O my Lord, my God, my tooth doth ache!'
  'Arise, O Peter, go thy way, thy tooth shall ache no more!'"
FOTHERINGHAM, p. 221.

The Wristing or Wresting Thread.—The following charm was used for the cure of sprains. A linen thread is tied around the injured part, after the solemn repetition of the charm:

> " Our Saviour rade,
> His fore-foot slade ;
> Our Saviour lichtit down.
> Sinew to sinew, vein to vein,
> Joint to joint, and bane to bane,
> Mend thou in God's name !"

During the time of repeating this charm nine knots must be tied on the thread, at regular distances, and to ensure success the charm should be repeated at every knot.

FOTHERINGHAM, p. 221.

Shetland. When a person has received a sprain, it is customary to apply to an individual practised in casting the 'wresting thread.' This is a thread spun from black wool, on which are cast nine knots, and tied round a sprained leg or arm. During the time the operator is putting the thread round the affected limb, he says, but in such a tone of voice as not to be heard by the bystanders, nor even by the person operated upon :

> " The Lord rade,
> And the foal slade ;
> He lighted.
> And he righted.
> Set joint to joint,
> Bone to bone,
> And sinew to sinew.
> Heal in the Holy Ghost's name !"

New Stat. Acct., Shetland, p. 141.

Orkney. A thread, having on it nine knots, was tied round the sprained part. As the thread was being tied the following Incantation was muttered :

> " Nine knots upo' this thread,
> Nine blessings on thy head;

> Blessings to take away thy pain
> And ilka tinter of thy strain."
>
> MACKENZIE, p. 73.

For Knots *cf.* I. *g*, " *Against Eagles.*"

Unst. *Nightmare Charm or Spell against the Mara.*— Pulling from my head the longest hair it possessed, and then going through the pantomime of binding a refractory animal, [the nurse] slowly chanted this spell:

> " De man o' meicht
> He rod a' neicht,
> We nedder swird
> Nor faerd nor leicht,
> He socht da mare,
> He fand da mare,
> He band da mare
> Wi' his ain hair,
> An' made her swear
> By midder's meicht,
> Dat shö wad never bide a neicht
> Whar he had rod, dat man o' meicht."

. . . There are different versions of this incantation, and I [Mrs. Saxby] forget which it was that the old nurse used on the occasion mentioned. Therefore I have given the one which is most familiar to me.

EDMONSTON and SAXBY, pp. 186, 187.

Shetland. [The following version is given by Mr. Karl Blind :]

> " Arthur Knight
> He rade a' night,
> Wi' open swird
> An' candle light.
> He sought da mare ;
> He fan' da mare ;
> He bund da mare
> Wi' her ain hair.
> And made da mare
> Ta swear :
> 'At she should never
> Bide a' night
> Whar ever she heard
> O' Arthur Knight."
>
> BLIND, *Nineteenth Century*, 1879, p. 1106.

Sanday, Orkney. *Telling out the Swey.*—The pain occasioned by a burn or scald is here [in Sanday] called

Swey or *Sweying*. To relieve the Swey this charm is employed, and must be repeated by a wise one in private:

> "A dead wife out of the grave arose,
> And through the Sea she swimmed;
> Through the Water made to the cradle;
> God save the Bairn burnt sair!
> Het fire, cool soon in God's name!"
>
> FOTHERINGHAM, p. 221.

Burn.—To cure a burn, the following words are used:

> "Here come I to cure a burnt sore;
> If the dead knew what the living endure,
> The burnt sore would burn no more."

The operator, after having repeated the above, blows his breath three times upon the burnt place. The above is recorded to have been communicated to a daughter who had been burned, by the spirit of her deceased mother.

New Stat. Acct., Shetland, p. 141.

Shetland. *Ringworm.*—The person afflicted with ringworm takes a little ashes between the forefinger and thumb, three successive mornings, and before having taken any food and holding the ashes to the part affected, says:

> "Ringworm! ringworm red!
> Never mayest thou either spread or speed;
> But aye grow less and less,
> And die away among the ase."

At the same time, throwing the little ashes held between the forefinger and thumb into the fire.

New Stat. Acct., Shetland, p. 141.

Orkney. *Stemming blood.*—For suppressing hemorrhage, as spitting of blood, bleeding from the nose, bleeding from a wound, &c., the following charm is solemnly repeated once, twice, or oftener, according to the urgency of the case, by some old man or woman accounted more sagacious than their neighbours. It is not to be repeated aloud, nor in the presence of any one but the patient:

> "Three Virgins came across Jordan Sand,
> Each with a bloody knife in her hand ;
> Stem blood, stem ! tetherly stand !
> Bloody Nose (or Mouth, &c.) in God's name mend !"
>
> FOTHERINGHAM, p. 221.

They have a Charm, whereby they stop excessive blooding in any, whatever way they come by it, whether by or without External Violence. The name of the Patient being sent to the Charmer, he saith over some words (which I heard) upon which the Blood instantly stoppeth, tho' the blooding Patient were at the greatest distance from the Charmer. Yea upon the saying of these words, the Blood will stop in the blooding Throats of Oxen or Sheep, to the astonishment of Spectators.

BRAND, p. 61.

A young woman who was troubled with the toothache [received] from an old beldame a little paper parcel which was warranted to effect a cure. The afflicted one was requested to wear the charmed packet round her neck, and on no account to open or examine it. She obeyed the instructions of the "wise woman," and an immediate cure was the result. But this young daughter of Eve yielded to the spirit of curiosity when relieved of her pain, and proceeded forthwith to open the mysterious packet. It contained an account of a miracle ascribed to Christ, but not to be found in the New Testament. No sooner, however, had she satisfied her curiosity at the expense of her promise than the toothache returned with aggravated pain, and the desecrated charm was found to have lost its healing virtue.

Notes & Queries, 7th Ser., v. v. p. 262 (citing the *Orkney Herald*).

Shetland. A Finn came ow'r fra Norraway,
Fir ta pit töth-ache away—
Oot o' da flesh an' oot o' da bane;
Oot o' da sinew an' oot o' da skane;
Oot o' da skane an' into da stane;
An' dare may du remain!
An' dare may du remain!
An' dare may du remain!
BLIND, *Contemporary Review*, vol. xl. p. 403.

Orkney. This incantation was also common in Orkney but beginning thus:

T'ree Finnmen cam' fae der heem i' de sea,
Fae de weary worm de folk tae free,
An' dey sall be paid wi' de white monie!
MACKENZIE, p. 59.

CHARMS.

Casting of the Heart.—They have a charm also whereby they try if persons will be in a decay or not, and if they will die thereof; which they call Casting of the Heart.
BRAND, p. 62.

Shetland. They firmly believe that if any person is emaciated by sickness, or other accidental causes, that his or their heart is worn away; and they have a method of investigating whether it is so or not, or whether it shall be restored; which is this, they melt a piece of lead and throw it in cold water, and according to the shape it takes, so they form their judgment; if it takes the shape of a heart (their imaginations are pretty quick in helping out this and other kinds of augury both here and in Orkney), the person is not altogether gone, and he will recover, if otherwise, *vice versa.*—LOW, p. 82.

When people are afflicted with consumptive complaints in Zetland, they imagine that the heart of the person so affected has been wasted away by the enchantment of the fairies, or witchcraft of some other evil beings. Old women, and sometimes men, profess to cure this disease. The patient must undergo the following curious and very ridiculous operation: He is directed to sit upon the bottom of a large cooking-pot, turned upon its mouth; a large pewter dish is placed, or held upon his head; upon the dish a bason or bowl is set nearly full of cold water; into this water the operator pours some melted lead through the teeth of a common dressing comb. A large key is also employed in this operation. All this is performed with many strange incantations and gesticulations. If the lead falls into a shapeless lump, they declare that the heart and the lungs of the patient are completely wasted away, that they will have infinite trouble, and perhaps, after all, will not be able to bring back the heart and lungs to their natural and healthful form. The lead is again melted, and run into the water through the teeth of the comb; it most likely assumes some shape, which the operator assures the spectators is the exact form of the patient's heart in its diseased state. The lead is repeatedly melted, and poured through the comb into the water; every time it is asserted to be more and more like the natural heart and lungs, and the bewitchment, of course, is rendered weaker and weaker. The patient undergoes this three times, with some days between each operation. When the last cast of the lead is over, the operator shews it round, and points out how exactly every part of the heart and the lungs are restored to their natural and proper shape; if the patient dies (perhaps his death is hurried on by the fatigue and agitation occasioned by this mummery), his death is ascribed to some oversight in the strict performance of all the relative parts of this casting of the heart. The moon must be a certain age, and it must be performed at a certain turning of the tide and hour of the night; numberless other things must be attended to. The operator will take anything they please to give, if it should be the half of their goods and chattels, but he must not touch money. He appoints, however, a particular place, where a Danish coin, worth fivepence, current in Zetland, is to be laid (as many as they like—the more the better, no doubt); this money is for the fairies, who come, it is asserted, and take it away; but the poor, honest operator must not, and will not finger it, otherwise his trouble would come to nought, and the spell which bound the patient would be firmer than ever. This operation of casting the heart is performed to this day in some parts of the Zetland Isles, and implicit belief placed in its efficacy. The patient must wear the lead, which has been used, in his bosom, for some time after the operation.

Note to *Harley Radington*, a novel, illustrative of Shetland manners, published about 1820. Quoted by HIBBERT, p. 603.

See also I. e, " *Trial of J. Knarstoun.*"

Jaundice.—About the Walls of these old Chappels are found Snails, called Shell-Snails, which they dry and pulverize, mingling the dust with their drink for the Jaundice, by which means these who labour under their sickness in 3. or 4. days time will recover of the same, but if they let this dust ly for a Year, without making use of it, it turneth into small living Creatures or Vermine, which they dry and bray over again, if they make any further use of it.

BRAND, p. 108.

See also I. a, " BUILDINGS."

Yell, Shetland. *Cure of King's Evil.*—As a substitute for the actual living finger of royalty, a few crowns and half crowns of the coinage of the first Charles, carefully handed down from father to son, have been effectual both here, and in every other parish in Shetland, towards removing this disease, and that to an extent which may appear somewhat incredible to many. . . . Be this as it may, there are few localities in Shetland in which a living evidence is not to be found of one said to have been "cured by the coin," and who would instantly be pointed at as a sufficient evidence to warrant confidence in its efficacy, should it happen that a doubt at any time rested thereon.

New Stat. Acct., Shetland, p. 85.

Foula, Shetland. *Churchyard Mould, etc.*— A much-respected dissenting clergyman, still alive, called at this cottage [Leraback, in Foula] to inquire for a poor woman who was dying of consumption. On hearing she was no better, he inquired if they had used means to aid her recovery : " Yah," said her aged mother, " we gaed to the kirkyard, and brought *mould* frae the grave o' the last body buried, an' laid it on her breast. As this had nae effect, we gaed to the brig ower which the last corpse was ta'en, an' took some water frae the burn below, an' made her drink it. This failed too, an' as a last resource, we dug a muckle hole i' the grund, an' put her in't."

REID, pp. 22, 33.

Shetland. *Cure for Stitch.*—In Shetland a stitch in the side was cured by applying to the part mould from a grave, and heated in a saucepan. Mould to be so used, it was held essential, should be taken from and returned to the grave after sunset.—ROGERS, vol. iii. 226.

Stone for Cure of Sterility.—Through the kindness of Mr James Shand of the Union Bank of Scotland, Edinburgh, I am enabled to exhibit an egg-shaped pebble of quartz, 2 inches in length by 1½ inch in greatest diameter, which was formerly used in Shetland as a cure for sterility. In a letter to me, Mr Shand gives the following account of the method of using the stone :

The charm-stone which I handed to you was for many years used in the west division of Sandsting parish, Shetland, as a cure for sterility in women. It was given to the lady from whom I received it by an old woman who had actually known it in use. The *modus operandi* was for the would-be mother to wash her feet in burn (*i.e.* "running") water, in which the stone was laid. I rather think there were some other formalities, but these I have unhappily forgotten. The stone was said to have been brought from Italy originally—this, no doubt, being calculated to make it seem more valuable. Unlike most charms, it was not preserved in one family, but passed from the hands of one wise woman to another, the trust being only relinquished when the holder was on her death-bed."—GEO. F. BLACK in *Proceed. Soc. Ant. Scotland*, vol. xxvii. pp. 452, 453.

See also I. *a*, "BUILDINGS."

Orkney. *Eelskin.*—[The skin of an eel] is stripped off and worn to prevent the cramp.—BARRY, p. 302.

Shetland. *Three Waves.*—Water taken from the tops of three waves was in Shetland believed to cure toothache.
ROGERS, vol. iii. p. 217.

See also " Sea, *Third Wave.*"

Dog's Saliva.—If a cow is off her food, or a calf does not take kindly to chewing the cud, some wise woman is sent for who works up a dough ball of oatmeal, and after placing it in a dog's mouth, compels the cow or calf to swallow it.—TUDOR, p. 169.

Kirkwall and St. Ola. *Transference.*—In the time of sickness or danger they often make vows to this or the other favourite saint, at whose church or chapel in the place they lodge a piece of money as a reward for their protection; and they imagine that if any person steals or carries off that money, he will instantly fall into the same danger from which they, by their pious offering, had been so lately delivered.—*Old Stat. Acct.*, v. vii. p. 560.

See also I. *e*, "*Trial of K. Grant,*" etc. See also *ante*, "*Spitting,*" "*Cure for Stitch.*" For Leechcraft, *see also* I. *a*, "HOLY WELLS," "BUILDINGS"; I. *d*, *passim*; I. *e*, "*Da Witch's Fee,*" and *passim*.

(g) MAGIC AND DIVINATION.

Northmavine. "*Thunderbolts*" (*Stone Axes*).—A few of the people are in possession of the ancient battle-axe, which is carefully concealed in some part of the house, and superstitiously preserved, and it is commonly called a thunderbolt. The writer of this paper has one in his possession, which was obtained from a parishioner, as a great favour.—*New Stat. Acct.*, Shetland, p. 75.

Shetland. The smooth stones termed thunder-bolts—a supposed safeguard against lightning—are still possessed by one or two, and highly prized.—REID, p. 31.

Thunderbolts—or battle-axe heads . . . are occasionally dug up. . . . I lately purchased a good specimen of this ancient stone weapon. The good-wife of the house, who parted with it most reluctantly, and only after a pretty good price had been offered, informed me it had been dug up in the common, a short time before, where it had fallen from the skies during a thunderstorm, and that her husband, who was from home, would be very angry with her for selling the thunderbolt, as it brought good luck to the house.—COWIE, pp. 296, 297.

Shetland. [A stone axe, 9¼ inches long, now in the Scottish National Museum of Antiquities, Edinburgh, was] found in the valley of Tingwall near Scalloway, Shetland, in the end of last century. It was acquired by the donor from an aged peasant woman in Scalloway who believed it to be a "thunderbolt," and of efficacy in averting evil from the dwelling in which it was kept.
Pro. Soc. Ant. Scot., v. xii. p. 599.

Shetland. *A "Trow's Sword."*—[On 10th April 1876, there was presented to the Scottish National Museum of Antiquities] a small bronze knife or dagger, with tang, 4 inches in length, found at Nordhouse, Sulem, Northmavine, Shetland, and long used as a "trow's sword" for magical purposes. [No further particulars given.]

Pro. Soc. Ant. Scot., v. xi. p. 471.

STORM-RAISING.

Shetland. *Abonjinit, Abonjinit.*—On another occasion a vessel of suspicious appearance was observed nearing the same island. She did not anchor, but when she had got close enough a boat's crew of armed men was sent on shore. The freebooters scoured the island, and seized all the fowls—ducks, hens, and geese—that they could come across. Some of the inhabitants ventured to remonstrate but the men replied:

"It's ducks and hens to-day; but it'll be oxen and cows to-morrow." They then returned to their ship, and she stood off the shore.

The islanders knew they could make no resistance. In their despair they sent two of the most influential men to an old woman, who was known occasionally to do something in the black art, though she did not court the reputation of a witch. They told their tale and she replied:

"Abonjinit, abonjinit! I canna dü ony güd, an I canna dü muckle herm; bit ye can geng an tell da folk ta mak fast dir boats and tak weel aboot dir grains o corn." The men departed and secured their boats, stacks of corn, and all loose property about the island. That night a wild storm burst on the Atlantic, and in the morning the islesmen saw the dreaded vessel founder in the offing.

BURGESS, p. 103.

Cf. I. *a*, "*Nouphead Rock.*"

Witches' Mode of Wrecking Ships.—Mr. George Sinclair, now of Dunedin, New Zealand, writes to me of Shetland stories about "witches on the shore, who, by means of wooden cups, wreck boats at sea. The cups are put into a tub of water; each cup means a boat; and the witch names them. Then she violently agitates the water, and the number of upset cups corresponds to the number of wrecked boats,

KARL BLIND, *Gentleman's Magazine*, 1882, p. 479.

Da Stakka Baa.—One day late in the autumn of a year now distant a small war-vessel came into a "voe," in an island on the West Coast of Shetland, and dropped anchor. The crew were seen cleaning guns and getting ready weapons, apparently for the purpose of attacking the inhabitants and plundering the island. In spite of the consternation this occasioned, a fat cow or "mert" was being slaughtered at a place called Nort-hus.

An old woman who was known in the island as a "wise wife" came to Nort-hus and offered to lift the Stakka Baa, a sunken rock out in the voe, and overturn the foreign ship, if the owner of the cow would only give her the piece of it named locally "da stickin collop." The man promised, and the "wise-wife" forthwith got to work. After some preliminary incantations she placed herself upon the lower step of a stair in Nort-hus and sat there, muttering for a little. Then she slowly raised herself to the second step. The "Baa" out in the "voe" rose up a bit. Step by step the "wise-wife" backed herself upstairs, and bit by bit the sunk rock neared the surface of the sea till, all at once it struck the bottom of the fated vessel. The foreigner capsized and all on board were drowned.—BURGESS, p. 103.

MISCELLANEOUS.

Shetland. *Storm-laying.*—Placing himself on the "brigstane" with his face towards the east, and taking his staff in his left hand, [the man] raised his right arm, and pronounced the following incantation, sawing the wind with his arm as he spoke:

"Robbin cam ower da vaana wi' a shü nü; Twabbie, Toobie, Keeliken, Kollickin, Palktrick alanks da robin. Güid sober da wind."—STEWART, p. 200.

Rain Charm.—When a peat fire is nearly consumed, some of the brands often remain standing in an upright in the light white ashes by which they are surrounded. And it was the fancied resemblance which those brands bore to persons, animals, ships, &c., which furnished the fire-reader with the means of foretelling events. One solitary upright brand, resembling a man or woman, was always called a "guest," *i.e.* a stranger or visitor from a distance. If it could be guessed who the person might be, and if welcome, the brand was lifted in the tongs and placed in the centre of the fire, and other brands heaped around it; but if the person was looked upon as an intruder, the brand was dipped in a tub of water, so that the individual represented might get a drenching of rain if he or she attempted the journey.—STEWART, pp. 235, 236.

Taking away and recovering Milk and Butter Profits.—That a person may take away and procure for herself the summer profits of her neighbour's cows, it is the practice to go clandestinely and pluck an handful of grass from the roof of the byre, and give it to her own cows, thereby supposing that the milk and butter which should have been her neighbour's, will by this means become hers. And, in order to regain the profits which are supposed to have been taken away, it is usual to milk in private a cow belonging to the person who is suspected of having taken them, and thereby to get them back.

New Stat. Acct., Shetland, p. 142.

Harvest.—In *Scapha* about a mile from Kirkwall to South-West it is said there was kept a large and ancient cup, which they say belonged to *St Magnus, King of Norway* . . . with which full of some strong drink, their Bishops at their first Landing were presented; which if they drank out they highly praised him and made themselves to believe that they should have many good and fruitful years in his time. This *Buchannan* relates and as Mr *Wallace* observes is still believed there.—BRAND, p. 46.

For other charms see I. *a*, "BUILDINGS"; I. *c*, "*Turbot*"; I. *d*, "*Elfshot*"; I. *e*, "TRIALS"; I. *h*, "SEA"; II. *a*, "YULE."

For silence during magical ceremonies *see* I. *a*, " HOLY WELLS."

SPELLS.

Unst. The following verse it is said would preserve young people from being led by evil spirits into the way of sinners :

"Clapa, clapa süda
Boochs ina schöl ina Bjöda
Bauta deema kjota schin
Swala clovena vjenta in
Roompan pöman söda."

EDMONDSTON and SAXBY, p. 201.

The following is or rather was a potent spell against malediction :

"Bis, Bis, Byo !
Bulva reeka tyo
Tak laigen,
Slogan veggin ;
Bulva reeka tyo."

Ibid., p. 201.

Papa Stour. "*Sparrow Telling.*"—In Papa Stour the sparrows are very destructive to the corn, and the Papa Stourians believed that the beadle of the kirk had the power of " telling " the sparrows away so as never to return, for which they paid him a fee. The "Sparrow Beadle" still lives in the island, though he has not been employed in his " sparrow-telling" capacity for a few years. It must have been rather an amusing sight to have seen and heard him going round the corn-fields using a variety of strange gesticulations, crying "Coosh-sh-sh, Hoosh-sh-sh awa' fra dis toon, an' never come again."—REID, p. 25.

See also I. e, " *Trial of H. Isbister.*"

Shetland. *Against Eagles.* — There are also in this Countrey, as well as in *Orkney* many Eagles which destroy their Lambs, Fowls, &c. For the preventing of which, some when they see the Eagles catching or fleeing away with their prey, use a Charm by taking a string whereon they cast some knots, and repeats a form of words, which being done the Eagle lets her prey fall, though at a great distance from the Charmer, an instance of which I had from a Minister, who told me, that about a Month before we came to Zetland, there was an Eagle that flew up with a Cock at Scalloway, which one of these Charmers seeing, presently took a string, (his garter as was supposed,) and casting some knots thereupon with the using the ordinary words, the Eagle did let the Cock fall into the Sea.

BRAND, p. 117.

See also I. d, "*Da Trow's Dart*"; I. e, "*Transformation Formula,*" I. f, "LEECHCRAFT"; and *ante*, "*Rain Charm,*" etc.

COUNTER CHARMS.

Orkney. *Churning.*—" Three heated stones" and "nine Ave Maryes" were a charm used in the churning of butter. [The allusion is obscure.]—EMERSON, p. viii.

South Ronaldsay and Burray. The existence of fairies and witches is seriously believed by some, who, in order to protect themselves from their attacks, draw imaginary circles, and place knives in the walls of houses. The worst consequence of this superstitious belief is, that when a person loses a horse or cow, it sometimes happens that a poor woman in the neighbourhood is blamed, and knocked in some part of the head, above the breath, until the blood appears.—*Old Stat. Acct.,* v. xv. p. 311.

Shetland. The only safeguard against the malice of witches is to "flight wi' dem," that is, draw them into a controversy and scold them roundly; or, more effectual still, scratch them "abune der breath." A man did so to his cousin who was a witch, and who had bewitched his wife so as to make her lame. He succeeded in scratching the reputed witch on the forehead, and *drew blood*, which is the essential part of the proceeding, and his wife got better *for a time*, "though she deed o' the trouble no lang after." That man and that witch are still [1888] alive.

EDMONDSTON and SAXBY, p. 206.

[*Cf.* I. *c*, "*Gull.*"]

Rowan Tree.—A practice which was at one time very prevalent, [consisted] of wearing a small piece of the branch of the roan-tree, wrapped round with red thread and sewed into some part of the garments, to guard against the effects of an "evil eye," or witchcraft,

> "Roan-tree and red thread
> Will drive the witches a' wud."
> *New Stat Acct.*, Shetland, p. 142.

To the lonely wanderer at nights among the bleak, Shetland hills, it was recommended that he should carry about his person the Sacred Scriptures as a shield to screen him from the attacks of demons and fairies. The Sacred Volume was also employed in detecting theft and the ceremony of "turning the key." The Bible was reputed one of the high points of witchcraft.

Frazer's Mag., p. 49 n.

Spitting.—In Shetland it is held that when a sick person describes his ailment, the listener is apt to have the distemper conveyed to himself, except he spit covertly.

ROGERS, vol. iii. p. 227.

For Spitting, *cf.* I. *e*, "*Trial of H. Wallas.*"

Papa Stour. *Iron.*—To ward off the "dark power" an old razor is kept in the byre, and a piece of steel fastened to the cow's head is supposed to have a benign result.

REID, p. 24.

See also I. *a*, "STONES"; I. *h*, "SEA, *Noggle, Charms*" II. *a*, "YULE."

For other counter charms *see* I. *d*, "*Da Trow's Dart.*"

DIVINATION.

Shetland. *Turning the Sieve.*—(6 *Aug.* 1602.) Jonat Archbald is dempt to quite hir selff with the saxter aithe for the turning of ane siff and riddill for ane pair scheiris quhilk wes tane fra hir guidman and failyeing thairof to pay sax merkis and to underley the law thairfoir as witchcraft.—Minutes of District Court held at Sumburgh, Dunrossness, quoted in GOUDIE, pp. 185-6.

(7 *Aug.* 1602.) Nicole in Culyesetter is dempt to quite himselff of the turning of sieue and the scheiris and that with the saxter aithe and failyeing thairof to pay vj merkis and to underly the law thairfoir as witchcraft.

Ibid., p. 187.

"*Sifting your Siller.*"—Take a sieve, keys, a pair of scissors, a comb and a bit of silver. Open two or three doors, and all the better if there are four, and if they are opposite each other. The person who wants to see his or her future husband or wife looks out the outer door, and then turns the sieve three times with the sun, and then three times against the sun, repeating the following each time they turn it:

> I sift, I tift; I sift, I tift,
> I sift dis night for dee,
> And he (or she) it is to be my true love,
> Let them appear presently.

MS. communication from Rev. THOMAS MATHEWSON, Burravoe, Yell, dated June 19th, 1893

Divination.

Turning the Sleeve.—J. D. was married to C. T.: they had a daughter called May, who had a number of sweethearts, but she loved an Unst lad the best. One night she and another girl went to the barn, shut the door, and put a large stone to the inside, wet their shirt sleeves, hung them to the fire, and went to bed. About midnight there was a great noise at the door, but it was secure, and after a while, the appearance of two men came in through the roof, turned the shirt sleeves, and went out again through the roof. The one that turned May's sleeve was T. M. After that May had no more love for her Unst lad; and ultimately she and T. M. were wed.—MS. communication from Rev. THOMAS MATHEWSON, Burravoe, Yell, dated June 19th, 1893.

Fey Folk.—It is a practice with some to burn the straw on which a corpse has lain, and to examine very narrowly the ashes, from a belief that the print of the individual's foot, who is next to be carried to the grave, will be discovered. The straw is set on fire when the body is lifted and the funeral company are leaving the house.

New Stat. Acct., Shetland, p. 141.

See also, I. e, "*Trial of M. Greive*," and "*Trial of M. Skebister*"; and *ante* "*Rain Charm.*"

(*h*) *SUPERSTITIONS GENERALLY.*

Sandsting. Innumerable instances of superstition yet remain among the people of the lower class, *e.g.* some of them neither eat nor drink on Sunday till after divine service. Others believe that if two infants, that have got no teeth, meet in the same room, one of them will die immediately after. If you praise their children or call them fat, they think you their worst enemy, and such children are certainly doomed to die.—LOW, p. 81.

Orkney. There are many other particulars of this kind of folly still remaining among the more ignorant vulgar, as charming diseases from one to another; foretelling events by dreams; deaths by deathlights, death-drops, and death watches, or by Ghosts here called Ganfers.—LOW, p. 8.

Eynhallow. *Time after Sunset.*—Fabulantur hic antiqui quod, si metantur segetes post solis occasum, subito manat cruor de calamis frumentorum (cf. under " Holy Places "); alii dicunt si equus ligatus fuerit sole decidente facile vagatur undique per noctem fine alicujus . . . si vero non . . . cernere hic posses eorum fictitias et fabulosas traditiones.—JO. BEN *apud* BARRY, p. 442. [The gaps are in the MS.]

For time after Sunset *cf.* I. *e*, " *Trial of K. Grant.*"

Damsay. *Eye Brows.*—Fabulantur quod aliquando supercilia auferuntur inter spatium unius horæ, deinde vero restituuntur.—*Ibid.*, p. 443.

Orkney. *Lucky Days and Months.*—Some days of the week are more fortunate to begin any business of importance; others would spoil it completely; and, in this respect, even some months are much preferable to others.

BARRY, p. 348.

See also II. *b*. "WEDDINGS"; "SEA," below, "*Luck and Unluck.*"

Shetland. *Counting.*—Counting the number of sheep, of cattle, of horses, of fish, or of any of a man's chattels, whether animate or inanimate, has always been considered as productive of bad luck.—TUDOR, p. 173.

Unst. *Name taboo.*—It was considered very rash—even sinful—to mention the name of a dead person, as the individual was likely "to appear" to the one who had named him. Also it was considered unsafe to name people who were believed to have dealings with the unseen world.

EDMONDSTON and SAXBY, p. 187.

Papa Westra. *St. Tredwels Loch.*—It is said that it will appear like Blood before any disaster befall the Royal family.—WALLACE, 1883, p. 24.

[Not in the original ed.]

South Ronaldsay and Burray. *Theft.*—Petty theft is very frequent. There are no Justices of Peace to punish this vice; and if there were, it would be extremely difficult to convict the delinquent; because there is a very general belief, that whoever is concerned in bringing the guilty to punishment, will never thrive.

Old Stat. Acct., v. xv. p. 311.

Baptism.—Within these last seven years the minister has been twice interrupted in administering baptism to a female child, before the male child, who was baptised immediately after. When the service was over, he was gravely told, that he had done very wrong, for as the female child was first baptised, she would, on her coming to the years of discretion, most certainly have a strong beard, and the boy would have none.

Old Stat. Acct., v. xv. p. 311.

For Omens *see* I. *a*, "HOLY WELLS"; "BUILDINGS"; "SEA," below.

For Luck *see* I. *d*, "TROWS."

For Magic Power of Smiths *see* I.*f.*

Orkney. *The Moon.*—The men here kept the observations of the moon in so far that they stall their marts at the waxing of the moon, affirming that they grow in the barrell.

From an entry "Of the Husbandry used by the Orchadians" at the end of Jo. Ben's MS. but in another and later hand.—BARRY, p. 451.

They would think the meat spoiled were they to kill the cattle when that luminary is wanting.

Old Stat. Acct., v. viii. p. 560.

If they kill cattle, they must do it at the growing of that luminary; from an idea that if delayed till the waning, the meat will be of an inferior quality.—BARRY, p. 348.

[They firmly believe] that if they did otherwise, the beef would dwindle in the pot.

New Stat. Acct., Orkney, p. 143.

See also III. *b*, "WEDDINGS."

Shetland. *Freemasonry.*—Freemasonry is almost universally believed, by the lower classes of people in Zetland, to confer on the possessors of the secret the rare faculty of detecting theft. Some curious occurrences of this kind have taken place, where a general threat of applying to a master-mason to discover the culprit, has been followed by restitution, during the night, of the things which had been stolen.—EDMONDSTON, *Shetland*, v. ii. p. 78.

The following document, which the minister obtained possession of at the church door, before it was made public, was issued and signed by four members of the Morton Lodge of Freemasons in Lerwick :

" At a meeting held in Morton Lodge, at Lerwick, upon the 18th day of August 1815, it was reported and faithfully declared upon oath, by M. B. in Easting parish in Shetland, that an woollen web, the property of M. B., shirts and other things also of great value belonging to M. B. ; as also, many suits of mutches, which belonged to M. B. ; all these, as above stated, has been stolen from the green of C. during the first part of this present month. Notice is hereby given, that cruelty forms no part of masonry, yet justice to the injured party must be done, and that if these things so stolen are not returned back before the next meeting of masons upon that business, or at furthest, in fifteen days from this date, a calamity of a severe nature may fall on all that parish in which the present crop may be blasted by storm, and the person or persons guilty shall be publickly led throw the parishes in the neighbourhood on day light, and that by evil spirits not seen by others. This paper to be intimated at the kirk door, that none may plead ignorance. Given under our hands at Lerwick, by authority of the Morton Lodge."—*New Stat. Acct.*, Shetland, p. 143.

Weather Prognostics.—Everything looks large in an east wind.

In severe winters the white swan visits the Orkneys. Its coming foretells continued severity.

When hens are observed to pick and pluck themselves more than usual, rain is near.

" An honest man and a north-west wind generally go to sleep together."

Note.—This is a common saying, and implies that if the wind is from the north-west in the early part of the day, it will veer or fall in the evening. The Westing appears to be important, for in Orkney the saying is : *The west wind is a gentleman, and goes to bed.*—SIR ARTHUR MITCHELL, *Popular Weather Prognostics of Scotland.*

Shetland. A cat " gaanin i' da lift," that is, looking up into the sky, foretells wind. " Sleepin' upo' her harns," that is, sleeping with the back of her head turned down, indicates a calm.—BLIND, *Gent.'s Mag.*, 1882, p. 361.

Vats-gaarin, a halo around the sun, perihelion, supposed to indicate bad weather, especially rain.

EDMONDSTON, *Glossary*, s.v.

Cats-crammacks, clouds over the sky having something of the appearance of hairs streaming from an animal's tail.

Ibid., s.v.

SEA AND FISHING.

Shetland. *Luck.*—On no subject are they more superstitious than in what relates to fishing. Some of the more skilful prophets can foretel, from the knots in the bottom boards of a boat, whether it will be lucky to fish or not ; and whether it will be overset under sail, or be otherwise cast away; and boats have been rejected, and torn up, in consequence of such a prophecy. When they go to the fishing, they carefully avoid meeting any person, unless it be one who has long enjoyed the reputation of being lucky; nor, when the boat has been floated, is it deemed safe to turn it but with the sun. If a man treads on the tongs in the morning, or be asked where he is going, he need not go to the fishing that day. When at sea, the fishermen employ a nomenclature peculiar to the occasion, and scarcely a single thing then retains its usual name. Most of their names are of Norwegian origin, for the Norway men were reported to have been successful fishers. Certain names must not be mentioned while they are setting their lines, especially the minister and the cat; and many others equally unmeaning.

EDMONDSTON, *Shetland*, vol. ii. pp. 73, 74.

Charms.—It is quite a common practice among the Zetland fishermen, when out at the *haaf* or deep-sea fishing, to stick the blade of their knives into the mast to bring luck. Another plan is to spit into the mouth of the last caught cod; and the consequence, they say, is that it will be followed by a fish equally large or larger. Sometimes it is rather amusing to hear an old grey-haired fisherman exclaim, while hauling for cod, "Pu' doon cod!" "come on cod!" or interjections of similar import.

FERGUSSON, p. 169.

Papa Stour. The fishermen consider a piece of steel or silver coin about their boat or lines a valuable safeguard against witchcraft.—REID, p. 24.

See also I. *f*, "*Forespoken Water.*"

Shetland. Our fishermen . . . instead of pouring a cup of ale into the sea to *forespeak* good luck, merely use significant toasts at convivial meetings. "Death to da head dat weers nae hair" (the fish).

Frazer's Mag., p. 497.

Foula, Shetland. *Supernatural Creatures.*—A few old men tell of a wondrous journey they once made over to the mainland, on which occasion they were surrounded by a legion of strange beings—a very host of monsters—who rose out of the sea and threatened to devour them. These old Foula men still grow pale and become unnerved when they tell of that hideous array, which they describe as containing every animal, created and uncreated, with "horrible combinations of bird and beast, and fish and human."—REID, p. 31.

Third Wave.—A vast number of our superstitious beliefs especially those that are, or rather were, connected with forecasts, luck, injuring neighbours by witchcraft, or spells used to counteract such craft, have a direct connection with the Sea—though sometimes also with fire. Water out of the "third die," that is, the wavelet that reaches your feet when you come to the "shoor-mil," namely, the edge of the water, was reckoned of great virtue, and could be used, either in working mischief, or preventing it, or in retaliation. But only the initiated could safely use it, as it was a two-edged weapon.

BLIND, *Gentleman's Magazine*, 1882, p. 363.

See also I. e, "*Trial of K. Grant.*"

Cat Ominous.—It is a good omen if a cat runs before a fisherman on his way to the fishing; a bad omen if she crosses his path—which latter, of course, is a sign that he should give up his intention for that day. Again, if she is observed running to the boat's "nust" before a fisherman returns from sea, it indicates a good catch.

BLIND, *Gentleman's Magazine*, 1882, p. 358.

Orkney. *Sunways Turn.*—In preparing for a voyage, when leaving the shore they always turn their boats in the direction of the sun's motion; and in some places they never fail to utter a short prayer on such occasions.

BARRY, p. 348.

Kirkwall and St Ola. In many days of the year they will neither go to sea in search of fish, nor perform any sort of work at home. . . . On going to sea they would reckon themselves in the most imminent danger were they by accident to turn their boat in opposition to the sun's course.—*Old Stat. Acct.*, v. vii. p. 560.

Orkney. In going to sea they turn the boat in the direction of the sun's course. To move in the opposite way would be considered improper if not dangerous.

New Stat. Acct., Orkney, p. 143.

Shetland. The fishermen, when about to proceed to the fishing, think they would have bad luck, if they were to row the boat "withershins" about. They always consider it necessary to turn her with the sun. Neither do they give the same name to most of the things in the boat, and to several on shore, by which they are usually known.

New Stat. Acct., Shetland, p. 141.

Orkney. The fishermen observe the curious practice of turning their boats in the direction of the sun, when they launch it; avoid whistling, and the mention of the minister's name, as unlucky omens, and instantly desist from their intention of fishing if questioned as to the direction in which they are going.

TEIGNMOUTH, vol. i. p. 286.

See also III. *b*, " WEDDINGS."

Unst. *Luck and Unluck.*—[The people here] dont like their way should be crossed when they go a fishing, particularly by the minister.—LOW, p. 162.

Shetland. Saturday is looked upon as a lucky day for the smacks to sail for the Faroe fishing.—TUDOR, p. 166.

The Sea a Witch.—One of my Shetland correspondents writes:—"'The sea,' said an old woman who was regarded as a good authority in our occult lore, 'is the greatest witch in all the world.'"

BLIND, *Gentleman's Magazine*, 1882, p. 365.

Sea and Fishing.

Tides.—An old man named John Georgeson gave his version of the cause of the tides. Namely, that away far out in the sea, near the edge of the world, there lived a monstrous Sea-Serpent that took about six hours to draw in his breath, and six hours to let it out; which sufficiently accounted for the rise and fall of the waters.

BLIND, *Gentleman's Magazine*, 1882, p. 362.
See also III. *b*, " WEDDINGS."

Drowning Persons.—Two things may be mentioned which are to this day believed in and acted on by living men. At any rate, within living memory they have in numerous cases been known as certainly as anything can be. One of these is the belief that it is "unlucky," or more correctly, "forbidden," to save a person from drowning. The real grounds on which this belief rests are difficult to ascertain. Sir Walter Scott and some others account for it by the explanation, that it was imagined that the rescued would afterwards injure his rescuer, and that he was fated to do so. But from what I have with difficulty learned, I rather believe the notion is that the man who prevents another from drowning will himself perish instead —that the sea will have its prey, and if a man deprives it of its victim, he himself must supply the victim's place. This is clearly a pagan belief pure and simple. The evil spirit—or the god of the sea, good or evil—must have his sacrifice; if you hinder him, you awake his anger, which another victim alone can appease. It is told how a man not only declined to put off his boat to rescue another drowning close inshore, but took the oars out so as to prevent it being used for this purpose; how three men stood and looked at their neighbour drowning before their eyes, and then turned around and walked homewards; how another pulled past a floating woman and paid no heed. These things have happened within forty years, and many other similar cases in every district of the country.— LAURENSON, *Proceed. Soc. Ant. Scot.*, vol. x. pp. 713, 714.

Word-taboos.— A peculiarity in fishermen's observances is their custom of proscribing certain words and names of persons or things as forbidden to be uttered while at sea. Prominently among these are the ordinary terms relating to the church, the minister, or his abode; and from this the inference may be drawn that at an early period it was believed that the mention of the new faith and its priests was hateful to the sea-god, and likely to bring his displeasure on those who named it. Later, when the English tongue was displacing the Norse of the islands, the old words were employed instead of the new when it was necessary to mention those forbidden or unlucky things, and thus, as in a dead language, these fishermen's words and phrases were preserved and handed down to the present day.—LAURENSON, *Proceed. Soc. Ant. Scot.*, vol. x. p. 714.

See also ante, " *Luck*," and I. *c*, " *Turbot.*"

To use ordinary words brings ill-luck [at sea]. Then the sea has to be called "holy toyt." A boat is spoken of as a " fair."—*New Rev.* p. 621.

For other fishing customs, etc., *see* I. *f*, " LEECHCRAFT," II. *a*, " *Fishermen's Foy.*"

SELKIES.

Orkney. In Orkney, selkie was the popular name for seal. Seals were popularly divided into two classes; namely, first, the common seal, here called tang fish, which had no power to assume the human form. These, like other inhabitants of the sea, were called fish. To the other class belonged all seals larger in size than the *Phoca vitulina*; such as the great seal, rough seal, Greenland seal, crested seal, and gray seal,—all of which have been seen in Orkney waters. And it was this class of larger seals that were called "selkie folk," because they had the power of assuming the human form. The believers in this myth were never at a loss to account for its existence; but the causes assigned for the origin of this amphibious human race, so far as known to me, must have been imagined since the introduction of Christianity. Some say the selkie folk were fallen angels, who, for a more trivial fault than that of those consigned to the infernal regions, were condemned to their present state. Others held that the selkie folk were human beings, who, for some grave misdemeanour were condemned to assume the seal's form, and to live in the sea, and were yet allowed to take human form and shape when on dry land. "And who kens," said one of my old gossips, "but they'll maybe some day get leave to come back tae their auld state?"

It was believed that males among the selkie folk sometimes held secret and illicit intercourse with females of the human race. Sometimes these marine gallants became the paramours of married women. The ballad which I hope later on to give is an instance of such connection. And however ungainly the appearance of these gentlemen when in the sea, on assuming human shape they became in form fair, attractive, and in manner winning; and by their seductive powers the female heart seems to have been easily conquered. And if the selkie gentlemen were attractive in the eyes of earth-born women, the selkie females were no less charming in the estimation of men.

Indeed, to see a bevy of these lovely creatures, their seal skins doffed, disporting themselves on a sea-side rock, was enough to fire with admiration the coldest heart.

Let it be noted that the selkie nymphs always appear in groups; they never sit alone combing their hair like the mermaid; and, unlike her, are not represented as wearing long golden hair. And, unlike the mermaid, the selkie folk were never represented as dwelling in "Finfolk-a-heem."

The only home of the selkie folk was some far outlying skerry, or sea-surrounded rock. Indeed, my old informants regarded the selkie folk as a wholly different race of beings from the Finfolk.

Writers on the subject, trusting to incorrect versions of old stories, have often confounded mermaids and seals together, and have often treated the two as identical.

Hibbert in his valuable work on Shetland has fallen into this error, and has been followed by most others whose writings on the subject I have seen. This error is easily accounted for. Most of those writers were unfamiliar with, and had not from childhood lived among the peasantry; had not sat for long winter evenings by the cottage fireside listening to the often tedious and long-winded, but spontaneous flow of old tales, from the lips of men and women who believed in the truth of what they told; and, more essential still, those narrators had not a doubt but that their fireside hearers believed in what they heard.

No Orcadian peasant would lay bare the treasures of his wild lore before the eyes of a stranger. The peasant believed, often correctly, that educated people held his lore in contempt. When they asked questions on old subjects, he suspected their only object was to make him and his stories objects for amusement. In asking for old lore among the Orkney peasantry, I suspect the proverb must be read, " Seek and ye shall not find it."

But to return, the seals when in human shape were generally seen on a dry, but sea-surrounded rock, where in groups they lay basking in the sunshine, or gambolling about in the sunny atmosphere, with their seal skins lying beside them on the rock. The moment that any disturbance arose, or alarm was given, the whole flock flung their sea garments on, and leaped into the sea.

It was only at certain periods and conditions of the tide in which the seals had power to assume the human shape. But these periods were a subject of dispute among my oral authorities.

Versions of the story I am now to tell were at one time rife in every Orkney island; and some of them have already appeared in print. The man who told me this tale was a native of North Ronaldshay, was well read in English literature, and so familiar with Shakespeare that any six lines of that author you quoted he would tell you from what play your quotation was taken. Though above superstitious belief in, he possessed an inexhaustible store of old-world tales. He often assisted me in clearing up some difficulty in Orkney folk-lore.

The goodman of Wastness was well-to-do, had his farm well-stocked, and was a good-looking and well-favoured man. And though many braw lasses in the island had set their caps at him, he was not to be caught. So the young lasses began to treat him with contempt, regarding him as an old young man who was deliberately committing the unpardonable sin of celibacy. He did not trouble his head much about the lasses, and when urged by his friends to take a wife, he said, "Women were like many another thing in this weary world, only sent for a trial to man; and I have trials enouch without being tried by a wife." "If that ould fool Adam had not been bewitched by his wife, he might have been a happy man in the yard of Edin to this day." The old wife of Longer, who heard him make this speech, said to him, "Take doo heed de sell, doo'll may be de sell bewitched some day." "Ay," quoth he, "that will be when doo walks dry shod frae the Alters o' Seenie to dae Boar of Papa."

Well, it happened one day that the goodman of Wastness was down on the ebb (that portion of the shore left dry at low water), when he saw at a little distance a number of selkie folk on a flat rock. Some were lying sunning themselves, while others jumped and played about in great glee. They were all naked, and had skins as white as his own. The rock on which they sported had deep water on its seaward side, and on its shore side a shallow pool. The goodman of Wastness crept unseen till he got to the edge of the shallow pool; he then rose and dashed through the pool to the rock on its other side. The alarmed selkie folk seized their seal skins, and, in mad haste, jumped into the sea. Quick as they were, the goodman was also quick, and he seized one of the skins belonging to an unfortunate damsel, who in terror of flight neglected to clutch it as she sprang into the water.

The selkie folk swam out a little distance, then turning, set up their heads and gazed at the goodman. He noticed that one of them had not the appearance of seals like the rest. He then took the captured skin under his arm, and made for home, but before he got out of the ebb, he heard a most doleful sound of weeping and lamentation behind him. He turned to see a fair woman following him. It was that one of the selkie folk whose seal skin he had taken. She was a pitiful sight; sobbing in bitter grief, holding out both hands in eager supplication, while the big tears followed each other down her fair face. And ever and anon she cried out, "O bonnie man! if there's onie mercy i' thee human breast, gae back me skin! I cinno', cinno', cinno' live i' the sea without it. I cinno', cinno', cinno' bide among me ain folk without my ain seal skin. Oh, pity a peur distressed, forlorn lass, gin doo wad ever hope for mercy theesel'!" The goodman was not too soft-hearted, yet he could not help pitying her in her doleful plight. And with his pity came the softer passion of love. His heart that never loved women before was conquered by the sea-nymph's beauty. So, after a good deal of higgling and plenty of love-making, he wrung from the sea-lass a reluctant consent to live with him as his wife. She chose this as the least of two evils. Without the skin she could not live in the sea, and he absolutely refused to give up the skin.

So the sea-lass went with the goodman and stayed with him for many days, being a thrifty, frugal, and kindly goodwife.

She bore her goodman seven children, four boys and three lasses, and there were not bonnier lasses or statelier boys in all the isle. And though the goodwife of Wastness appeared happy, and was sometimes merry, yet there seemed at times to be a weight on her heart; and many a long longing look did she fix on the sea. She taught her bairns many a strange song, that nobody on earth ever heard before. Albeit she was a thing of the sea, yet the goodman led a happy life with her.

Now it chanced, one fine day, that the goodman of Wastness and his three eldest sons were off in his boat to the fishing. Then the goodwife sent three of the other children to the ebb to gather limpits and wilks. The youngest lass had to stay at home, for she had a beelan foot. The goodwife then began, under the pretence of house-cleaning, a determined search for her long-lost skin. She searched up, and she searched down; she searched but, and she searched ben; she searched out, and she searched in, but never a skin could she find, while the sun wore to the west. The youngest lass sat in a stool with her sore foot on a cringlo. She says to her mother, "Mam, what are doo leukan for?" "O bairn, deu no tell," said her mother, "but I'm leukan for a bonnie skin, tae mak a rivlin that wad ceur thee sare fit." Says the lass, "May be I ken whar hid is. Ae day, whin ye war a' oot, an' ded tought I war sleepan i' the bed, he teuk a bonnie skin doon; he gloured at it a peerie minute, dan folded hid and led hid up under dae aisins abeun dae bed." (Under the aisins—space left by slope of roof over wall-head when not beam-filled.)

When her mother heard this she rushed to the place, and pulled out her long-concealed skin. "Fareweel, peerie buddo!" (a term of endearment), said she to the child, and ran out. She rushed to the shore, flung on her skin, and plunged into the sea with a wild cry of joy. A male of the selkie folk there met and greeted her with every token of delight. The goodman was rowing home, and saw them both from his boat. His lost wife uncovered her face, and thus she cried to him : " Goodman o' Wastness, fareweel tae thee ! I liked dee weel, doo war geud tae me ; bit I lo'e better me man o' the sea!" And that was the last he ever saw or heard of his bonnie wife. Often did he wander on the sea-shore, hoping to meet his lost love, but never more saw he her fair face.

Not only did females of the finfolk sometimes become the temporary wives of men, but males of the watery race frequently formed illicit connection with fair ladies on land. These gentlemen never abode for any length of time on shore. They only came on land to indulge unlawful love. And as when divested of their sea skins they were handsome in form and attractive in manners, they often made havoc among thoughtless girls, and sometimes intruded into the sanctity of married life.

Many wild tales were told of the amorous connection between fair women of earth and those amphibious gentlemen. If a young and fair girl was lost at sea, she was not drowned, but taken captive by selkie folk or finfolk. And in olden times mothers used to sin, that is, to paint the sign of the cross on the breasts of their fair daughters before going by sea to the Lammas Fair. If a beautiful girl grew up to womanhood without the enjoyment of matrimonial bliss, she sometimes indulged in illicit amours with one of the selkie folk. Again, if a married woman found her husband unfaithful to her, she would revenge herself by secret intercourse with a marine lover.

Among many wild tales of the kind, I give one said to have happened in the last bygone century. The name only of our heroine is changed, because her descendants are still among us ; and if any of them should read these lines, let them not think that aught offensive is intended. If the lady was their ancestor, she was also a near relative of ancestors of mine.

Selkies.

Ursilla was the daughter of a laird belonging to one of the oldest families in Orkney. She was handsome and pretty, but had a sternness of manner, and that firmness of features which often presents a masculine exterior in females of Norse blood, and often hides, as with a film of ice, a loving heart within.

Ursilla was not one to wait patiently till some one turned up to offer himself as her husband. Indeed, had any one presumed to approach her as a lover, she would have treated him with haughty disdain, regarding his bold presumption as sufficient ground for his rejection. She determined not to be chosen, but to chose for herself. Her choice fell on a young handsome fellow, who acted as her father's barn-man. But she knew that any disclosure of her passion would mortally offend her old father and bitterly mortify his family pride, and might lead him to disinherit her. So she locked up her love in her own breast ; kept watchful eye on the object of her love, and treated him to a full share of the scoldings she daily bestowed on the servants.

When, however, her father died, and her tocher was safe, she disclosed her passion to the young man, and commanded him to marry her—a command which he was too gallant to disobey. Her marriage excited among the gentry great indignation : to think that one of their class should marry a farm servant ! Ursilla treated their contempt with indifference ; she made a good housewife, managed her house well, and also, it was said, managed her husband and the farm.

So far I have given what I believe to be a true account of Ursilla, having had it from descendants of her relatives. What follows I believe to be an imaginary tale, invented by gossips, in order to account for a strange phenomenon visibly seen on her descendants : and it is only given to illustrate one of the popular beliefs.

Yes, Ursilla was married, and all went well and happy, so far as outward appearances showed ; yet Ursilla was not happy. If disappointed in her husband, she was far too proud to acknowledge it, knowing that the gentry would only say in derision, "She shaped her own cloth, let her wear her ill-fitting dress." Whatever the cause might be, there was a terrible want—a want that Ursilla felt bitterly. And she was not the woman to sit down and cry over sorrow; she determined to console herself by having intercourse with one of the selkie folk.

She went at early morning and sat on a rock at high-tide mark, and when it was high tide she shed seven tears in the sea. People said they were the only tears she ever shed. But you know this is what one must do if she wants speech with the selkie folk. Well, as the first glimpse of dawn made the waters gray, she saw a big selkie swimming for the rock. He raised his head, and says he to her, "What's your will with me, fair lady?" She likely told him what was in her mind; and he told her he would visit her at the seventh stream (spring tide), for that was the time he could come in human form. So, when the time was come, he came; and they met over and over again. And, doubtless, it was not for good that they met so often. Any way, when Ursilla's bairns were born, every one of them had web hands and webbed feet, like the paws of a selkie. And did not that tell a tale? The midwife clipped the webs between every finger, and between every toe of each bairn. "She showed the shears that she used to my grandmother." So said the narrator. And many a clipping Ursilla clipped, to keep the fins from growing together again; and the fins not being allowed to grow in their natural way, grew into a horny crust in the palms of the hands and soles of the feet. And this horny substance is seen in many of Ursilla's descendants to this day.

Whatever may be thought of this tale, its last sentence is quite true. The horn still appears in feet and hands of some of the lady's descendants. One, two, or three in a family may show the abnormal horny substance; while brothers and sisters are entirely free from the troublesome horn.

Some ten years ago, while engaging a harvest hand, I said to one of these men, " Of course, you can do all kinds of harvest work?" "Oh na, sir," said he, "hid's nae use tae tell a lee about hid; but 1 cinno' bind a sheaf wi' this plaguid horn in me livs." Another of the same family told me that when, through the growth of the horn, he was unable to walk or work, he would, with hammer and chisel, cut off large slices of horn from the soles of his feet. This growth is by no means confined to those engaged in manual labour. I have felt it on the hands of one of the same race who followed a profession where manual labour was not required.

This curious phenomenon seems well worthy of careful investigation by the physiologist. Pity it could not be traced to the seal; we might then be in sight of the missing link.

Many wild tales were told of the offspring of such strange parentage who had webbed hands and feet; but the foregoing will serve to illustrate a once popular belief.

DENNISON in *Scottish Antiquary*, v. vii. pp. 171-177.

Shetland. Of mermen and merwomen, many strange stories are told. Beneath the depths of the ocean, an atmosphere exists adapted to the respiring organs of certain beings, resembling, in form, the human race, who are possessed of surpassing beauty, of limited supernatural powers, and liable to the incident of death. They dwell in a wide territory of the globe far below the region of fishes, over which the sea, like the cloudy canopy of our sky, loftily rolls, and they possess habitations constructed of the pearly and coraline productions of the ocean. Having lungs not adapted to a watery medium, but to the nature of atmospheric air, it would be impossible for them to pass through the volume of waters that intervenes between the sub-marine and supra-marine world, if it were not for the extraordinary power that they inherit, of entering the skin of some animal capable of existing in the sea, which they are enabled to occupy by a sort of demoniacal possession. One shape that they put on is that of an animal human above the waist, yet terminating below in the tail and fins of a fish, but the most favourite form is of the larger seal or Haaf-fish; for, in possessing an amphibious nature, they are enabled not only to exist in the ocean, but to land on some rock where they frequently lighten themselves of their sea-dress, resume their proper shape, and with much curiosity examine the nature of the upper world belonging to the human race. Unfortunately, however, each merman or merwoman possess but one skin, enabling the individual to ascend the seas, and if, on visiting the abode of man, the garb should be lost, the hapless being must unavoidably become an inhabitant of our earth.—HIBBERT, p. 566.

Ve Skerries, Shetland. The Ve Skerries are, according to popular belief, the particular retreat of the fair sons and daughters of the sea, where they are defended by a raging surf, that continually beats around them, from the obtrusive gaze and interference of mortals; here they release themselves from the skins within which they are inthralled, and, assuming the most exquisite human forms that ever were opposed to earthly eyes, inhale the upper atmosphere destined for the human race, and, by the moon's bright beams, enjoy their midnight revels.

As the green-haired denizens of the ocean are mortal, the visits that they pay the upper world are not always unattended with peril. But the greatest danger to which these rangers of the sea seem liable are from the mortal hurts that they receive, upon taking on themselves the form of the larger seals or Haaf-fish; for when shot under this shape, the blood no sooner issues forth from the wound, and mixes with the ocean's brine, than it possesses the supernatural power of causing an awful swell and break of the sea, in the vicinity of the spot where the victim, from a sense of the pain inflicted, has been seen to dive. On the Ve Skerries the inhabitants of submarine depths are liable to considerable peril, whenever the natives of Papa Stour repair thither, at certain times of the year, for the purpose of attacking the seals, as they lie in the hollow of a certain crag. A story is told of a boat's crew that landed with this design at one of the Stacks;—they stunned a number of these animals, and, in this state, stripped them of their skins, with the fat attached to them,—left the carcases on the rock, and were about to set off for the shore of Papa Stour, when such a tremendous swell arose, that every one flew quickly to the boat, and were successful in entering it, except one man, who had imprudently lingered behind. The crew were unwilling to leave a companion to perish on the skerries, but the surge increased so fast, that after many unsuccessful attempts to bring the boat close in to the stack the unfortunate wight was left to his fate. A stormy night came on, and the deserted Shetlander saw no prospect before him but of perishing with cold and hunger, or of being washed into the sea by the breakers which threatened to dash over the rocks. At length, he perceived many of the seals, who in their flight had escaped the attack of the boatmen;—they approached the skerry, disrobed themselves of their amphibious hides, and appeared like the sons and daughters of the ocean. Their first object was to assist in the recovery of their friends, who, having been stunned by clubs, had, in this state, been deprived of their skins. When the fled animals had regained their sensibility, they assumed their proper form of mermen or merwomen, and began to lament in mournful lay, wildly accompanied by the storm that was raging around, the loss of their sea-dress, which would prevent them from enjoying their native azure atmosphere, and coral mansions that lay below the deep waters of the

Atlantic. But their chief lamentation was for Ollavitinus, the son of Gioga, who, having been stripped of his seal's skin, would be for ever parted from his comates, and condemned to be an outcast inhabitant of the upper world. Their song was at length broken off, by observing one of their enemies viewing, with shivering limbs, and looks of comfortless despair, the wild waves that dashed over the stack. Gioga immediately conceived the idea of rendering subservient to the advantage of her son the perilous situation of the man. She addressed him with mildness, proposing to carry him safe on her back across the sea to Papa Stour, on condition of receiving the seal-skin of Ollavitinus. A bargain was struck, and Gioga clad herself in her amphibious garb; but, the Shetlander, alarmed at the sight of the stormy main that he was to ride through, prudently begged leave of the matron, for his better preservation, that he might be allowed to cut a few holes in her shoulders and flanks in order to procure, between the skin and the flesh, a better fastening for his hands and feet. The request being complied with, the man grasped the neck of the seal, and committing himself to her care, she landed him safely at Acres Gio in Papa Stour; from which place he immediately repaired to a skeo at Hamna Voe, where the skin was deposited, and honourably fulfilled his part of the contract by affording Gioga the means whereby her son could again revisit the ethereal space over which the sea spread its green mantle.

HIBBERT, pp. 567-569.

Shetland. *The Great Silkie of Sule Skerry.*—Another version of the foregoing story is given by Capt. F. W. L. Thomas, according to which the silky who rescued the man was not the mother but the mate of the one whose skin was to be restored. Two holes are cut in the Silky's skin by the rescued man to hold on by, and the truth of his story is proved some weeks afterwards to the incredu-

Selkies.

lous people by the body of a large seal being found upon the shore, having the two holes in the skin by which the fisherman had held. Capt. Thomas continues: Such is one of the legends of the Shetlanders, as related to me during my residence among the natives of these northern Isles; and which may serve as an illustration of the popular belief in which the following ballad originated. The ballad itself is too regular and well constructed to be very old, but it may prove interesting to the Society as a graceful record of Scandinavian romance. I must not forget to add that it was sung to a tune sufficiently melancholy to express the surprise and sorrow of the deluded mother of the Phocine babe.

> An eart'ly nourris sits and sings,
>   And aye she sings "Ba lily wean;
> Little ken I my bairnis father,
>   Far less the land that he staps in."
>
> Then ane arose at her bed fit,
>   An' a grumly guest I'm sure was he;
> "Here am I thy bairnis father,
>   Although that I be not comelie.
>
> "I am a man upo' the lan',
>   An' I am a Silkie in the sea;
> And when I'm far and far frae lan',
>   My dwelling is in Sule Skerrie."
>
> "It was na weel," quo' the maiden fair.
>   "It was na weel, indeed," quo' she;
> "That the Great Silkie of Sule Skerrie,
>   S'uld hae come and aught a bairn to me."
>
> Now he has ta'en a purse of goud,
>   And he has pat it upo' her knee;
> Sayin' "Gie to me, my little young son,
>   An' tak' thee up thy nourris fee.
>
> "An' it sall come to pass on a simmer's day
>   Quhen the sin shines het on evera stane,
> That I will tak my little young son,
>   An' teach him for to swim the faem.

> "An' thu sall marry a proud gunner,
> An' a proud gunner I'm sure he'll be;
> An' the very first schot that ere he schoots,
> He'll schoot baith my young son and me."

Capt. F. W. L. Thomas in *Proceedings of the Society of Antiquaries of Scotland*, 1851, vol. i. pp. 86-89.

See III. *c*, Ballads, "*Ballad o' de Lathie Odivere.*"

Unst, Shetland. Sometimes mermen and merwomen have formed connubial attachments with the human race. A story is told of an inhabitant of Unst, who, in walking on the sanday margin of a voe, saw a number of these beings dancing by moonlight, and several seal-skins strewed beside them on the ground. At his approach they immediately fled to secure their garbs, and taking upon themselves the form of seals, plunged immediately into the sea. But as the Shetlander perceived that one skin lay close to his feet, he snatched it up, bore it swiftly away, and placed it in concealment. On returning to the shore he met the fairest damsel that was ever gazed upon by mortal eyes, lamenting the robbery, by which she should become an exile from her submarine friends, and a tenant of the upper world. Vainly she implored the restitution of her property; the man had drunk deeply of love, and was inexorable,—but offered her protection beneath his roof as his betrothed spouse. The merlady, perceiving that she must become an inhabitant of the earth, found that she could not do better than accept of the offer. This strange connubial attachment subsisted for many years, and several children were the fruits of it, who retained no further marks of their origin than in the resemblance which a sort of web between their fingers, and a particular bend of their hands, bore to the forefoot of a seal,—this peculiarity being possessed by the descendants of the family at the present day. The Shetlander's love for his merwife was unbounded; but his affection was coldly returned. The lady would often steal

Selkies.

alone to the desert strand, and on a signal being given, a large seal would make his appearance, with whom she would hold, in an unknown tongue, an anxious conference. Years had thus glided away, when it happened that one of the children, in the course of his play, found concealed beneath a stack of corn a seal's skin, and, delighted with the prize, ran with it to his mother. Her eyes glistened with rapture,—she gazed upon it as her own,—as the means by which she could pass through the ocean that led to her native home,—she burst forth into an ecstasy of joy, which was only moderated when she beheld her children, whom she was now about to leave, and, after hastily embracing them, fled with all speed towards the sea-side. The husband immediately returned,—learned the discovery that had taken place,—ran to overtake his wife, but only arrived in time to see her transformation of shape completed,—to see her in the form of a seal, bound from the ledge of a rock into the sea. The large animal of the same kind with whom she had held a secret converse soon appeared, and evidently congratulated her, in the most tender manner, on her escape. But, before she dived to unknown depths, she cast a parting glance at the wretched Shetlander, whose despairing looks excited in her breast a few transient feelings of commiseration. "Farewell," said she to him, "and may all good attend you. I loved you very well when I resided upon earth, but I always loved my first husband much better."

These inhabitants of a submarine world were, in the later periods of Christianity, regarded as fallen angels, who were compelled to take refuge in the seas: they had, therefore, the name of Sea-Trows given to them, as belonging to the dominion of the Prince of Darkness.

HIBBERT, pp. 569, 570.

Shetland.—From their shyness, their great strength, and the singular intelligence of their aspect, the Shetland fishermen imagine seals to be fallen spirits in metempsychosis, enduring in the form of seals a mitigated punishment. For this reason, however eagerly they may be killed for the sake of their valuable skins and blubber, it is generally done not without compunction and misgivings, it being supposed that they are both powerful to injure and malevolent to revenge. [A young fisherman caught one and skinned it, afterwards tossing the carcase into the sea; thereafter joining his companions who were waiting for him.] Meanwhile the seal having only been stunned and stripped, soon revived to feel particularly cold, and still more disconsolate at his changed and disfigured condition. Sad and miserable he wandered through the waters lamenting, and in this plight he retired to the neighbourhood of a coral bower, where a mermaid had her abode. The latter overheard the sad plaint of the cruelly used seal, and after kindly soothing, asked if she could help him. *Selkie* imagined she might, but only by regaining for him the covering of which he had been so ruthlessly bereft. Whereupon, the kind and gentle being darted off on her compassionate and friendly errand.

Now the spoiler's conscience had by this time sorely smitten him for having destroyed the seal that morning; he believed some evil would assuredly overtake him; he muttered many a prayer and many a vow, and carefully concealed his fault from his comrades, giving them to understand, that he had obtained the much coveted skin from an animal found dead on the shore. How horrified then was he, when a hook on their fishing-lines drew into their boat a mermaid!

Eagerly he implored the other men to release her instantly; but they over-ruled his wishes, from the conviction that they would obtain a considerable reward for such an extraordinary capture. The mermaid was therefore consigned to a secure place in the boat, and laid carefully on *the skin of the seal,* that very prize for which she had thus risked her life. After a few plaintive cries, the self-devoted maiden of the sea began to feel, that out of her native element she could not long survive, and that she would soon indeed fall a victim to her friendship; but at the same time, she well knew, the demons of the deep would avenge her, and that when the boat had sunk to the caves and groves below, though all too late for her, the seal would find his robe again. It so proved accordingly. The mermaid had hardly gasped her last, when a sudden and teriffic storm arose. In the hurry and alarm of the moment the men forgot their late prey; but the murderer of the seal believed firmly his hour was come, and that the associates of the "fallen angel" [the seal, a name by which the animal is known in Shetland] were busy at their demon work of revenge. The boat was lost with all her crew. When she sunk in the whelming billows, the unhappy seal recovered his clothing, but had to lament over the dead body of his devoted friend. For this reason, the seals have ever since constituted themselves the especial guardians of the mermaiden race. They watch them with grateful solicitude,—often supply them with dainties from dangerous deeps, where mermaids may not venture; and while frequently themselves charmed listeners of the sea-maids' wondrous songs, never remit a vigilant guard over their safety, or neglect to give prompt alarm should danger approach. Indeed, it often happens, that seals fall victims to this self-imposed task, thus repaying the dearly displayed devotion of a mermaid to one of their race.

EDMONDSTON, *Sketches*, pp. 79-82.

Quarff, Shetland. *Mermen and Mermaids.*—About two Years and an half or three Years ago, there was a Boat passing with several Gentlemen of the Countrey in it, and by the way in the Voe of Quarf, through which they went, there appeared something unto them with its Head above the Water, which as they could discern, had the Face of an old Man, with a long Beard hanging down; first it appeared at some distance from them, and then coming nearer to their Boat, they had a clear sight of it; The sight was so very strange and affrighting, that all in the Boat were very desirous to be on Land, tho the Day was fair and the Sea calm; a Gentleman declaring, (as a Minister in Company with them, and saw this sight informed me), that he never saw the like, tho he had travelled through many Seas.

I heard another remarkable story like unto this, that about 5 Years since, a Boat at the Fishing drew her Lines, and one of them, as the Fishers thought, having some great Fish upon it, was with greater difficulty than the rest raised from the Ground, but when raised it came more easily to the surface of the Water upon which a Creature like a Woman presented it self at the side of the Boat, it had the Face, Arms, Breasts, Shoulders, &c. Of a Woman, and long Hair hanging donn the Back, but the nether part from below the Breasts, was beneath the Water, so that they could not understand the shape thereof: The two Fishers who were in the Boat being surprised at this strange sight, one of them unadvisedly drew a Knife, and thrust it in her Breast, whereupon she cryed, as they judged, *Alas*, and the Hook giving way she fell backward and was no more seen: The Hook being big went in at her Chin and out at the upper Lip. The Man who thrust the Knife into her is now dead, and, as was observed, never prospered after this, but was still haunted by an evil Spirit, in the appearance of an old Man, who, as he thought, used to say unto him, *Will ye do such a thing who Killed the Woman*; the other Man then in the Boat is yet alive in the Isle of Burra. This a Gentleman and his Lady told me, who said they had it from the Baillie of that place to which the Boat did belong: It being so strange I enquired at severals thereanent, which tho many were ignorant of, yet some said that they had heard thereof, and judged it to be very true.

BRAND, pp. 113, 114.

Shetland. A mermaid had the ill-luck once to be caught on a hook, and dragged into a boat. She begged for liberty, and promised, if the men let her go, that any wish they might chose should be granted. The skipper thereupon dropped the mermaid over the gunwale, and as she dived to her home she sang gleefully :

> " Muckle gude I wid you gie,
> And mair I wid ye wish,
> There's muckle evil in the sea,
> Scoom weel your fish."

" Cheated, and by a mermaid! " cried the skipper, and only one of the six men belonging to the boat took any notice of the sea-maiden's injunction. But one *did* scoom weel his fish, and found a splendid pearl among the scooming.

EDMONDSTON and SAXBY, p. 228.

Sometimes they catch with their Nets and Hooks *Tritons*, they call them *Shoupiltins* and Mermaids, but these are rare and but seldom seen.—SIBBALD, p. 9.

Shetland. "*Noggle.*"—There is a "trow" called a "Neogle," somewhat akin to the water-kelpie of other lands, who makes his appearance about mills, particularly when grinding, in the shape of a beautiful poney [*sic*]. That he may attract the attention of the person who acts the part of the miller, he seizes and holds fast the wheel of the mill; and, as is natural, the miller goes out to examine into the cause of the stoppage; when, to his astonishment, a beautiful poney, saddled and bridled, is standing, and ready to be mounted; who but an old miller could let slip such a fair opportunity for a ride? But if he should neglect warnings, and unguardedly put his foot in the stirrup, his fate is sealed. Neither bit or bridle avail him anything. Off goes the poney, bog or bank arrest not his course, till in the deep sea he throws his rider, and himself evanishes in a flash of flame. But some millers are proof against the temptation, having been taught caution by the fate of others; and instead of taking a ride, salute his Neogleship with a fiery brand through the lightning-tree hole, which makes him immediately scamper away.—*New Stat. Acct.*, p. 142.

With regard to the legendary attributes of the Nuggle, he was believed to be more deceitful than courageous; and his sole bent seemed to be to play mischievous pranks on the human race. I am not aware of any Shetland word that connects the name with water, but the tradition is that the Nuggle was never found at any distance from the water; generally frequenting a footpath near a loch or a burn on which water-mills were built. The object the Nuggle had in frequenting footpaths near a loch, was to offer his services to any unsuspecting wayfarer who might feel disposed to take advantage of them, in order to facilitate his progress, if likely to be benighted. In form he was exactly like a pony, with the exception of his tail, which was said to resemble the rim of a wheel, but which he cunningly kept concealed between his hind legs, when he meant to victimise any pedestrian; and woe be to the man who bestrode him without examining that appendage! It was not stated whether he used his tail as a means of locomotion or not; but no sooner had he felt the weight of his victim, than with lightning speed he flew into the water, and the equestrian found himself submerged beyond his depth, and if he ever gained the shore, it was no fault of the Nuggle. He did not, however, attempt attack; but it is said when the rider got his head above water, he saw him disappear in cloudy vapour or blue flame.

This was one of his pranks, the other was alleged to be played on people grinding corn at the water-mill. All of a sudden the mill would stand still, while the water was running on the wheel, or "tirl" in full power. This was very unpleasant to an individual who was alone in the mill in the night—perhaps a mile from the nearest habitation. The cure for this was to throw a fire-brand down the "lighting-hole" in the "looder." It appears the miscreant can't stand fire, for no sooner is the cure, applied than he lets go his hold of the "tirl," and the machinery is again in motion. Numerous instances are recorded, illustrating both these phases of his propensity to work mischief.

[From Mr. Laurenson Mr. Blind obtained an account of a man who had "quite recently" seen the "Nuggle." Mr. Laurenson says :]

"The Man is a very worthy, 'decent' man (as they call a sensible well-behaved person here), and well known to me from childhood. But I certainly never would have supposed that he believed in the 'Njuggle,' had we not accidentally come on the subject. He told me that, when a young man, one night his sister and he were coming down by a 'burn,' each carrying a lighted brand, to show them their way, a very common mode of lighting up the path in the Shetland country districts in winter. The night was very dark. Some sparks from their brands blew into the water, and that moment 'a creature like a Shetland horse' rose in the middle of the burn, rushed down stream, straight out the mouth of the burn, and away into the sea. They were then near the sea; and they saw it vanish therein. Then they knew it was the 'Njuggle,' because, when fire touches the water, he rushes off. My informant had a friend who one night was grinding in his mill. Suddenly the mill stopped. He suspected it was the 'Njuggle,' and slipped a lighted brand down the shaft hole of the mill. When it touched the water, the wheel went round again, as before, the Njuggle having let it·go. He is of a grey colour."

In an account of the Nuggle obtained from another correspondent it is stated that:

"The Water Nuggle — also called in some parts of Shetland, the Shoepultie—resembles the Scotch Water Kelpie strongly in almost every particular, save the tail, . . . which he knew how . . . to use on certain occasions as a propeller."

BLIND, *Contemporary Review*, 1881, pp. 189-191.

An ancestor of George Henderson, of Burravoes, who dwelt in Unst, was wont to rise early. One morning he rose early, and went out for a walk. On his way home, he was coming along the edge of a loch, and wished that he had something to ride on. And he soon came to a white mare, and he jumped on her, and rode her along the loch, and she always sought towards the loch, and he tried to keep her from it. But as they rode along, she grew so persistent that he came off, and she went on the loch and over the water in a blue "low."

KARL BLIND, *Gentleman's Magazine*, 1882, p. 369.

Foula, Shetland. One noted spirit,—the "Nygel," or "Nigle" was supposed to appear near streams of running-water, and particularly about water-mills, where, in the night, he seized and held fast the water-wheel with his teeth, until he was driven away by brands of fire thrown at him. In colour and size he varied, but behoved always to be shaped like a quadruped,—to have glaring eyes, terrible teeth, and a tail like the rim of an immense wheel turned up over his back. It is said that he once entered a dwelling and expelled the inmates, after which the place was not occupied for thirty years.—REID, p. 31.

[Mr. G. F. Black has been informed by a native of Foula that until within recent years it was common for mothers in putting their children to bed at night to caution them: "Now be good or the Noggle will come and take you away."]

Selkies.

Delting, Shetland. "Dey wir great stories aboot da Nyugl whan I was young. Dey said 'at da Nyugl wid stop da water mills. He wid grip hed o' da fedirs o' da tirl an' stop da mill. An' dey wid slip fire doon da lightneen' tree-hole, ir stik a knife ita da groti. (Da widen busheen i' da understeen, 'at da spindle kam up troo, dey caad dat da groti.) An as syün as da knife kem ita da groti, da Nyugl wid slip an' flee. An' dey wid see him too. He wiz lek a horse; gre, ir some colour lek dat. An' dey wid see him upo' da daylight. If dey wir gyain' alang a loch, he wid come ta dem, gyain' da sam way. An' he wid come upo' dem; an' some wiz fül enough to ride him. An' if dey did, he ran upo' da loch wi' dem, an' dey got a dookin'. Ir if dey said da neem o' Gyüd, he wid vanish. He aye vanished in a fire."—KARL BLIND, *Gentleman's Magazine*, 1882, p. 370. Written down from the recitation of an old man in Delting, Shetland.

Whalsay, Shetland. There was a man in Whalsay, who did not believe in Nyogles, or fairies, or spirits. And one night he was at the *kreigs* at Skura, and had drawn his *büdi* of piltaks. And ere long, on his way home, he came to a black horse, and he went on him. And the horse began to run, until he was going so fast that the man did not know whether he was on the earth *or in the air*. At last he took his knife and drove it into the horse, and he went from under him, and went over the banks *in a blue* "*low*."—KARL BLIND, *Gentleman's Magazine*, 1882, pp. 369-70.

See also II. *a*, "YULE."

PART II.

TRADITIONAL CUSTOMS.

(a) *FESTIVAL CUSTOMS.*

Shetland. Their Festivals are Christmas, Newyearsday, Uphaliday (the last day of Yule), Bonny Sunday, Peace Sunday (Easter), Johnsmass (J. Baptist's), Lambmass, Candlemass, Hallowmass, etc., and to each of these they annex particular ceremonies mostly drawn from the Papish times.—LOW, p. 82.

Holy Days.—Besides the well-known festivals still recognised, and the legal term-days of Christmas, Candlemas, Lammas, Whitsunday, Martinmas, Pasch-Sunday, and St. John's Day (December, 27), there are still dated Lawrence Mass (August 23), Korsmas (3d May and 14th September), Fastern Eve (before Lent), Catherine Mass (22nd December), Boo Helly (fifth day before Christmas), Bainer Sunday (first day before Christmas), Antinmas (twenty-fourth day after Christmas), or Uphellia Day, Solomon's Even (3d November), Sow-day (17th December), Martinbullimas (St. Swithin's Day), Johnsmass (24th June).

LAURENSON, *Proceed. Soc. Ant. Scot.*, vol. x., p. 716.

Saints' Days.—Several of the Isles have their Saints' Days which some do superstitiously observe. There is one day in Harvest, on which the more ignorant, especially in Rousa, say, if any work the Ridges will blood.

BRAND, p. 61.

(Cf. I. *a*, "HOLY PLACES," I. *h*, "SUPERSTITIONS GENERALLY.")

Mainland. *Crosskirk.*—The superstitious Commons of old used to frequent [this] in the silence of the night, each carrying their candles with them, and there feasted, and sported until day, but this Superstitious Custome is now banished.—SIBBALD, p. 72.

Lady Parish, Orkney. *New Year.*—Formerly it was customary for companies of men, on New Year's morning, to go to the houses of the rich, and awake the family, by singing the New Year's song, in full chorus. When the song was concluded, the family entertained the musicians with ale and bread; and gave them a smoked goose or a piece of beef.—*New. Stat. Acct.*, Orkney, p. 142.

See also III. *c.* "SONGS."

Sandwick. *Mar. 3rd. June 29th.*—The people do no work on the 3d day of March, in commemoration of the day on which the church of Sandwick was consecrated; and as the church was dedicated to St Peter, they also abstain from working for themselves on St Peter's day (29th June), but they will work to another person who employs them.—*Old Stat. Acct.*, vol. xvi. pp. 460, 461.

For Lent and Easter *see* I.*a*, "BUILDINGS."

Sandstiney & Aithstiney. *June 24th. Fishermen's foy.*—Johnsmas (24th June, O.S.) is regarded by the fishermen as a holiday. Again, before striking their tents at Lammas, and bidding adieu to the busy, bustling, perilous occupations of the summer, the fishermen who have been accustomed to associate together during the season, meet and take a parting cup, when the usual toast on this occasion is, "Lord! open the mouth of the grey fish, and haud thy hand about the corn." This meeting is known by the name of the fishermen's foy.

New Stat. Acct., Shetland, p. 132.

[For Allhallows *see* I.*e*, "*Trial of J. Sinclair*," and I.*f*, "*Forespoken Water.*"]

Shetland. Solomon's-Avon (Even), November 3d.; a superstition of ill-omen connected with this day.

EDMONDSTON, *Glossary*, s.v.

Sowday.—In a part of the parish of Sandwick, every family that has a herd of swine, kills a sow on the 17th day of December, and thence it is called Sow-day. There is no tradition as to the origin of this practice.

Old Stat. Acct., vol. xvi. p. 460.

Westray. *Yule.*—One custom in this parish, and common to Orkney at large, is that of allowing the servants four or five days liberty at Christmas, to enjoy themselves. Only the most necessary part of domestic work, with due attention to the bestial on the farm, is done on these days. The master of the house has, also, to keep up a well furnished table for all his servants at that season.

Another practice peculiar to this place is, that of observing punctually those days in the Roman calendar, on which eating and drinking are practised with more liberality than usual.—*New Stat. Acct.*, Orkney, p. 127.

Shetland. . . . Yule was not one festival, but a series of them, and that period is still named by the Shetlanders "the Yules."

The Yules began with Tul-ya's e'en, which was seven days before Yule-day. On that night the Trows received permission to leave their homes in the heart of the earth and dwell, if it so pleased them, above ground. . . . One of the most important of all Yule-tide observances was the "saining" required to guard life or property from the Trows. If the proper observances were omitted the "grey-folk" were sure to take advantage of the opportunity.

At day-set on Tul-ya's e'en two straws were plucked from the stored provender and laid, in the form of a cross, at the steggie leading to the yard where the stacks of hay and corn, &c., were kept. A hair from the tail of each cow, or "beast o' burden," was plaited together and fastened over the byre door, and a "lowing taand" was carried through the barn and other out-houses.

Helya's night followed Tul-ya's e'en. On Helya's night milk brose was partaken of, and children were committed to the care of "Midder Mary."

A Shetlander told me she remembered when she was a little girl seeing this ceremony performed by her old grandmother. "Minnie raise up frae the fire and gaed to the cradle where our infant was sleeping. She spread her hands ower the cradle-head and said, loud out—

> 'Mary midder had de haund
> Ower aboot for sleepin'-baund,
> Had da lass and had da wife,
> Had da bairn a' its life.
> Mary midder had de haund
> Round da infant's o' oor laund.'

Then Minnie came to the bed and said the same ower us, and a' the time she was doing sae, auld da' was standing raking the peats back and fore upon the hearthstane, and saying some words; but we never got to ken what it was he said."

Dec. 20th.—Thammasmass e'en was five nights before Yule-day, and this evening was supposed to be peculiarly holy. No work of any kind was done after day-set, and—unlike all other evenings of Yule-tide—no amusements were allowed. The smallest deviation from what was considered orthodox on this occasion was sure to bring bad luck.

> "The very babe unborn
> Cries oh dul! dul!
> For the breaking o' Thammasmass nicht,
> Five nichts afore Yule."

Byana's Sunday.—The Sunday preceding Yule-day was called Byana's Sunday. That evening half a cow's head was boiled and eaten for supper. The fat skimmed off the water was made, with burstin into brose. The skull was carefully cleaned, a candle stuck in the eye-socket, and then it was set aside for use later in the season. Yule e'en was the great time of preparation for the crowning festival of all. Though the family might be very poor indeed, they always contrived to have a piece of "flesh-meat" to cook on Yule e'en.

After the ordinary bread was baked, a round oatcake was kneaded for each child, differing in size as the young ones differed in age. These cakes were pinched into points round the outer edge, and a hole was made in the centre, and they were named emphatically *the* Yule-cakes. . . . Each member of the family washed their whole person, and donned a clean (if possible, new) garment, in which they slept that night. When the hands or feet were put into the water "three living coals were dropped into the water, else the Trows took the power o' the feet or hands."

Cf. I. *e*, "TRIALS."

The house was carefully tidied, "no unkirsn things left in sight," and all soiled water thrown away. All locks were opened, a lamp was left burning all night, and an "iron blade" was laid on a table near the door.

Before daylight on Yule morning the gudeman of the house got up and lit the candle, which had been stuck in the eye-socket of the cow's skull. Then he proceeded with this unique candlestick to the byre and fed the beasts, giving to all a little better food than usual, which they were expected to eat by the light of that candle. The next thing the gudeman did was "to go round to the folk of the house with drams," and even the bairns were bound to "taste, if nae mair," while to all he said—

"Yule gude and yule gear
Follow de trew da year."

Breakfast was eaten by artificial light, and on this occasion many a bit of hoarded candle was produced by the youngsters, who had secreted those morsels for months that they might have a fine lighting up on Yule morning.

No work of any kind was done upon Yule-day, for the old rhyme said—

> "Nedder bake nor brew,
> Shape nor shew,
> Upon gude Yule,
> Else muckle dul
> Will be dy share
> Dis year and mair."

A girl who, "wishful to show contempt for auld ways (and moreover needing sair to finish a pair o' socks that the laird was to buy frae her), took ta her wires [knitting-needles] upon Yule-day. A' folk telled her to be wise, and some said she was see! And, puir lass! she never saw another Yule."

Football was the amusement of the men, while the brief day lasted; dancing the amusement of the evening. Trows are excessively fond of dancing, and always try to join the revels, but this they can only do in the disguise of a mortal. Woe-betide the man, woman, or child who has forgotten to be "sained," and by such omission given the Trows power to do as they will.

EDMONDSTON and SAXBY, p. 136.

Once a merry young couple desired to share in the merriment in a neighbour's house one Yule evening. They did not wish to be encumbered by their little ones, so they bribed the boys (two in number, aged four and five) with extra cakes and sweets to go early to bed, and as soon as the little ones' eyes were closed in slumber, the youthful parents stole away to join the dancers in the next house, which was not much more than a stone's-throw from their dwelling.

The big barn had been cleared for the dancing, and after a few hearty reels the couple adjourned to the "ben-end o the hoose" to partake of refreshment. Shortly after they disappeared there glided into the barn two tiny creatures, scantily attired, with wide-open eyes, bare feet, and smiling lips, which said never a word. A shout arose from the youths and maidens assembled, and the older folks laughed, while one fisherman called out, " Come awa' my lambs, and ye sall hae a reel as weel as the best o' wis." The fiddler struck up the "Shoals o' Foula," and the two little uninvited guests tripped merrily up and down, their small bare feet keeping wonderful time and executing such marvellous steps that the merry-makers declared they must have been taught by the Trows. When the reel was at its height, the dancing fast and furious, the young mother returned to the barn, and no sooner did she catch sight of the tiny couple than she exclaimed: "Guid save me, the bairns!" No trow can remain visible when a pious word is spoken. No sooner had the "Guid save me" passed her lips than the little strangers vanished through the crowd at the door. Of course, some jokes were tossed at the mother, who, however, declared that she had left her boys asleep in bed, and never dreamt of their following her. There was snow on the ground, and snow was falling, although it was a moonlight evening. An ancient dame muttered: "The lambs 'ill take cauld"—a remark which of course touched the young mother's heart, and she hastened after her children. But when she reached her own house they were not there. No, nor were they to be found in any neighbouring house. And for half an hour the parents and all the merry party searched for the children, but without success. Then folk began to whisper to one another of the wonderful steps the little couple had danced, and of the curious silence they maintained though evidently enjoying the dance. At last an aged woman asked the weeping mother if she had "looked weel to da saining?"

"I never thought of that," cried the terrified girl; and then "a' folk kent it was Trows that had ta'en the form o' Jock's peerie boys."

There was no more dancing that night. "No, nor for many Yules after in that toon," for next morning the baby boys were found dead in each other's arms in a great, soft snowdrift which filled a ravine not many hundred yards from their home. And every one affirmed that the calamity occurred through the parents having omitted to *sain* their offspring on Yule e'en.

One Yule a large party had assembled at the Moolapund, "after the evening was half spent they found that the drink was aboot done, for double the number o' folk had come than was expected." "Lads," said the man of the house, "some o' you will hae to gang ower the hill for some liquor." " And ye'll meet the Trows about the Moola-burn!" cried a saucy damsel.

"Is du no feared ta speak o' the grey-folk?" whispered a youth in her ear. "No' I," said the lass.

"Then come wi' me to the Moola-burn," he said, "and see them linking ower the braes." . . . As they left the house an old woman muttered: "Gude preserve them; it was a fule thing o' Breeta [the young woman's name] to speak like yon about them that is oot this night."

Long, long did the folks wait, and many were the wrathful words uttered at Josey's delay. At last he came—and came alone. Nay, more, he reeled in, flourishing two empty whisky bottles and shouting madly: "The Trows hae got the drink, and they've got the lass as weel!" . . . Vainly did the men strive to elicit information from Josey. He was utterly mad with drink, and could only shout, "The Trows hae taen my lass!"

"And" (said she who told the story) "Josey spakd the wird o' truth for a' that; for puir Breeta was lying in the Molla-burn, weet and wan, when her brithers fand her. She had in her hand a bulwand, and that ye ken is what the grey-folk use for horses. She was dead, puir lass, and a' for speaking lichtly o' them that has power at sich times. As for Josey, he never did mair gude frae that nicht, and afore the Yules cam' round again he was dead too."

Yule week proper is the period between Yule-day and New'r'day, and during that week no person ought to prosecute their ordinary employment; the penalty for so doing is bad luck for a year.

Some fishermen went to sea on the fourth day o' Yule, and the first thing they brought up on their lines was a hideous monster—half fish, half horse. This creature told them that—

> "Man wha fished in Yule week
> Fortune never mair did seek."

On New'r'day work of every kind was begun. Men went to the fishing, if only for an hour; girls began sewing and knitting if only for a few stitches; a bit of simmond was woven; a turf was turned; a stone set up; a shilling laid by; a torn garment was mended; a new one shaped; the byre was cleaned out; the fishing gear was repaired; "everything pertaining to thrift was got under weigh to begin the year weel."

From that day until "Twenty-fourth night" work and play went hand in hand, and the merry season sped to its end amid much enjoyment. On Twenty-fourth night the small family parties became enlarged, and lost much of their domestic as well as superstitious element. The young people of many hamlets clubbed together and spent the evening in the house of some one who owned a large barn, where dancing was vigorously carried on. An old rhyme warned the young men to

> "Mak' the maist o' ony chance,
> Yule is time to drink and dance.
> New'r'mas lucky lines sood bring.
> Twenty-fourth night, get the ring.
> Gie the lass a kiss, and mind
> Time and time are easy tined."

On Twenty-fourth night the doors were all opened, and a great deal of pantomimic chasing and driving and dispersing of unseen creatures took place. Many pious ejaculations were uttered, and iron was ostentatiously displayed, "for Trows can never abide the sicht o' iron." The Bible was read and quoted. People moved about in groups or couples, never singly, and infants were carefully guarded as well as sained by vigilant and learned "wise women." . . . When day dawned after Twenty-fourth night the Trows had vanished and the Yules were ended.

EDMONDSTON AND SAXBY, pp. 136-146.
See also "MARRIAGE CUSTOMS."
For Trows at Yule *see* I. *e*, "*Trial of K. Jonesdochter.*"

Lerwick. *Guizing.*—The Christmas season, which has always been held with more than ordinary merriment in Scandinavia, is still kept in the good old Norse fashion by the Lerwegians. With the outset of winter, the ingenuous youths of Lerwick commence preparation for Yule, taking care to observe the strictest secrecy. On Christmas Eve, the 4th January,—for the old style is still observed—the children go *a guizing*, that is to say, disguising themselves in the most fantastic and gaudy costumes, they parade the streets, and infest the houses and shops, begging for the wherewithal to carry on their Christmas amusements. One o'clock on Yule morning having struck, the young men turn out in large numbers, dressed in the coarsest of garments, and, at the double-quick march, drag huge tar barrels through the town, shouting and cheering as they go, or blowing loud blasts with their "louder horns." The tar barrel simply consists of several—say from four to eight—tubs filled with tar and chips, placed on a platform of wood. It is dragged by means of a chain, to which scores of jubilant youths readily yoke themselves, They have recently been described by the burgh officer of Lerwick as "fiery chariots, the effect of which is truly grand and terrific." In a Christmas morning the dark streets of Lerwick are generally lighted up by the bright glare, and its atmosphere blackened by the dense smoke, of six or eight tar barrels in succession. On the appearance of daybreak, at six A.M., the morning revellers put off their coarse garments—well begrimed by this time—and in turn become guizards. They assume every imaginable form of Costume—those of soldiers, sailors, Highlanders, Spanish Chevaliers, &c. Thus disguised, they either go in pairs, as man and wife, or in larger groups, and proceed to call on their friends, to wish them the compliments of the season. Formerly, these adolescent guizards used to seat themselves in crates, and accompanied by fiddlers, were dragged through the town. The crate, however, has for some years fallen into disuse. After the revels of the morning, they generally grow pretty lanquid ere evening arrives. Old New Year's Day (12th January), is kept similarly to Christmas, but the rejoicings it calls forth are usually on a smaller scale.

COWIE, pp. 136, 137.

Shetland. Christmas day, old style, called *Yule day*, is held in great veneration by all the peasantry of Zetland. No individual will then engage in any kind of labour, and if a drop of spirits can be obtained by any sacrifice, it must be had to hail the morn of that happy day. Long before daylight, the fiddlers present themselves at the doors of the houses, playing a tune called the *day dawn* [See III. c]. . . . This tune has long been consecrated to Yule day, and is never played on any other occasion. The first day of the New Year, old style, is also much respected, but not in so enthusiastic a manner as the former.

EDMONDSTON, *Shetland*, ii., pp. 66, 67.

In the olden time, on the last night of the old year, five young lads, consisting of a "gentleman," a "carrying horse," and three others, all disguised, went from house to house, singing what they called a "New'r Even's Song," and collecting provisions for a banquet on New Year's night. The "gentleman" wore a cap made of straw, with his name lettered on the front, a collar of straw round his neck, a belt of straw round his waist, and a band of straw round his right arm. It was his duty to sing, which he did standing outside the door; and when the song was finished, if invited, he would enter the house and introduce himself as Vanderdigan come from Drontheim, pronounced Dornton.

For this song *see* III. *c*, " SONGS."

For guizards *see also* II. *b*, " WEDDINGS."

On Christmas Eve, New Year's Eve, and Uphelya—the twenty-fourth day after Yule and that on which the Holy or Holidays are supposed to be "up"—the youths of Lerwick, attired in fantastic dresses go "guising" about the town in bands, visiting their friends and acquaintances. . . . On one or other of these occasions a torchlight procession forms part of the revelry. Formerly blazing tar-barrels were dragged about the town, and afterwards, with the first break of morning, dashed over the knab into the sea.—RAMPINI, in *Good Words*, 1884, p. 747.

The Straw Suits are still in some parts of Scotland worn by the peasantry in order to disguise themselves when going from house to house at Hallowmas or Martinmas and at Christmas. Those disguised are sometimes termed in Scotland "gyzarts" and also in some localities "skeklers," but I have not ascertained the meaning of the latter term. The straw helmet is usually ornamented with long streamers of ribbons of different colours. One of the pieces surrounds the neck and covers the shoulders, the larger covers the middle and the narrow bits are anklets. The face is covered partially with a coloured handkerchief. The maskers go from house to house, and if possible accompanied by a fiddler, performing the most grotesque dances, expecting a dram or small gratuity. The custom is fast dying out; it is not easy to procure a complete suit. The dresses exhibited were made in the town of Fetlar.

T. EDMONDSTON, in *Proc. Soc. Ant. Scot.* [1868-70], viii. 471.

(b) CEREMONIAL CUSTOMS.

WEDDING CUSTOMS.

Shetland. When a courtship is somewhat advanced, the lover pays a visit to his mistress on Saturday night, and generally remains a day or two in the house. This is considered as an open avowal of his intentions, and it is occasionally repeated until the marriage ceremony gives to his arms the object of his choice. The weddings generally take place in the winter time, and as the guests come from a distance, the entertainment sometimes lasts for several days in succession. It is a common practice for several young men to disguise themselves, and visit the company thus assembled. Such a party is known by the appellation of *Guizards*. Their faces are masked, and their bodies covered with dresses made of straw, ornamented with a profusion of ribands. Each of them has a particular character to support, but none speak, so that the performance is a kind of pantomimical masquerade. The person who directs their movements is called the *Skudler*, and he is always the best dressed of the party. They are kindly received, and dance with every person present, in succession. As the accommodation of the Zetland Cottar houses is by no means great, the mode of lodging the company during the night is sufficiently simple, and I believe peculiar. A quantity of straw and some blankets are spread over the floor of the barn, and all lie down and repose together like the children of the same family.

EDMONDSTON, *Shetland*, vol. ii., pp. 64, 65.

Before describing a Shetland wedding, we may step aside into a cottage by the banks of a quiet voe in the parish of Walls. The family of our humble heroine, Mary, whom the occasion has invested with a temporary importance, is awaiting the visit of her Jamie, who is coming that night to "speer" for her. The house and its inmates are in the best of order; and while all are seated round the fire, a tap is heard at the door, which is opened by the youngest member of the family, who, by dint of listening and reasoning, has formed a pretty correct idea of what is about to take place. In walks Jamie, remarkably confused. He does not know what to say, or where to look; but if he can at all manage it, he makes an awkward sally on the floor, and slips a small bundle into a box-bed which stands opposite the door—a bundle which everybody knows to be a bottle of excellent whisky, the "speering bottle." He advances to the fire, and shakes hands with all except Mary, whom he does not seem to notice, while she, covered with blushes, does not seem to notice him. Tea over, every facility is put in his way for having an interview with the father; but he takes no hint, and appears blind to all the little plans and arrangements which Mary's sisters have made and are making. However, as the night advances, one of the sisters whispers to him, that if he "wants to speak to da," he would better do so now, as he has just gone to the barn to thrash the straw for the cow's supper. Go now he must; but when face to face with the man whose consent he must ask, his former awe of him having painfully increased, his mind becomes a blank, and he forgets every word of the neat little speech he had prepared to deliver, and can only stammer out bluntly that he and Mary are going to marry, and he wishes to ask his consent. When the father consents, and wishes them many happy days, Jamie comes jumping out of the barn, feeling as light as if a hill had been rolled off his shoulders, and is for the remainder of the night the heartiest, happiest, chattiest fellow alive. The bottle is drunk at breakfast next morning (Sunday); and in a few hours the whole district is informed that "Jamie O'Houll speered for Mary O'Clingrigarth thestreen."

All weddings in Shetland must commence with new

moon, otherwise the marriage will be an unlucky one. The week succeeding the "speering," after which the young couple are called bride and bridegroom, they proceed to Lerwick to purchase their "wedding needs." The bride's eldest brother, and bridegroom's eldest sister, accompany them. Jamie is no miser on such an occasion: he has, perhaps, had a successful season at Davis' Straits, or returned home from a voyage to Australia or California and is in possession of money. He buys a white muslin dress, white shawl and two beautiful caps, tastefully trimmed with ribbons, for his bride, with some "braw" for each of his and her sisters, and a suit for himself. He will think nothing of laying out £20 on his wedding. "It is a poor heart," he says, "that never rejoices; let the money go; as long as I keep my health, I have no fear." On Saturday, the bridegroom's family and friends meet by invitation at the house of the bride's father, to celebrate the "contract feast." The bride awaits their arrival, and must kiss every invited guest as they enter. The sumptuous "tea" which follows, consists of bread, butter, and fresh mutton, two or three fat sheep having been killed that morning. The bottle is sent round freely. The night is spent discussing the crops, the fishing, and the condition of the country in olden times. Tales of voyages and shipwrecks, and of hair-breadth escapes on returning from the haaf, are told; and after a late but plentiful supper, they separate.

The wedding-even at the bride's house is a day of great bustle and preparation. Two women are employed from morning till night baking oatmeal cakes—vast ones, about three feet in circumference, and cut in halves,—care being taken, in setting them on the wedding table, to have their cut edges next the fire. The men are engaged in bringing home sheep from the hill, and slaughtering them; and the young women in cleaning up the house, and putting the finishing touches to their caps and dresses.

The "best man" must sleep with the bridegroom on the wedding even. About six o'clock, the "aff-gang," or bridegroom's breakfast, is put on the table, and his men, who have been invited, assemble; and about the same time the bride's maidens, twelve or fifteen in number, meet at her house. Breakfast over at the bridegroom's (generally a work of three hours), he and his men walk to the bride's house, draw up in line before the door, and fire a shot. The door is shut, and no response is made. A second shot is fired; still silence. After a third shot, the door is opened, and the bride, leading all her maidens in single file, walks to the spot where the bridegroom and his men are standing, when every lad must kiss every lass. On re-entering the house, an ancient and peculiar custom is observed. The bride, with her maidens, on coming out of the house, does not walk direct to the spot where the bridegroom is standing, but turns to the left, and goes so as to form a half-circle, following the course of the sun; and on re-entering, the circle is completed. Observing an order of procession as old as the hills, they walk to the manse. There is a married couple at every wedding called the "honest folk," whose duty it is to walk before the bride and bridegroom in procession, and attend to the comforts of the whole company. There is also a fiddler, who walks at the head of the procession on every occasion, playing energetically. On the conclusion of the ceremony, which is generally performed in the manse kitchen, the "honest man" goes round with a bottle of wine or brandy, offering each of the company a glass, and the "honest woman" follows with a basket of biscuit or cake. There is always a "gunner" in every company; and on returning from the manse shots are fired as fast as the gun can be loaded, while with every shot there issues from the throat of each man a vociferous "hip—hip—hurrah." As they approach the bride's house, her mother and one or two female relatives meet her, carrying in a clean white cambric napkin a cake baked with seeds and sugar, called the "bride's-cake," or "dreaming-bread," broken into small pieces, which she throws over the head of the bride.

Dinner is now on the table—a dinner, I believe, peculiar to Shetland weddings. The fire has been removed from the centre of the floor, and the table, formed of chests, extends the whole length of the house, and is covered with white cotton. The dinner consists of a savoury dish of "stove," made of five or six fat newly-slaughtered sheep, cut into small pieces with an axe, and boiled in the largest "kettle" in the neighbourhood; it is seasoned with salt, pepper, and carraway seeds, and served boiling hot in huge dishes, around each of which are laid a number of cow's-horn spoons. The company are seated each opposite his own partner; grace is said; and fortunate is he who has secured a spoon with a long handle, since in a few minutes the short-handed ones become encased in a mass of mutton-fat. Oat-cakes are eaten along with the "stove," and a glass of whisky concludes the repast. Tea, or the "bride's piece," is generally over about six o'clock: the floor is cleared, the fiddler is elevated on the top of a chest, and dancing commences. About nine o'clock, commotion and whispering being observed among those nearest the door, the fiddler stops, dancing ceases, and the "honest man" informs the company that the "guisers" have arrived. On the best man announcing that there is plenty of both meat and drink for all comers—five gallons of whisky it may be yet untouched—the fiddler is told to "play up the guisers' spring," when in walks a tall, slender-looking man, called the "scuddler," his face closely veiled with a white cambric napkin, and on his head a cap made of straw, in shape like a sugar-loaf, with three loops at the upper extremity, filled with ribbons of every conceivable hue, and hanging down so as nearly to cover the cap. He wears a white shirt, with a band of ribbons around each arm, and a bunch of ribbons on each shoulder, with a petticoat of long clean straw, called "gloy," which hangs loosely. The moment he enters he gives a snore, and having danced for a few minutes, another enters, called the "gentleman," somewhat similarly attired: he, too, having danced, a third, called the "fool," appears, and so on till all are in. And it is really a strange sight to see six tall young men dressed thus fantastically, and dancing with so much earnestness. They are careful to speak not a word lest they reveal their identity; and not a sound is heard but the music of the fiddle, the rustle of the straw petticoats, the thud of their feet on the eartheran floor, the laughter of the "fool," and the whispers of the bride's maidens guessing who the guisers may be. Dancing is kept up by the company till far on in the small hours, and supper is at last announced—a simple repast of sowans and milk; after which they retire for the night. About ten a.m. they reassemble, have breakfast, walk in procession for two or three hours, take dinner, and then finally separate.—REID, pp. 60-62.

[This description of a Shetland marriage was written by Mr. Robert Jamieson, Schoolmaster of Sandness.]

Orkney. During the winter season, it was customary to carry on a perpetual succession of merry-makings, called balls. Every marriage was the occasion of two—the bride's friends being at the expense of the wedding-feast, and the best man feeling himself called upon to give *the back-feast*, which occurred a month or two after the wedding, and in which he was assisted by contributions from some of the other young men in the immediate neighbourhood. Besides these regular meetings, a great many more were added to fill up the void.

New Stat. Acct., Orkney, p. 113.

Shetland. The country weddings take place in the winter time, and are attended by a large number of persons from all parts of the neighbouring districts.

Dancing begins in the evening, and is continued till the small hours of the morning are getting large again, interrupted by brief but frequent intervals for drinking. The festivities over for the night, the dancers instead of returning to their homes, adjourn to the barn of their host's cottage, which serves as a dormitory, the members of each sex being alternately ranged along the floor, on a huge couch of straw. Until very recently these festivities were continued over three days, but now they are confined to one. The people enter quite innocently into these "barn bundlings," as they are termed, and both statistics and the testimony of respectable persons who have taken part in them, prove that nothing immoral occurs.—COWIE, p. 102.

Orkney. There was a custom among the lower class of people in this country which has entirely subsided within these twenty or thirty years. Upon the first day of every new year the common people, from all parts of the country, met at the Kirk of Stainhouse [Stennis], each person having provision for four or five days; they continued there for that time dancing and feasting in the kirk. This meeting gave the young people an opportunity of seeing each other, which seldom failed in making four or five marriages every year; and to secure each other's love, till an opportunity of celebrating their nuptials, they had resource to the following solemn engagements:—The parties agreed stole from the rest of their companions, and went to the Temple of the Moon, where the woman, in presence of the man, fell down on her knees and prayed the god Wodden (for such was the name of the god they addressed upon this occasion) that he would enable her to perform all the promises and obligations she had and was to make to the young man present, after which they both went to the Temple of the Sun, where the man prayed in like manner before the woman, then they repaired from this to the stone marked D, and the man being on one side and the woman on the other, they took hold of each other's right hand through the hole, and there swore to be constant and faithful to each other. This ceremony was held so very sacred in those times that the person who dared to break the engagement made here was counted infamous, and excluded all society.—Low, *Intro.*, p. xxvi.

Flotta. The wedding seems generally to have taken place on a Thursday, and at the wedding feast a sort of loving-cup was handed round called "the bride's cog" or "leem."—TUDOR, p. 334.

Shetland. Marriages, which are chiefly contracted during winter, serve to draw together a large party, who not many years ago, used to meet on the night before the solemnity took place. It was then usual for the bridegroom to have his feet formally washed in water by his men, though in wealthy houses wine is used for the purpose. A ring is thrown into the tub—a scramble for it ensued, the finder being the person who would be first married. On the eve before the marriage the bride and bridegroom were not allowed to sleep under the same roof; and on the wedding night the bridegroom's men endeavoured to steal the bride from her maidens, and a similar design on the bridegroom was made by the bridesmaids—kisses being the usual forfeiture exacted from the negligent party. Last of all took place the throwing of the stocking. The bride, when in bed, threw the stocking of her right foot over her left shoulder and the individual on whom it fell, was predicted to be the first who should be married.

HIBBERT, p. 554.

It is no uncommon thing for neighbours who have not been invited to the marriage to dress in disguise and participate in the festivities of the evening. The usual way they disguise themselves is by rolling the body up in straw rope and blacking the face. The maskers have usually all the privileges of bidden guests and are treated with great civility. At the end of every dance every man must *kiss* his female partner.—*Chambers's Journal,* 1859, p. 384.

South Ronaldsay and Burray. No couple chuses to marry except with a growing moon, and some even wish for a flowing tide.—*Old Stat. Acct.,* v. xv., p. 311.

Orkney. The people never marry but when the moon is growing. Were they to do so, when it is waning, the marriage bed would be barren. . . . Thursday is the day generally fixed for marriage.
New Stat. Acct., Orkney, p. 143.

Kirkwall and St. Ola. They do not marry but in the waxing of the moon. . . . They would consider it as an unhappy omen were they, by any means, disappointed in getting themselves married, or their children baptized on the very day which they had previously fixed in their mind for that purpose.—*Old Stat. Acct.,* v. vii., p. 560.

Shetland. Among the peasantry in Shetland marriages almost invariably take place on Thursday.
MACKENZIE, p. 74.

Orkney. Thursdays and Fridays are the days in which they incline to marry; and they anxiously and scrupulously avoid doing it at any other time than when the moon is waxing.—BARRY, p. 348.

Divorce.—It was likewise usual, when husband and wife could not agree, that they both came to the Kirk of Stainhouse [Stennis], and after entering into the kirk the one went out at the south and the other at the north door, by which they were holden legally divorced, and free to make another choice.—LOW, *Intro.,* p. xxvi.

A. The old church of Stennis.
B. Maesbowe.
C. Ring of Stennis, called "the Temple of the Moon," where the "rites of Odin" were celebrated.
D. "Stone of Odin," used for the solemnization of contracts, which is indicated by the betrothing compact into which a man and woman are represented as entering, by the ceremony of joining hands through the perforation, or "stone-ring of Odin." At the Temple of the Moon, C, the woman is invoking the king of the gods, on her knees, to enable her to fulfil her promise. The man performs the same ceremony at the Temple of the Sun, marked F.
E. Pillar Stone at Bridge of Brogar.
F. Ring of Brogar, called "the Temple of the Sun."

Archæologia Scotica, vol. iii., p. 122.

FUNERAL.

Orkney. Funeral ceremonies in Orkney are much the same as in Scotland. The corpse is laid out after being stretcht on a board till it is coffined for burial. I know not for what reason they lock up all the cats of the house, and cover all looking glasses as soon as any person dies.—Low's *History of Orkney* (MS.) quoted in GOUGH, *Sepulchral Monuments*, II. ccv.

Unst. *Funeral custom.*—When they see a funeral, they lift three clods and throw them one by one after the corpse, but can assign no reason for so doing.—LOW, p. 162.

(c) *GAMES.*

Shetland. *Forfeits.*—The following description of a game of forfeits, which used to be played on winter evenings, not however so far as the authors are aware, special to any particular day of the year, or to any festival, heathen or christian. A lowan taund (a blazing peat), or anything that would do duty as a lighted torch, was held forth by No. 1 of the players towards No. 2, the following being the form of rhyme passing between them :

> "No. 1. Whaul buy me Jocky-be-laund?
> No. 2. What an' he dees ata me haund?
> No. 1. De back sall bear da saidle baund,
>   Ower stocks an' stanes
>   An' dead men's banes,
>   An' a sall lie upon dy heed at anes,
>   If do lets me janty Jocky edder dee or fa !"

This is repeated with the utmost rapidity, and if concluded before the torch goes out, No. 2 must instantly seize it. He then turns to No. 3 with the same interrogatory, "Whaul buy me Jocky-be-laund?" replied to as before. He in whose hand the torch goes out pays the forfeit, whatever may have been fixed. I [Rev. B. Edmondston] rather think there was a special form of forfeit in the shape of piling a lot of rubbish on the back of the unfortunate person who chanced to hold the torch when it went out— he standing on all fours to represent a horse. It was a sort of saddling and burdening him.

EDMONDSTON and SAXBY, pp. 198, 199.

"*A King making captives:*"

> "Heetem, peetem, penny pie,
> Baba lonie jenkem jy
> A' day doot,
> Stand doo king oot."

This form of words was commonly used by children to decide who was to be king, in the play of "A King making captives." The game was usually played among stacks of corn after the harvest. The children stood in a semi-circle while one repeated the formula, giving to each child consecutively a word; and on whomsoever the last word fell, he became king, or pursuer. All the others were fugitives, to be made captives, if the king were able to catch them and put his hand on each of their heads.—From Mr. A. K. WILLIAMSON, Leith, a native of Shetland.

Ronin the Bee.—A rude game: a cazzie is unexpectedly thrown over the head of a person; the victim is then pressed down, and buckets of water thrown upon the cazzie until the person beneath is thoroughly saturated.

EDMONDSTON, *Glossary*, s.v.

Luggie.—A game in which one is led around a circle by the ear, repeating a rhyme; if the party selected to repeat the rhyme makes a mistake he in turn becomes "luggie."—*Ibid.*, s.v.

Handy-croopen.—A game in which one of the players turns his face to the wall, his hands resting upon his back; he must continue in this position until he guesses who struck his hand, when the striker takes his place.

Ibid., Glossary, s.v.

King-come-a-lay.—A game played by boys: two sides strive for the mastery as to which party can secure most prisoners for the king.—*Ibid.*, s.v.

Foula. "*Putting the Stone.*"—In the Church-yard observed a large round stone which I could just easily lift, formerly of great use to the inhabitants. This was the Putting Stone of the island, and here the whole community met on Sunday afternoon, the younger sort to try their strength, at putting, the elders as spectators and reciters of ancient matches at putting, nay sometimes mixed in the diversion. They have a fixed stone, which is the standing goal, and I observed several marks, by driving stones into the earth, which they told me was the distance where such and such an old man, now gone, threw the Putting Stone, at the same time lamenting that now none in the isle could come up with them.—LOW, p. 114.

Unst. There is one species of dance which seems peculiar to themselves, in which they do not proceed from one end of the floor to the other in a figure, nor is it after the manner of a Scotch reel; but a dozen or so form themselves into a circle, and taking each other by the hand, perform a sort of circular dance, one of the company all the while singing a Norn Visick.—LOW, p. 163.

(*d*) *LOCAL CUSTOMS.*

Shetland. *Wattle.*—The wattle was a tax imposed on every family, paid in barley to the fond or bailie. It is said to have had its origin from presents made to a pious lady, sent over by the Bishop of Orkney to bless the pastures, in order to the increase of the flocks.

New Stat. Acct., Shetland, p. 63.

"*Riding the Hāgrie.*"—The heritors of a parish are said to "ride the Hāgrie" when examining the scattald marches.—EDMONDSTON, *Glossary*, s.v.

Tingwall, Whitness, and Weisdale. *Beating the Bounds.*—The Bailie, or chief magistrate, went along the marches, accompanied by some of the most respectable people of each parish, who were all well acquainted with the division, and with them some young boys, on whom they bestowed a good flogging at particular places, in order that they might remember the Marches, after which they received some little reward. I have heard some old people who were present, describe what took place at these ridings of the marches, called "riding the Hagra."

New Stat. Acct., Shetland, p. 64.

PART III.

TRADITIONAL NARRATIVES.

(a) *TALES*.

SAGAS.

Shetland. *How Women were promoted to the Place of Honour at the Table.*—A Danish rover, followed by a large number of fierce attendants, made a descent upon Unst, at a time when the greater number of the "fighting men" were from home. Those left were chained and compelled to act as slaves, while, hardest of all, the conqueror and his followers took possession of the Shetlander's houses and wives. But the women did not tamely submit to such a state of affairs. They concocted a plan and kept the secret till all was fully matured. Then, one night, at a preconcerted signal, they simultaneously murdered the sleeping Danes, and freed their lawful but enslaved husbands. As a reward for this action, and to commemorate the occasion when women kept a secret, the wife was henceforth to occupy the honoured post at the "top of the board."

EDMONDSTON and SAXBY, pp. 228, 229.

Weir. Vígr now Weir was the homestead of that famous Orkney-man Kolbein Hruga. . . . In the traditions [of the natives] Kolbein has become a fabulous personage, a giant who casts stones and rocks at churches.

P. A. MUNCH, in *Mem. des Ant. du Nord*, 1845-1849, p. 239.

Sagas.

Papa. In this Isle of *Papa*, belonging to *Waes*, there is an high Rock called *Frowa Stack*, that is, the Maiden Rock, divided from the land by a narrow Fork, upon the Top of which the Tradition is, that a certain *Norway* gentlewoman (in the time the *Norwegians* were masters of these Isles) having vowed perpetual Virginity, to preserve herself from the tempting Solicitations of Suitors, built a strong Tower, to which there was no ascent, but by the help of ropes, how it came to pass is unknown, she became with Child, and thereupon the Tower was demolished, the rubbish and vestiges of it are yet to be seen. [*Cf.* HIBBERT, p. 550.]

SIBBALD, p. 20.

Shetland. The first folks that ever were in our island were called Picts, and they were said to come from a place in France called Picardy. They had quarrelled there among themselves and some fled *by Scotland*, and some *spoored up* as far as Wick. They had no ships, only small boats, and they resolved to go on from shore to shore, till they go to the end of all land. When they reached the north of Shetland they said 'Yit-land, Yit-land' meaning outermost or last land and that was the way these isles came to be called Shetland. These Picts were not a seafaring folk at all. They were very small but strong and ingenious. They were very placable, kindly folk but lazy. They built brochs, which were always made so that one flat stone covered the top, and no one can tell how far down in the earth the lower rooms went; for the Picts after finishing the tops of the habitations, continued to add vaults and cells, passages innumerable underneath the ground. They never provided more food than what was required for ten days' wants, and after supper they always said—

'He that was in Bethlehem born
Will provide for us the morn.'

They brewed a kind of spirit from the heather flowers and this spirit was so much liked that many nations tried to make it, but the Picts kept the secret of how to do it themselves. By and by the Norsemen came unexpectedly and killed all the peace-loving Picts except one man and his son. They were spared that the conquerors might be instructed in the art of brewing spirits from heather-tops. At first both the Picts refused to tell but after torture was applied the father said, 'Kill the lad and then I'll tell you.' The Sea-kings did as the father desired. 'Now,' said he triumphantly, 'you can kill me, slow or fast; it is all one. You shall never learn the secrets of our race from the last of the Picts. My son might have been tempted to reveal them but there is no fear of that now:—

> 'Kill slow or kill fast,
> Death man come at last.'

And that was the end of the Picts in Shetland.

EDMONDSTON and SAXBY, p. 222.

MÄRCHEN.

Orkney. *Assipattle and the Mester Stoorworm.*

DOUGLAS, pp. 58-72. [*Cf.* also *Scottish Antiquary*, vol. v. pp. 130-31.]

Shetland. *Mind the Crooked Finger.*

DOUGLAS, pp. 123, 4.

Orkney. *Nuckelavee.*—DOUGLAS, pp. 160.

[*Nuckelavee.*—In plain English the name means "Devil of the Sea." Dennis in *Scottish Antiquary*, vol. v. p. 131.]

Rousay, Orkney. *Peerifool*—There was once a king and queen in Rousay who had three daughters. The king died and the queen was living in a small house with her daughters. They kept a cow and a kail yard; they found their cabbage was all being taken away. The eldest daughter said to the queen, she would take a blanket about her and would sit and watch what was going away with the kail. So when the night came she went out to watch. In a short time a very big giant came into the yard; he began to cut the kail and throw it in a big cubby. So he cut till he had it well filled.

The princess was always asking him why he was taking her mother's kail. He was saying to her, if she was not quiet he would take her too.

As soon as he had filled his cubby he took her by a leg and an arm and threw her on the top of his cubby of kail and away home he went with her.

When he got home he told her what work she had to do; she had to milk the cow and put her up to the hills called Bloodfield, and then she had to take wool, and wash and tease it and comb and card, and spin and make claith.

When the giant went out she milked the cow and put her to the hills. Then she put on the pot and made porridge to herself. As she was supping it, a great many peerie yellow-headed folk came running, calling out to give them some. She said:

"Little for one, and less for two,
And never a grain have I for you."

When she came to work the wool, none of that work could she do at all.

The giant came home at night and found she had not done her work. He took her and began at her head, and peeled the skin off all the way down her back and over her feet. Then he threw her on the couples among the hens.

The same adventure befell the second girl. If her sister could do little with the wool she could do less.

When the giant came home he found her work not done. He began at the crown of her head and peeled a strip of skin all down her back and over her feet, and threw her on the couples beside her sister. They lay there and could not speak nor come down.

The next night the youngest princess said she would take a blanket about her and go to watch what had gone away with her sisters. Ere long, in came a giant with a big cubby, and began to cut the kail.

She was asking why he was taking her mother's kail. He was saying if she was not quiet he would take her too.

He took her by a leg and an arm and threw her on the top of his cubby and carried her away.

Next morning he gave her the same work as he had given her sisters.

When he was gone out she milked the cow and put her to the high hills. Then she put on the pot and made porridge to herself. When the peerie yellow-headed folk came asking for some she told them to get something to sup with. Some got heather cows and some got broken dishes; some got one thing, and some another, and they all got some of her porridge.

After they were all gone a peerie yellow-headed boy came in and asked her if she had any work to do; he could do any work with wool. She said she had plenty, but would never be able to pay him for it. He said all he was asking for it was to tell him his name. She thought that would be easy to do, and gave him the wool.

When it was getting dark an old woman came in and asked her for lodging.

The princess said she could not give her that, but asked her if she had any news. But the old woman had none, and went away to lie out.

There is a high knowe near the place, and the old woman sat under it for shelter. She found it very warm. She was always climbing up, and when she came to the top she heard someone inside saying " Tease, teasers, tease; card, carders, card; spin, spinners, spin, for peerie fool, peerie fool is my name." There was a crack in the knowe, and light coming out. She looked in and saw a great many peerie folk working, and a peerie yellow-headed boy running round them calling out that.

The old woman thought she would get lodging if she

went to give this news, so she came back and told the princess the whole of it.

The princess went on saying "peerie fool, peerie fool," till the yellow-headed boy came with all the wool made into claith.

He asked what was his name, and she guessed names, and he jumped about and said " No."

At last she said, " Peerie fool is your name." He threw down the wool and ran off very angry.

As the giant was coming home he met a great many peerie yellow-headed folk, some with their eyes hanging on their cheeks, and some with their tongues hanging on their breasts. He asked them what was the matter. They told him it was working so hard pulling wool so fine. He said he had a good wife at home, and if she was safe, never would he allow her to do any work again.

When he came home she was all safe, and had a great many webs lying all ready, and he was very kind to her.

Next day when he went out she found her sisters, and took them down from the couples. She put the skin on their backs again, and she put her eldest sister in a cazy, and put all the fine things she could find with her, and grass on the top.

When the giant came home she asked him to take the cazy to her mother with some food for her cow. He was so pleased with her he would do anything for her, and took it away.

Next day she did the same with her other sister. She told him she would have the last of the food she had to send her mother for the cow ready next night. She told him she was going a bit from home, and would leave it ready for him. She got into the cazy with all the fine things she could find, and covered herself with grass. He took the cazy and carried it to the queen's house. She and her daughters had a big boiler of boiling water ready.

They couped it about him when he was under the window, and that was the end of the giant.

Taken down from the recitation of an Orkney woman by Mr. D. J. ROBERTSON. Printed in *Longman's Magazine*, vol. xiv. pp. 331-334.

Lunna, Shetland. *Thorn and Willie.*

DOUGLAS, pp. 134-137.

For stories of Swan-maiden type *see* I. *h*, "SELKIES."

CUMULATIVE TALES.

Shetland.

DA FLECH AN' DA LOOSE SHACKIN DIR SHEETS.

Da Flech an' da Loose lived tagedder in a hoose;
An' as dey shook dir sheets,
Da Flech shü snappered, an' fell i' da fire,
An' noo da Loose she greets.

Da Crook he saw da Loose greetin', an' says he ta da Loose:—"Loose! Loose! why is du greetin'?"

"Oh! da Flech an' I wer' shackin' wir sheets.
Da Flech shü snappered an' fell i' da fire.
Noo what can I du bit greet?"

"Oh! dan I'll wig-wag back an' fore!" says da Crook. Sae da Crook wig-waggit, an' da Loose she grett.

Da Shair saw da Crook wig-waggin'; an' says he ta da Crook:—"Crook! Crook! why is du wig-waggin'?"

"Oh! da Flech and da Loose wer' shackin' dir sheets;
Da Flech shü fell i' da fire an' brunt.
An' noo da Loose she greets, an I wig-wag."

"Oh! dan," says da Shair,
"I'll jump o'er da flör."

Sae da Shair she jimpit; da Crook wig-waggit; an' da Loose she grett.

Cumulative Tales.

Da Door he saw da Shair jimpin'; an' says he ta da Shair:—"Shair! Shair! why is du jimpin' o'er da flör?"

"Oh! da Flech an' da Loose wer' shackin' dir sheets;
Da Flech fell i' da fire, an' da Loose she greets.
Da Crook wig-wags, an' so I jimp."

"Oh! dan I'll jangle upo' my harrs."

Sae da Door jingle-jangled; da Shair he jimpit; da Crook wig-waggit; an' da Loose she grett.

Da Midden he saw da Door jinglin'; an' says he ta da Door:—"Door! Door! why is du jingle-jangling upo' dy harrs?"

"Oh! da Flech an' da Loose wer' shackin' dir sheets,
Da Flech fell i' da fire, an' da Loose she greets.
Da Crook wig-wags; da Shair he jimps;
An' I jingle-jangle upo' my harrs."

"Oh! dan," says da Midden, "I'll scrieg o'er wi' maeds."

Sae da Midden he scriegit; da Door jingle-jangled; da Shair he jimpit; da Crook wig-waggit; an da Loose she grett.

Da Burn he saw da Midden scriegin', an' says he ta da Midden:—"Midden! Midden! why is du scriegin' o'er wi' maeds?"

"Oh! da Flech an' da Loose wer' shackin' dir sheets,
Da Flech fell i' da fire, an' da Loose she greets;
Da Crook wig-wags; da Shair he jimps;
Da Door jingle-jangles; an' sae I scrieg o'er wi' maeds."

"Oh! dan I'll rin wimple-wample."

Sae da Burn ran wimple-wample; da Midden he scriegit; da Door he jingled; da Shair he jimpit; da Crook wig-waggit; an' da Loose she grett.

Da Loch saw da Burn rinnin' wimple-wample, an' says

he ta da Burn :—" Burn! Burn! why is du rinnin' wimple-wample?"

"Oh! da Flech an' da Loose wer' shackin' dir sheets,
Da Flech fell i' da fire, an' da Loose she greets.
Da Crook wig-wags; da Shair he jimps;
Da Door jingle-jangles; da Midden scriegs o'er wi' maeds—
An' sae I rin wimple-wample."

"Oh! dan I'll swall o'er my brim."

Sae da Loch he swalled an' he swalled; da Burn ran wimple-wample; da Midden he scriegit; da Door he jingled; da Shair he jimpit; da Crook wig-waggit; an' da Loose she grett—when doon comes da Flüd, an' sweeps awa' da Hoose an' da Loose, da Crook an' da Shair, da Door an' da Midden, wi' da maeds, a' doon i' da müddow whare da Burn ran wimple-wample. An' sae ends da storie o' da Flech an' da Loose.—Communicated by Mr. KARL BLIND to the *Archæological Review*, vol. i. pp. 346-352.

(c) *BALLADS, SONGS, AND MUSIC.*

BALLADS.

Foula, Shetland. *The Earl of Orkney and the King of Norway's Daughter.*—The following song is the most entire I could find, but the disorder of some of the stanzas will show that it is not wholly so. The subject is a strife between a King of Norway and an Earl of Orkney, on account of the hasty marriage of the Earl with the King's daughter in her father's absence. Here it is worthy to be observed that most of the fragments they have are old historical Ballads and Romances, this kind of Poetry being more greedily swallowed and retentively preserved by memory than any others, and most fitted to the genius of the Northerns. In this ballad I cannot answer for the orthography; I wrote it as the old man pronounced it, nor could he assist me in this particular. This man (William Henry, a farmer in Guttorm in Foula) has the most knowledge of any I found; he spoke of three kinds of poetry used in Norse, and repeated or sung by the old men —the Ballad (or Romance, I suppose); the Vysie or Vyse, now commonly sung to dancers; and the simple Song. By the account he gave of the matter, the first seems to have been valued here chiefly for its subject, and was commonly repeated in winter by the fireside; the second seems to have been used in public meetings, now only sung to the dance; and the third at both. Let it be remarked that the following ballad may be either written in two long line or four short line stanzas:

> Da vara Jarlin d'Orkneyar
> For frinda sin spur de ro
> Whirdi an skildè meun
> Our glas buryon burtaga.

> Or vanna ro eidnar fuo
> Tega du meun our glas buryon
> Kere friendè min yamna men
> Eso vrildan stiendi gede min vara to din.

> Yom keimir cullingin
> Fro liene burt
> Asta Vaar hon fruen Hildina
> Hemi stu mer stien.

> Whar an yaar elonden
> Ita kan sadnast wo
> An scal vara kundè
> Wo osta tre sin reithin ridna dar fro.

> Kemi to Orkneyar Jarlin
> Vilda mien sante Maunis
> I Orknian u bian sian
> I lian far diar.

An gevè Drotnign kedn puster
On de kin firsane furu
Tworare wo eder
Whitranè kidn.

In kimerin Jarlin
U klapasse Hildina
On de kidn quirto
Vult doch, fiegan vara moch or fly din. *1

Elde vilda fiegan vara
Fy min u alt sin
Ans namnu wo
So minyach u ere min heve Orkneyar kinge ro. *

Nu di skall taga dor yochwo
And u ria dor to strandane nir
U yilsa fy minu avon
Blit an ear ne cumi i dora band.

Nu Swaran Konign
So mege gak honon i muthi
Whath ear di ho gane mier
I daute buthe.

Tretti merkè vath ru godle
Da skall yach ger yo
U all de vara sonna less
So linge sin yach liva mo.

Nu linge stug an konign
U linge wo an swo
Wordig vaar dogh mugè sonè
Yacha skier fare moga so minde yach angan u frien rost wath comman mier to landa.[2]

[1] Stanzas marked thus * seem to be confused, some having too much, others too little to render the verse complete.

[2] This verse seems to be part of an intermediate stanza, perhaps to be placed between 12 and 13.

Ballads.

Nu swara Hiluge
Hera geve honon scam
Taga di gild firre Hildina
Sin yach skall liga dor fram.

Estin whaar u feur fetign
Agonga kadn i sluge
Feur fetign sin gonga
Kadn i pluge.

Nu steinderin Jarlin
U linge wo an swo
Dese mo eke Orknear
So lunge san yach lava mo.

Nu eke tegaran san
Sot Koningn fyrin din
U alt yach an Hilhugin
Widn ugare din arar.

Nu Swarar an frauna Hildina
U dem san idne i fro
Di slo dor a bardagana
Dar comme ov sin mo.

Nu Jarlin an genger
I vadlin fram
U kadnar sina mien
Geven skeger i Orkneyan.

Han u cummin
In u vodlerdin
Fionde fans lever
Vel burne mun.

Nu fruna Hildina
On genger i vadlin fram
Fy di yera da ov man dum
Dora di spidlaiki mire man.

Nu sware an Hiluge
Crego gevan a scam
Gayer an Jarlin frinde
Din an u fadlin in.

Nu fac an Jarlin dahuge
Dar min de an engin gro
An east ans huge ei
Fong ednar u vaxhedne more neo.

Di lava mir gugna
Yift bal yagh fur o lande
Gipt mir nu fruan Hildina
Vath godle u fasta bande.

Nu bill on heve da yals
Guadnè borè u da kadn
Sina kloyn a bera do skall
Fon fruna Hildina verka wo sino chelsina villya.*

Hildina liger wo chaldona
U o dukrar u grothè
Min du buga till bridlevsin
Bonlother u duka dogha.

Nu Hildina on askar feyrin
Sien di gava mier livè
Ou skinka vin
Ou guida vin.*

Duska skinka vin, u guida vin
Tinka dogh eke wo
Jarlin an gougha here din.*

Watha skilde tinka
Wo Jarlin gouga herè min
Hien minde yagh inga forlskona
Bera fare kera fyrin min.

Ballads.

Da gerde on fruna Hildina
On bar se mien ot
On soverin fest
Fysin u quarsin sat.

Da gerde un fruna Hildina
On bard im ur
Hadlin burt sien on laghde
Gloug i otsta jatha port.

Nu iki visti an Hiluge
Ike ov till do
Eldin var commin i lut
U stor u silke sark ans smo.

Nu leveren fram
Hiluge du kereda
Fraun Hildina du
Gevemir live u gre.

So mege u gouga gre
Skall dogh swo
Skall lathi min heran
I bardagana fwo.

Du tuchtada lide undocht yach
Swo et sa ans bugin bleo
Dogh casta ans huge
I mit fung u vexemir mise meo.

Nu tachtè on heve fwelsko
Ans bo vad mild u stien
Dogh skall aldè misè Koningnsens
Vadne vilda mien.

A literal translation of the above I could not procure, but the substance is this :—" An Earl of Orkney, in some of his rambles on the coast of Norway, saw and fell in love with the King's daughter of the country. As their passion happened to be reciprocal he carried her off in her father's absence, who was engaged in war with some of his distant neighbours. On his return, he followed the fugitives to Orkney, accompanied by his army, to revenge on the Earl the rape of his daughter. On his arrival there Hildina (which was her name) first spied him, and advised her now husband to go and attempt to pacify the King. He did so, and by his appearance and promises brought the King so over as to be satisfied with the match. This, however, was of no long standing; for as soon as the Earl's back was turned, a courtier called Hiluge took great pains to change the King's mind, for it seems Hiluge had formerly hoped to succeed with the daughter himself. His project took, and the matter came to blows; the Earl is killed by Hiluge, who cut off his head and threw it at his lady, which she says vexed her even more than his death, that he should add cruelty to revenge. Upon the Earl's death Hildina is forced to follow her father to Norway, and in a little time Hiluge makes his demand to have her in marriage of her father; he consents, and takes every method to persuade Hildina, who with great reluctance agrees, upon condition that she is allowed to fill the wine at her wedding. This is easily permitted, and Hildina infuses a drug which soon throws the company into a deep sleep, and after ordering her father to be removed, sets the house on fire. The flame soon rouses Hiluge, who piteously cries for mercy; but the taunts he had bestowed at the death of the Earl of Orkney are now bitterly returned, and he is left to perish in the flames."

Such is the subject of the ballad, which might have been built on a true story, though now lost. It however shows the genius of the people, that though they were cut off from the rest of the world they had amusements, and these correspondent to the manners of the Northerns. . . . Most or all of their tales are relative to the history of Norway:

they seem to know little of the rest of Europe but by name; Norwegian transactions they have at their finger ends.

LOW, pp. 107-114.

[Mr. Black has succeeded in restoring nearly the whole of the above text in Icelandic, and hopes to publish it with a translation at an early date.]

Orkney. *The Play of the Lady Odivere.*—This ballad was at one time represented as a drama. This fact influenced me in adopting one of its old names, namely play, in preference to other names, by which the ballad was known —such as rhyme, ballan, teel. The ballad was always divided into fits, but I have been told that its divisions were once called by another name, which I have been unable to discover.

A few stanzas of the ballad appeared in the transactions [*sic*, Proceedings] of the Scottish Antiquarian Society, communicated by Captain Thomas, R.N., and heard by him in Shetland.

It is now well-nigh fifty years since I first heard parts of this ballad, for forty years I have been gathering up fragmentary scraps of it from many old people in different parts of Orkney.... It is right to say, that while the utmost care has been taken to preserve the original, and to select the best from the versions recited to me, I have often had to fill in a word, sometimes a line, in order to make the sense clear or to complete the stanza.... If the ballad contains any moral, it is probably the enforcement of an old belief once current here. The belief that to swear the Odin oath was sure to bring success to the swearer in the first place, and was most certain to bring on bitter disappointment in the end. I may say here, it is not likely that Christ is meant by the phrase, "him that hung on tree"; but rather that Odin is intended.

THE PLAY O' DE LATHIE ODIVERE.

First Fit.

In Norawa a lathie bed,
   A bonnie lass in muckle gare ;
An' hid wus soothly sung an' said,
   Shü wus a lathie sweet an' fair.

They cam fae aest an' west i' pride,
   An' some cam sailan ower de sea ;
An' a' tae win her for a bride ;
   Bit never a bride wade de lathie be.

Shü bad dem gang heeme an' mend deir clais,
   Dat dey had worn in comin' sae far ;
Shü ca'd dem füls, shü ca'd dem flaes,
   Set stooks on dem, an' gae dem a skar.

Der wis a man baith stoor an' strang,
   An' he wus neemed Odivere ;
He lo'ed de sword, he lo'ed de sang,
   Bit aye he lo'ed de lasses mair.

Dis Odivere fell on his knee,
   An' vooed a voo apo' his life,
An' swore bae Him dat hang on tree,
   Tae mak dis lathie fair his wife.

He's coorted her, he's waded her ;
   An' dey wür blyth an' blissfu' baith ;
An' aye he bragged near an' far,
   He wan his wife bae Odin's aith.

He's left her i' his boorly ha',
   A greetan sare dat dolefu' day ;
Tae Guthaland he's geen awa',
   Dae muckle pagan loons tae slay.

As he cam back fae Guthaland
  I' Muckle Gerth he bed a while;
An' foy's an' fiechtins hed tae hand
  For lathies fair düd him beguile.

At muckle Gerth he terried lang,—
  Black sight on him, for biddan dare!
While sat i' dool her maids amang
  Wi' tearfu' ee his lathie fair.

An' aft shü boonied hersel sae bra',
  An' aft her gouden hair wad keem,
An' dan luk ower de castle wa'
  Tae see her ain gude-man co' heem.

An' aye shü looked an' lipened lang,
  For minay a dowie day an' year;
Bit Odivere, he düd no come,
  Nor word o' Oddie could shü hear.

Second Fit.

Ae enen i' de mirkin o'd,
  A stately knight cam tae her ha';
Fu lood he chapped on de yet
  An' loodly at de yet düd ca'.

"A boon, a boon! ye porter loon,
  Bed me this nicht within your ha',
Me vista's lang, the nicht is mirk,
  An' heem an' haudin far awa'."

"Begone, begone, awa, awa!
  Tae bed ye here that may no' be;
Nae stranger sleeps within dis ha,
  While my gude lord's ayont de sea."

"Gin ye wad no find de weight o' me hand,
  Gae tell your lathie mistress fair,
Dat I hae come fae Guthaland,
  An' bare her word o' Odivere."

De yet was apened at his word,
  An' baldly strode he i' de ha';
An' de wemen roon him said,
  A stoorer knight dey never saw.

An' he's taen aff his silken cap,
  An' he's geen doon apo his knee,
An' he's laid a goud ring on de lathie's lap,
  Dat shü was unco fain tae see.

"A token fae dee husband dear,
  I bring tae dee mae lathie fair;
I left him weel, i' jolly cheer;
  Dey ca' him noo, Sir Odivere.

"An' weel he's win his knight's degree,
  Bae slaying miny a soldier stoor,
An' mackan hosts o' pagans flee,
  Afore his sword sae sharp an' door."

Whin shü de gouden ring hed seen,
  Shü tük nae tent o' what he said;
Bit drew her kerchief ower her een;
  An' colour fae hir fair face fled.

Bit syne her bonnie face grew bright,
  An' blithely blinked her bonnie ee.
"Rise up, rise up, ye valyent knight,
  For uncons gude ye bring tae me.

"A stately bülie i' de ha',
  Poo oot de best o' blude reed wine,
Wi' futh o' a' dats gude an' bra',
  Dat dis brave knight fu' weel may dine."

An' miny a teel he tald dat nicht,
    O' tulyes faucht for lathies fair;
An' a' aboot dat worthy wight,
    I' Guthaland, Sir Odivere.

He minted aye, to he never said,
    An' skeeted aye i' ilka teel,
Dat Odivere wus a rovin' bled,
    An' liked de lasses ower weel.

An' whin de bülie wus fairly dün,
    An' a' de servents gaen tae bed,
An' de twa dem sels wur left alane,
    De lathie tae de stranger said:

"Why bring ye back dat gouden ring
    Dat brings tae me sare dool an' pain,
Dat minds me o' de blithsam days,
    Whin I o' dee wüs ower fain?"

"Ye ken fair dame, tae me aye dear,
    Lang syne ye gae dat ring tae me;
An' on dis ring i' de mün-licht clear,
    Ye swüre forever mine tae be.

"An' I i' dool hae geen sin syne,
    A lanely man on land an' sea;
An' never a face hae seen bit dine,
    Dat I could speer me wife tae be."

"Noo wheesht, noo wheesht, ye faus tongued knight
    Your words will wark me muckle skaith,
Fu' weel ken ye, what sindered is;
    Hid wüs de dowie Odin's aith."

He's taen her white hand i' his stately nave;
    An' fain wüs shü, an' fain wüs he;
What happened neest, ye need no speer;
    In sooth I wüs no dare to see.

The knight's awa' i' de mornin gray,
    He bed no for a fare weel foy,—
What nae bothie kens nae bothie can say,—
    Bit de lathie's left i' peerie joy.

Her bonnie een blinked so sae bright,
    Her reed an' white grew white an' gray;
An' ilka day shü wised for nicht,
    An' ilka nicht shü wised for day.

Third Fit.

I heard a lathie ba'an her bairn;
    An' aye shü rockit, an' aye shü sang,
An' teuk sae hard apo' de verse,
    Till de hert within her bothie rang.

"Ba loo, ba loo, me bonnie bairn,
    Ba lo lillie, ba loo lay,
Sleep du, me peerie bonnie budo!
    Du little kens dee mither's wae.

' Aloor! I dinno ken dee faither,
    Aloor, aloor! me waefu' sin!
I dinno ken me bairn's faither,
    Nor yet de land dat he lives in.

"Aloor, aloor! ca'd sall I be
    A wicked woman bae a' men,
Dat I, a married wife, soud hae
    A bairn tae him I dünno ken."

Dan ap an' spak a grimly gest,
    Dat stüd sae lech at her bed feet,
"O here am I, dee bairn's faither,
    Alto I'm no' dee husband sweet."

"Me bairn's faither I ken du are,
　　Na luve sae sweet I'll ever hae;
An' yet I hae a gude, gude man,
　　Dat's far awa' fae me dis day."

" I care no for dee wadded carl,
　　I wus his face I'll never see,
Bit whin sax munt is come an' gaen,
　　I'll come an' pay de noris fee.

" Hids no' be said du tint bae me,
　　A bodle wirt o' warly gare,
Sae whin I come, dus get dee fee,
　　An' I me bairn tae be me heir."

" Noo, for de luve I bür tae dee,
　　A luve dats brought me muckle sheem,
O tell me whar du heem may be,
　　An' tell me true du vera neem?"

" San Imravoe hid is me neem;
　　I gang on land; an' sweem on sea;
Amang de ranks o' selkie folk
　　I am a yarl o' hich degree.

" I am a man apo' de land,
　　I am a selkie i' de sea;
Me heem it is de Soola-Skerry,
　　An' a' dats dare is under me.

" Mair or a thoosan selkie folk,
　　Tae me a willan sarvice gae;
An' I am king o' a' de folk,
　　An' la' tae dem is what I say."

" O who can du de bairn tak,
　　An' who can du de bairn save?
I' de cald heem doo'l only mak
　　De grimly sea me bairn's grave."

" Me peerie bairn I'll safely ferry,
 To I hae nather ship or skift,
Wi' muckle care tae Soolis-Skerry,
 Afore de sin's hich i' de lift."

" Bit who sall I me young son ken,—
 An' who sall I me bairn know?"
" O' a' de selkies i' Soolis-Skerry,
 He's be de middlemaist o' dem a'.

His megs sall a' be black as seut,
 His croopan white as driven snaw,
An' I beside him, like the sam'
 I wüs tae die i' times awa'."

" Me ain gudeman a warrior prood,
 An' aye a stival nave his he;
An' he may prick or club me bairn,
 When he's a selkie i' de sea."

" I fear no dat, I fear bit dis,
 Dat cock-cra comes an' fiands me here;
Bit come what may, I come agen,
 An fetch me bairn i' ae half year.

" For dan he'll be a seeveneth stream,
 An' dan a man agen I'll be,
An' tak me bonnie peerie bairn
 A' tae de boons o' Soolis-Skerrie."

Whin de sax munts were come an' geen,
 He cam tae pay de noris fee;
The tane o' his hands was fu' o gowd,
 De tither fu' o' white monie.

De lathie's taen a gowden chain,
 Her wadin boon fae Odivere,
Shü tied hid roon her bairn's hars,
 Hid for her sake shü bade him wear.

"I'm come tae fetch me bairn awa;
　Fare weel, for doo'r anither's wife,"
"I wad dee wi' a gowden ring,
　An' bide beside dee a' me life."

"Doo wad no', whin I wad gudewife;
　I winno, whin doo'r willan noo,
Dat day doo tint doo'l never fiand;
　He's late, he's ower late tae rue."

De lathie lived a lanely life,
　An' aften looks apo de sea,
Still lipenan her first luve tae fiand,
　Bit jubish that can never be.

Fourth Fit.

Sae Odivere's come heem ageen,
　Wi' muckle store o' warly gare;
An' he, his lathie, an' his men,
　Mak helliedays wi' bülies rare.

Dey danced an' sang, dey tald deir teels;
　An' syne sat doon tae drink an' dine,
Wi' joles of flesh, fuman cogs,
　An' wallie horns o' blud-reed wine.

Ae day says Oddie tae his men,
　"I doobt gin here we langer link,
We'll a' grow fat as butter bas;
　An' dee wi' fouth o' maet an' drink.

"Hid's we'll enouch a peerie while;
　I kinno thole it lang ava,
Let's hunt de otters on de shore,
　An' start de morn at blink o' da."

Dey hunted otters on de shore,
    A selkie ran oot o' a geo;
An' Odivere he teuk no lang
    Tae fell him wi' a mester blow.

Den oot an' spak, een o' his men,
    "Far hae I sailed an' muckle seen,
Bit never gowd on selkie's hars,
    Till noo I see'd wi' baith me een."

Dae bür de selkie tae de ha';
    An' never a word said Odivere,
His face wüs black an' lowed his een,
    To he düd nather ban or sware.

"Co' doon, co' doon! Lathie Odivere
    Co' doon, an' see me farly fang,
Ye's read tae me dis riddle rae,
    Bae a' de sants dat ever sang!"

De lathie shü cam doon tae see,
    Dey meed sae muckle steer.
"Here's de gowd chain ye got fae me,
    Tell me, gudewife, who cam hid here?"

"Aloor, aloor! me bonnie bairn,
    Me bairn! What am I born to see?
Me malisen lie on de hand
    Dats wroucht dis deed o' blüd on dee!"

Dat lathie wi' her torn hair,
    Shü wüs a doleful sicht tae see,
Her greetin' lood an' saban sair,
    Her erms aroond de deed selkie.

"Your bairn! gudewife, nae bairn o' mine,
    An' yet ye wür me wedded wife,
I doobt, when I've been far fae heem,
    Ye'r led a wicked woman's life."

"An' gin I be de wedded wife,
    A wedded man wür du tae me;
Ye left me tae a lanely life,
    An' bed lang years ayont de sea."

" I left du wi' baith lands an' gare,
    An' meed du mistress o' dem a',
An' toucht du wad be true tae me,
    As I tae dee whin far awa."

" Black sicht apo' de lands an' gare!
    Du little kens a woman's hert,
Tae tink de gift o' wardly gare,
    Is a' de lovin' husband's pert."

" Whin doughty deeds wür tae be dün,
    Hid wüd hae been a bonnie pass,
Hed I line heem to culye dee,
    An' bore me fingers i' de ass.

" I could no' thole a slugerd life,
    An' lathie I wüd hae de ken,
Whin I tük dee tae be me wife,
    I düd no' want a cluckan hen."

" Gin I can cluck, saul du can craw,
    Ower a' de deeds wi' women dün;
Hoo ilka bonüie winch du saw,
    Du coorted her an' ca'd it fun.

" Bit ae deed bairn, aloon hae I !
    An' gif dis deed wüs wrang i' me,
Hoo miny bairns his doo tae sha,
    Hoo true a man doo's been tae me?

" Could I no' tak what cam tae me,
    Tae tempt me i' me langsam life,
While du wür skalan frank an' free
    De dearest tocher o' a wife?"

"Ye lee, ye yee, ye leean limmer!
   Whar er we drank abüne dem a',
Du weel fard face I toasted aye
   An' foucht wi' him dat said me na.

"An' whin i' battle's sairest pall,
   Me hert grew strang, when mest outmoucht
Bae tinkin' on me lovin' wife—
   Dat shü wüs faus I little toucht.

"Wi' selkie folk du's led a life!
   Awa ye limmer slut fae me!
I wadno hae dee for a wife,
   For a' de gowd i' Christindee!"

Shü's whiped de chain fae de selkie's hars,
   An' waped hid on Oddie's croon,
"Gae tak ye that, ye ill-tongued tike,
   An' keep hid for a pertin boon!"

De lathie dey pat i' a hich, hich toor,
   Wi' nae sweet licht, trow hole or bore;
Dey hae geen her meal an' water dare,
   An' steeked fest de iron door.

Fifth Fit.

The Ting has passed her awfu' doom,
   Dat for her fats an' sinfu' deed,
Shü s'ud be taen an' brunt tae ass,
   Withoot or mercy, or remeed.

"Aloor, aloor! de doolfu' day!
   Aloor! what am I born tae see?
I' de red het fire I man be brunt!
   O waes me hert an' waes me.

"O gin me faither been i' life,
  He wad hae doorly foucht for me.
Deid mither's ghest wul du no come
  An' set dy doolfu' dochter free?

"Whin I lay on dee cother breest
  An' du de peerie bairn düd rüs,
Du little toucht dy bonnie bairn
  Wad be a cinder i' de ass!"

Than up an' spak San Imravoe,
  An' a lood an' wallie cry gae he;
Ye selkie folk, to Norawa
  Ca' a' de whals i' de Nort Sea!"

De day afore dat lathie fair
  Wüs tae be brunt wi' muckle woe,
A cry wüs raised around de ha':
  "Whals, whals! i' ilka bay an' voe."

Dan Odivere an' a' his men,
  Ran tae de ca' wi' muckle speed;
An' dare wüs rowin', rootin', yowlin',
  An' noise dat micht hae raised de deed.

Dey rowed an' rooted a' de day,
  Bit never a whal got for der pains,
An' i' de mirkin heem dey geed,
  Wi' sweean laevs an' tiftan banes.

An' whin dat dey cam tae de ha',
  Dey got a gluf ye may be sür,
For ilka door stüd open wide,
  An' de door o' de toor lay on de flür.

An' dey ran ap, and dey ran doon,
  An' glowered aboot wi' a' deir een;
De lathie fair wüs clean awa',
  An' never mair bae mortal seen.

An' Odivere's a lanely man
  An' weary o' his sicker skathe;
An' aye an' sare he rues de day
  He ever tuk de Odin aith.

Tae menye-singers tanks we gae,
  Tae menye-singers drink we a';
Wür foys dey wür no wirt a strae,
  Withoot deir sangs an' ballans bra.

DENNISON, *Scottish Antiquary*, v. viii. pp. 53-58.

Unst, Shetland. *Unst Version of "King Orfeo."*—EDMONDSTON and SAXBY, pp. 194-198. It is unnecessary to reprint this ballad, which has been reprinted by the late Prof. Child in his Collection of "English and Scottish Ballads," pt. 1, p. 217.

See also Prof. BUGGE'S article, "Harpens Kräft" in the *Arkiv för Nordisk Filologi*, ny. följd, bd. 3, pp. 116-119.

SONGS AND MUSIC.

THE FOULA REEL.

Foula, Shetland.

[The Air set by MISS KEMP of Edinburgh, 1822.]

Songs and Music.

Weel, since ye are welcome to Yule, up wi't Lightfoot,
  link it awa', boys;
Send for a fiddler, play up Foula Reel; we'll skip as light
  as a maw, boys.

Chorus.

   The Shaalds of Foula will pay for a'—up wi't Lightfoot, link it awa', boys;
   The Shaalds of Foula will pay for a', the Shaalds
   will pay for a', boys.

The Awens are amang the cows in the byre—up wi't
  Lighfoot, link it awa', boys;
Link up the pot, and put on a gude fire; we'll sit till cocks
  do craw, boys.
   The Shaalds of Foula, &c.

Now for a light, and a pot of good beer—up wi't Lightfoot,
  link it awa', boys;
We'll drink a gude fishing against the next year, and the
  Shaalds will pay for a', boys.
   The Shaalds of Foula, &c.

   HIBBERT, *Shetland,* pp. 563, 564.

Unst. [Fragment of an "Odinic Song" recited by an Unst woman named Russlin to George Sinclair in 1865, and by him communicated to Mr. Arthur Laurenson.]

   " Nine days he hang pa da rütless tree;
    For ill wis da folk, in' güd wis he.
    A blüdy maet wis in his side—
    Made wi' a lance—'at wid na hide.

> Nine lang nichts, i' da nippin' rime,
> Hang he dare wi' his naeked limb.
> Some, dey leuch;
> But idders gret."
> BLIND, *Nineteenth Century*, 1879, p. 1093.
> Communicated by Arthur Laurenson.

It is well to note that the discoveries of "Odinic fragments" in the Shetlands are utterly illusory. A poem in a fragmentary and corrupt condition, in fact in an advanced stage of decomposition, is taken down in the twelfth century just as it is fading out of tradition; and it is believed that this very fragment (covering, it is to be observed, by a miraculous coincidence, a space included in the fragment we already have) can be still on record in the nineteenth century, a fragment which yields nothing new, no fresh word or idea.—Credat Judæus Apella! Let us remember, putting aside all other possibilities, that Resenius' printed text, with a Latin translation, has been accessible for more than two hundred years.

VIGFUSSON, *Corpus Poeticum Boreale*, v. i. Intro. p. lxxiv.

THE FINFOLK'S FOY SONG.[1]

O' blithe is de land dat's fae man far awa!
Whar wae smolie his lair, an' wae lauch at his la'.
Whar hens never kackel, and cocks never cra';
Whar nichts never mirken, an' days never da'.
Whar wolfs never wirry, an' winds never bla;
Whar frosts never sturtan an' rains never fa.
Whar baests never peris o' hunger i' sna;
For de grund's never kivered i' winter ava.
Whar music de saftest an sweetest o' a',

[1] [In a footnote Mr. Dennison says: "Among my juvenile papers I found a copy of the Finfolk's foy song; but as, when a boy, I added some lines to the oral original, and as I now, at a distance of nearly half a century, cannot distinguish between my tinkering and the original lines, it would be unfair to present the lines as a genuine product of tradition. However . . . I give it, such as it is. It is the only instance of continuous rhymes I have met with among our rude native verses."—*Scottish Antiquary*, vol. vii. p. 23.]

Floughs oot ever mair fae de Finfolk's ha',—
A right bonnie bigging withoot spot or fla',
O' crystal his reuf, and o' coral his wa.
Whar dance bonnie lasses weel buskit an bra,
Wi' faces de fairest dat een ever sa,'
An der no vero skakesem i' coortin ata' ;
An dat, gin ye try dem, dael vero senn sha'.
Whar wi' sorcery wae saften de Mester Fiend's cla',
An mester de poor o' his mesterfu pa',
Whar, wur flocks are de fishes wae foster an ca,
Wur flocks need nae beuls an wur baests need nae sta'.
Wae sleep tae de soond o' de sea's lullaba ;
Foo' saftly an sweet sings the sang o' his swa!
Wae fill no wur waems wi' what's rotten or ra',
Wae find no de wark and wae hae no de sca
For lice or for yuk nather kum wae nor cla.
Wur herts are no shilpid wi' envy or ga,'
Wae are bald jolly fellows ! An whatever befa'
Tae a brim feeman horn, wae sall never say na.
An noo, or wae bid ane anither ta ta,
Tae drink a geud nicht, sirs, wae sinno be sla,
Lets sipe oot wur horns, and a lang braeth weel dra,
To soopel wur wasans an open wur ja,
For de warld an her feuls, let us lauch a gae fa !
An for Finfolk aheem let us gae a ha ha !
An finis' wur sang wi' a wallie hurra !

    DENNISON in *Scottish Antiquary*, vol. vii. p. 81.

FRAGMENTS.

Shetland. Saina poba wer-a
          Leetra mavie, Leetra mavie,
          Saina poba wer-a
          Leetra mavie drengie.

          Daala stuy-ta stonga rara
          Oh—badeea, oh—badeea,

252   *Traditional Narratives.*

> Daala stuy-ta stonga rara
> Oh—badeea moynie.
>
> Wher der isno topshag
> Topshag, topshag,
> Where der isno topshag
> Shakda cole o Gamblie.

No Shetlander can tell what these lines mean.

> EDMONDSTON and SAXBY, pp. 199, 200.

> Bunye sits upo tappa tirl;—
> Calye inta bamba birl,
> Ba hilkie toonie;
> Ladyco hilka tilta,
> Roonin oondie cong ga loo!
> Ba hilkie toonie.
>
> EDMONDSTON and SAXBY, p. 200.

THE DAY DAWN.

[An Ancient Scandinavian Air preserved in Shetland, set by MISS KEMP of Edinburgh.]

Songs and Music.

HIBBERT, *Shetland*, p. 608.

NEW YEAR'S EVEN SONG.

Peace be to this buirdly biggin'!
   We're a' Queen Mary's men,
From the stethe unto the riggin',
   And that's before our Lady.

This is gude New Year's even nicht—
   We're a' Queen Mary's men;
An' we've come here to claim our richt,
   And that's before our Lady.

The morrow is gude New Years' day—
   We're a' Queen Mary's men;
An' we've come here to sport and play,
   An' that's before our Lady.

The hindmost house that we came from—
   We're a' Queen Mary's men;
We gat oat-cake and sowens' scone;
   The three-lugged cog was standing fou;
We hope to get the same from you,
   And that's before our Lady.

Gudewife gae to your kebbock-creel—
 We're a' Queen Mary's men,
And see thou count the kebbocks weel,
 And that's before our Lady.

Gudewife gae to your gealding-vat—
 We're a' Queen Mary's men,
An' let us drink till our lugs crack,
 An' fetch us ane an' fetch us twa,
An' aye the merrier we'll gang awa',
 And that's before our Lady.

Gudewife gae to your butter-ark—
 We're a' Queen Mary's men ;
An' fetch us here ten bismar mark ;
See that ye grip weel in the dark,
 And that's before our Lady.

May a' your mares be weel to foal—
 We're a' Queen Mary's men,
And every ane be a staig foal,
 And that's before our Lady.

May a' your kye be weel to calve—
 We're a' Queen Mary's men ;
And every ane a queyock calf,
 And that's before our Lady.

May a' your ewes be weel to lamb—
 We're a' Queen Mary's men ;
And every ane a ewe and a ram,
 And that's before our Lady.

May a' your hens rin in a reel—
 We're a' Queen Mary's men ;
And every ane twal at her heel,
 And that's before our Lady.

Songs and Music.

> Here we hae brocht our carrying-horse—
> We're a' Queen Mary's men;
> A mony a curse licht on his corse;
> He'll eat mair meat than we can get;
> He'll drink mair drink than we can swink,
> And that's before our Lady.

It was the custom for companies of men to go from house to house on New Year's Eve singing in full chorus the [above] song.

At the conclusion of the song the minstrels were entertained with cakes and ale, and sometimes a smoked goose was set before the company. The singing-men at starting were few in number, but every house visited sent forth fresh relays, and the chorus waxed in volume as the number of voices increased. . . . The "carrying-horse," mentioned in the last verse, was the clown or jester of the party, who suffered himself to be beaten with knotted handkerchiefs, and received double rations as the reward of his folly.—GORRIE, pp. 334-37.

[Another version from the parish of Deerness, differing slightly from the above, is given by Chambers, in his *Popular Rhymes of Scotland*. He states that the song had been placed before him "in a form not the most satisfactory to an antiquary, but the best that circumstances admitted of—namely, with a number of verses composed as much from imagination as from memory, to make out something like the whole piece." On the conclusion of the song, Chambers adds: "The inner door being opened, a tremendous rush took place towards the interior. The inmates furnished a long table with all sorts of homely fare, and a hearty feast took place, followed by copious libations of ale, charged with all sorts of good wishes. The party would then proceed to the next house, where a similar scene would be enacted. Heaven knows how they contrived to take so many suppers in one evening! No slight could be more keenly felt by a Deerness farmer than to have his house passed over unvisited by the New-year singers."

CHAMBERS, pp. 166-168.]

The following are the words of the "New'r Even's Song" (*see* II. *a*, "YULE"), as remembered by an old dame in Shetland:

"Gude new'r even, gude new'r night—St. Mary's men are we;
We're come here to crave our right—before our leddie.

"King Henry he's a huntin' gane,—St. Mary's men are we,—
And ta'en wi' him his merry young men—before our leddie.

"I'll tell ye how our lady was dressed,—St. Mary's men are we,—
If ye'll gie tae us some o' yer best—before our leddie.

"She had upon her well-made head—St. Mary's men are we—
A crown of gold, an' it fu' braid—before our leddie.

"She had upon her middle sma'—St. Mary's men are we—
A silver belt an' it fu' bra'—before our leddie.

"She had upon her fingers ten—St. Mary's men are we—
Rings o' gold, fu' mony an ane—before our leddie.

"She had upon her weel-made feet—St. Mary's men are we—
Silver slippers, an' they fu' neat—before our leddie.

"Gude man, gang in your gauin-geel—St. Mary's men are we—
An' gie's a can or two o' ale—before our leddie.

"Gude wife, gang in your butter-kit—St. Mary's men are we—
An' gie's a spoon or two o' it—before our leddie.

"Likewise gang in your farrel-creel—St. Mary's men are we—
An' wale your farrels, an' wale them weel—before our leddie.

"Our spoon is made o' cow's horn,—St. Mary's men are we—
Open da door, an' let us in—before our leddie.

"We're standing here before da door,—St. Mary's men are we—
An' we'll pass in before a score—before our leddie."

REID, p. 59.

For Music *see also* I. *d*, "*Fairy Tunes.*"

(*d*) *PLACE LEGENDS AND TRADITIONS.*

Papa Stour. On a small level green, near the middle of the cultivated part, observed the marks of a circular enclosure, in which tradition says a Lord Terwil fought a duel with another gentleman, on some dispute or other, and afterwards accompanied by his eleven sons, went down on purpose to rob his neighbours, but together with his whole family perished on a rock, since called Terwil's Ba' or rock.

LOW, p. 123.

Sand House, Shetland. *Sand House Mansion.*—The beautiful old castle of Scalloway, built by Earl Patrick Stewart about 1600, was spoiled of much of its ancient grandeur, by having its dressed freestones torn from their place, to supply door and window jambs and lintels, and corner stones for this mansion. But the spoliation of the castle . . . was not permitted to proceed without a fearful warning.

While the work of demolition was busily going on, a voice, it is said, was heard to declare, " They might pull down and build up, but the fourth generation should never inhabit."—*New Stat. Acct.*, Shetland, p. 115.

Hoy. *Dwarfie Stone.*—Ingentissimus mons hic est, distat enim a terra in pari altitudine tribus miliaribus, ubi ascensus non est; alter est mons non admodum eo altus, inter quos lapis est admiratione dignus, magnus est et excelsus fabricatus a gigante suaque uxore: unus lapis est cameratus, in quo lectus est perquam artificiose factus in lapide viro et uxore; tempus camerationis foemina gravida fuit, ut lectus testatur; nam ea pars lecti in qua uxor cubuit effigiem habet ventri gravidi. In lapide pulvinar factum est duobus scuvialibus ex tumore lapidis, non tamen materie tenaci aliqua conjunguntur, sed unus est. Osteum habet obtrusum lapide; qui hoc fit, nescio. Fabulantur quod alter gigas in odium illum habebat quapropter lapidem fabricavit longitudine et latitudine ostei ut eos includeret, et ita fame perirent, tandemque ipso dominante insulam, ad suum usum lapidem hateret et retineret. Detulit tandem lapidem fabricatam in summitatem montis atque jaculo imposito summa vi brachiorum (atque dolore alterius prosperitatis) in ostium injunxit, gigante incluso evigilante auribus lupum tenebat exire nequiens suis maleis impluvium fecit per quod egressus est.

Jo. Ben *ap.* Barry, p. 449.

The *Dwarfie Stone* . . . is about 34 feet long, 16 or 17 broad, and 8 thick. . . . The common tradition among the people is that a giant with his wife lived in this Isle of Hoy, who had this stone for their castle.—Brand, p. 42.

Mainland. At the Loch of Stennis, in the mainland in that part thereof, where the loch is narrowest, both on the west and east side of the loch there is a ditch; within which there is a circle of large and high stones erected: the larger

Place Legends and Traditions.

Round is on the west side above 100 paces diameter. . . . On the other side of this loch . . . is another ditch, about half a mile from the former, but of far less circumference, within which also there are some stones standing, something bigger than the other stones on the west side of this loch, in form of a semicircle, I think, rather than of a circle, opening to the east. . . . Many of the countrey do say, that in the larger Round the Sun and in the lesser the Moon was worshipped by the old Pagan inhabitants of these Isles.—BRAND, pp. 43-44.

Papa-Stour. In the Church-Yard of *Papa-Stour*, in the Parish of *Waes*, lyeth a Stone 5 foot long, at the one end two, and at the other one foot broad, concave from one end to the other, of which the common Tradition goes, that this stone came ashore on that Isle with a dead Man tied to it, who lys buried there beside it.—BRAND, p. 109.

[From the description this appears to have been an ordinary stone coffin. Low also briefly describes this stone, and on p. 27 gives a rough drawing of it.]

South Ronaldsay. *Stone at Lady Kirk.*—South Ronaldsay habet templum juxta littus marinum, ubi lapis est durissimus, vulgus vocat (a grey whin), longitudine sex pedum, latitudine quatuor, in quo pressura duorum pedum nudorum insigitur, quam faber nullus quidem fabricari potest: fabulantur senes, quod Gallus quidam patria expulsus, locaque asyli, ingressus est navem quandam, ubi subita procella orta, periclitati, passique sunt naufragium, ipse tandem transiliens super tergum belluæ constitit suppliciter deum orans, quod si salvus portaretur ad terram, in memoriam &c. Mariæ Virginis ecclesiam construeret: Oratione audita; salvus ad littus appulit, adminiculo belluæ. Bellua tandem mutata in lapidem ejusdem coloris ipse in ecclesiam illam collocavit, ubi adhuc manet, ut supra dixi.

JO. BEN *apud* BARRY, p. 447.

In this old Fabrick of our *Lady's Church*, there is a Stone lying about 4 foot long, and 2 foot broad, but narrower and round at the two ends, upon the surface of which Stone, there is the print of two feet, concerning which the Superstitious People have a Tradition, that *St. Magnus*, when he could not get a Boat on a time to carry him over *Pightland Firth*, took this Stone, and setting his Feet thereupon, passed the Firth safely, and left the Stone in this Church, which hath continued here ever since.

BRAND, p. 60.

Sandsting. *Standing Stones at West Skeld.*—These two stones are said to be the metamorphosis of two wizards or giants, who were on their way to plunder and murder the inhabitants of West Skeld; but, not having calculated their time with sufficient accuracy, before they could accomplish their purpose, or retrace their steps to their dark abodes, the first rays of the morning sun appeared, and they were immediately transformed, and remain to the present time in the shape of two tall moss-grown stones of ten feet in height.—*New Stat. Acct.*, Shetland, p. 111.

Rousay. *Stone hurled by giant.*—Here may be noticed a huge slab of stone, not unlike those in the circle of Stenness, with a very wonderful history attached to it. In the days of miracles and other supernatural appearances there lived a mighty giant named Cubbierow beside the Fitty Hill of Westray. He seems to have had a feeling of enmity towards some unlucky individual, and was determined to punish him severely. Although his foe had fled to Rousay, a distance of about eight miles, the giant took up his position in Fitty Hill; and seizing the huge slab, he hurled it at his enemy across the intervening sound. . . . The marks of Cubbierow's fingers are to be seen upon that stone unto this day.—FERGUSSON, pp. 129, 130.

Unst. Saxie and Herman were two Unst giants— Saxie holding as his special territory the hilly promontory of Saxafiord on the east side, and Herman that of Hermaness on the west side, of Burrafiord, the geological formation of their respective domains being totally different. They seem to have quarrelled perpetually, and many stories of these quarrels are told. The most noteworthy seems to have been the occasion when, using the rocks for weapons, they contrived to leave a record of their exploits which will last for all time. A huge boulder which Saxie flung rises to the surface of the water close to the shore on the Hermaness side of the fiord, and is called "Saxie's Baa"; and the rock which Herman hurled at his foe is bedded in the cliffs of Saxfiord, and goes by the name of "Herman's Hellyac." Saxie's Kettle is a basin in the rock, into which the water rises from below, bubbling and hissing as if it were boiling. Once Herman asked the loan of this kettle in which to boil an ox, and Saxie said he would lend it only on condition that they should go halves. Said Herman,

"I'll radder reeve rüt
As gie da half o üt."

A pitched battle was the consequence of Herman's refusal to pay for the loan of Saxie's Kettle, but it is not known who got the best of it.

EDMONDSTON and SAXBY, pp. 225, 226.

Giant's Stepping-Stone.—Sigger-hill is benorth Colviedell, and on the slope there is a large flat stone eight to ten feet square. There was a giant who lived in that neighbourhood called Sigger, and he put a rock in the sea for a craig-seat—that is, a seat where he could place himself conveniently for fishing. But the water was deep, and the giant did not like wetting his feet, so he thought he would place a stepping-stone between the shore and Scarva-Skerry. He went up the hill, and found a large flat stone suitable for his purpose, but as he was returning staggering under the weight of the enormous stone, his wife (the guy-karl) came out, and seeing him, so burdened, exclaimed,

> "Oh, Siggie, Siggie,
> Mony an evil stane
> Has lain on dy riggie"!

With that the giant tripped and fell, and the stone on top of him—and he died there; and there he had to lie, for no one was able to take that stone off him.

EDMONDSTON and SAXBY, pp. 224, 225.

For Place Legends *see also* under I. *a*, "HOLY PLACES," "STONES," "BUILDINGS."

(*e*) *DRAMA.*

Shetland. *Sword Dance.*—*See* Sir Walter Scott, *The Pirate*, Note P, given as from an old manuscript, which also includes a description of the sword dance itself and the epilogue. For the Sword-dance *see also* Hibbert, *Description*, pp. 556-560.

PART IV.

FOLK SAYINGS.

(a) COUNTING-OUT RHYMES

Orkney.
Etem, petem, penny pie,
Popalorúm jinkum jie,
Esas, esink,
Peas, pottage,
Small drink,
Thu art once oot.
    Communicated by GILBERT GOUDIE, Esq.,
      of Braefield, Dunrossness, Shetland.

Shetland.
Etem, petem, penny pie,
Baaby loory, jinkum jie,
White fish, grey troot,
Gibby ga, du's oot.

Variant of third line:
Black fish, white troot.   *do.*

Shetland. Eenery, twaery, ockory, seven,
Alapa, crackapa, ten apo' 'leven ;
Peen pan, musky dan,
Eedlem, tweedlem, twenty-wan.   *do.*

(b) PROVERBS.

Shetland. A Shetlandic proverb remarkable for the reiteration of the word "cood."

A man considering himself unjustly blamed for not doing what he considered had been beyond his power, and so feeling aggrieved replied:

"Foo cooda quin a coodna?
Cooda dae mair or a cood, cooda?"

[Eng. "How could I when I could not? Could I do more than I could, could I?"]

Communicated to Mr. Black by Mr. A. K. WILLIAMSON, a native of Shetland.

Cunningsburgh. The people of this small spot, a stout hardy race, by all accounts the wildest in Shetland. Tradition scandalises them much with regard to their humanity, particularly in entertaining strangers. It became proverbial, when one wanted to dismiss a stranger, or thought he stayed too long, to use the Coningsburgen phrase in Norn: "Myrk in e Liora, Luce in e Liunga, Tim in e Guest in e guengna"; "It's (mark [mirk]) dark in the chimney, but it's light thro' the heath, it's still time for the stranger to be gone."—LOW, p. 180.

See also Appendix.

Orkney. There used to be a very common proverb circulating in these islands to the effect that "Giff Bessie say it is weill it is weill." The Bessie referred to was one Bessie Skebister, who had the power of informing fishermen and their wives whether any of their boats were in danger or not.... This woman was strangled and burned for various offences, one of which was that of riding on the back of a certain James Sandieson, and flying with him through the air to Norway and Zetland, with a bridle in his mouth.—FERGUSSON, p. 35.

Shetland. [The inhabitants of Sound, a village near Lerwick] pique themselves on inhabiting the exact spot of ground held by their ancestors for centuries, and look down upon the Lerwegians, exclaiming—

> "Sound was Sound when Lerwick was none,
> And Sound will be Sound when Lerwick is done."

COWIE, p. 130.

Selivoe . . . at a certain season, *i.e.* a week or two before Lambmass, swarms with such a glut of Mackrel in boatfulls. . . . In windy weather a bit of red rag is very good bait, which affords us a proverb that "women and mackrel are easily caught by a red clout."

LOW, p. 85.

Harray. "Let be and I'll let be, as the Harra-man said to the lobster."

The inland situation of the parish of Harra exposes its inhabitants to the imputation of ignorance of maritime affairs, and, consequently, to the ridicule of their brother islanders. A Harra man is said, when he saw for the first time a lobster which had just dropped from a basket, to have immediately laid his hand on it, when the animal seized him, and inflicted upon him a severe gripe. The exclamation which he made use of has passed into a proverb, and is employed when one man, quarrelling with another, wishes him to desist.

TEIGNMOUTH, vol. i. p. 274.

LOCAL TEE, TUE, OR NICKNAMES

Each district in the islands has its own *Tee-name*, or nickname. Tradition says that many of these names date from the building of the cathedral, and were given from the provisions the several detachments brought with them. Thus the Papa Westray folk are known as *Dundies* (poor cod), the Westray people as *Auks* (the common Guillemot), and the inhabitants of Walls as *Lyres* (Manx Shearwaters). Many of these names are of respectable antiquity.

TUDOR, p. 204.

Orkney. *List of Tee-names.*

Kirkwall—*Starlings.*
St. Andrew's—*Skerry Scrapers.*
Deerness—*Skate Rumples.*
Holm—*Hobblers.*
Orphir—*Yearnings.* Yearnings, the stomach of a calf used to curdle the milk in cheese-making.
Firth—*Oysters.*
Stromness—*Bloody Puddings.*
Sandwick—*Ash Patties.*
Harray—*Crabs.* [For the origin of this name *see* under "Proverbs."]
Birsay—*Dogs* or *Hoes* (species of small shark).
Evie—*Cauld Kail.*
Rendall—*Sheep Thieves.*

South Isles.

Hoy—*Hawks.*
Walls—*Lyres* (Manx Shearwaters).
Burray—*Oily Bogies.*
South Ronaldsay :
    Grimness—*Gruties.*
    Hope—*Scouties* (Richardson's Skuas).
    Widewall—*Witches.*
    Herston—*Hogs.*
    Sandwick—*Birkies.*
    South Parish—*Teeacks* (Lapwings).

Western Isles.

Gairsay—*Buckies* (the large whelk used for bait).
Veira or Wyre—*Whelks.*
Egilsay—*Burstin-lumps.* [Burstin is corn dried in a kettle over the fire.]
Rousay—*Mares.* The inhabitants of this island are so called, because, at least so says tradition, when they wanted to establish a breed of horses on the island,

they sent a Moses Primrose sort of fellow to buy at the nearest horse fair, who purchased a lot of mares, but forgot all about there being any need of stallions.

North Isles.

Shapinsay—*Sheep*.
Stronsay—*Limpets*.
Sanday—*Gruellie Belkies*, porridge and brose feeders.
North Ronaldsay—*Seais, Hides*, or *Hoydes*.
Eday—*Scarfs* (Cormorants).
Westray—*Auks* (Common Guillemot).
Papa Westray—*Dundies* (Spent Cod).

Shetland. Lerwick—*Whitings*.
Scalloway—*Sma' Drink*.
Tingwall—*Timmer Guns*.
Bressay—Men, *Sparks*; women, *Crackers*, from their being supposed to be great talkers.
Dunrossness—*Liver Coids*, Saith in their third year. From the favourite dish of the district, one of these fish cleaned, filled with liver, and roasted among hot peat ashes.
Sandsting—*Suck of legs*, from the poor people using in cold weather the upper parts of stockings or socks, of which the soles are past darning, to protect the tops of their feet and legs from cold.
Aithsting—*Smuicks* or *Smocks*. [Smuicks, a kind of shoe or slipper made of cloth, and cross-sewn on the soles, to prevent slipping.]
Walls—three divisions:
 Mid Waas, *Gentry*.
 Wast O'Waas, *Settlins*.
 Down O'Waas, *Dirt*.
Sandness—*Burstin Brunis*. [Burstin Brunis, cakes made of Burstin.]
Foula—*Nories* (from *Tammy Nories*, Puffins).

Weisdale and Nesting—*Gauts*, Cut Swine.

Lunnasting—*Hoes*, Dog-fish.

Delting—*Sparls*, from the intestines of a sheep filled with chopped meat and suet, heavily seasoned with pepper and salt, and smoke-dried.

Northmaven—*Liver Muggies* or *Ulie Coils*. "Muggies," from the stomach of a cod filled with its liver and then boiled.

Whalsay—*Piltocks* (Saith in their second year).

Yell—*Sheep Thieves*, or simply *Thieves*.

Fetlar—*Russie Foals*—Ungroomed year-old colts, with their first coats hanging in unkempt masses about them.

Unst—*Midden Slues*, meaning dirty and lazy people. They are also sometimes styled the *Honest Folk of Unst*, but this latter appellation must be considered sarcastic.—TUDOR, pp. 612-615.

APPENDIX.

1. *PHYSICAL CHARACTERISTICS.*

The Coningsburghers[1] present both physical and mental peculiarities, which entitle them to be considered a distinct tribe from the rest of the Shetlanders. Having harsher features, larger muscles, and a broader "build" than their countrymen, they are said more to resemble Saxons than Scandinavians. Tradition assigns to them a large proportion of Spanish blood. It may be difficult to recognise in him Iberian features, but there is no doubt the modern Coningsburgher has much of the excitable nature of the Spaniard.

COWIE, p. 119.

Noltland, Westray. Close to the shore I passed a hamlet, the dwellers in which are nick-named "Dons," being descended, it is averred, from seamen of the Spanish Armada, who were wrecked on Fair Isle, and who migrated to Westray. The families so designated have certainly a swarthy complexion and an Iberian cast of countenance.

GORRIE, pp. 182-3.

Weir, Orkney. [In the churchyard at Cubbierow] most of the [old] graves are seven feet long, which is not to be wondered at, since the present inhabitants . . . are many of them above the ordinary stature.

BARRY, pp. 65, 66.

---

[1] *See also* IV. *b.*

2. *NAMES.*

Orkney. In general, they have no family surnames, but to their own Christian name each of the sons and daughters joins that of the father; the former adding to it son, the latter daughter. This as may easily be conceived, is an awkward and most inconvenient custom, rendering it difficult, and frequently impossible, to establish their propinquity to any of their relations that die abroad.

HALL, *Travels in Scotland*, vol. ii. p. 525.

Shetland. The fore-name "Arthur" is common in Shetland now, but I rather think it is only a seventeenth or eighteenth century corrupt form of the Old Northern "Ottar." Last century "Otto," or "Otho," or "Ottie," was a frequent fore-name here; and now no case of it occurs. In our Northern Isles it has even been Judaised into "Hosea," so that "Otto Ottoson" was transmuted into "Hosea Hoseason"—so written but pronounced "Osie Osieson."

K. BLIND, *Nineteenth Century*, 1879, p. 1112, quoting Arthur Laurenson of Lerwick.

Sanday, Orkney. The oldest names among them are Torfs, Tullachs, Muirs, Swaneys, Feas.—BARRY, p. 59.

Orkney. A large proportion of the names of persons, as well as of places, are of Norwegian derivation. . . . In general, however, while family names indicate Norse lineage, the family faces exhibit more of the Scottish than the Scandinavian type.—GORRIE, p. 343.

GLOSSARY.

A', all.
Abeun, above.
Abhominable, abominable.
Affrayit, frightened.
Ahint, behind.
Als, alse, as.
Amas, alms.
Ammers, embers.
An', and.
Ance, anes, once.
Aquavite, whisky.
Ase, ass, ashes.
'At, that.
Ather, either.
Aucht, aught, possession; to own.
Aucht, aught, eight.
Auld, old.
Auld da, grandfather.
Awe-band, in a moral sense that which inspires awe or reverence.
A-whaaking, quaking.
Awin, own.
Ayont, beyond.

Baa, a sunken rock.
Bae, by.
Bair, bear, beir, barley (Hordeum vulgare).
Bait-coubbie, basket for bait.
Bald, bold.
Ballin, throwing stones at anything.
Beakned, beckoned.

Beat of lint, a sheaf of flax made up for the mill.
Bed, dwelt, lived.
Beelan, suppurating.
Beir shaues, sheaves of barley.
Bie, beey, bee.
Big, build.
Biggin, bigging, house; verb, building.
Bismar, an instrument for weighing, resembling a steelyard.
Bleud, blood.
Boisting, threatening.
Boit, boat.
Bokie, bugbear.
Boneshaw, beanschaw, sciatica.
Boorly. See *Buirdly.*
Bothie, person, individual.
Branks, bridle.
Braw, a trinket.
Brig, bridge.
Brint, burnt.
Brocht, brought.
Brute, bruit.
Büdie, a straw basket.
Bülie, banquet.
Büns, bones.
Buirdly, boorly, large, stately; applied to a house.
Bullering, a bellowing noise. Cf. "Bullers of Buchan."
Burstin, corn dried in a kettle over the fire.
Busome, broom.

But the hous, towards the outer apartment.
But-room, outer room.
Butter-ark, butter-tub.

Ca'd, called.
Cáft, bought.
Cald, cold.
Cald, vb. called.
Callowit, calved.
Cap, cappy, a small wooden cup.
Cashie, cassie, cazy, cazzie, a straw basket.
Ceur, cure.
Chaking, making a clinking noise.
Chapping-can, a quart pitcher.
Chappit, knocked.
Chirme and chirle, emitting mournful sounds.
Cinno (*c* hard), cannot.
Cla, to scratch.
Cloak, a beetle.
Clout, cloth.
Clowen, cloven.
Codd, a pillow.
Coft, caft, bought.
Cog, a circular wooden dish.
Coit, pettycoat.
Collie, an iron lamp.
Corbie, raven.
Corssis, crosses.
Cother, warm, snug.
Couped, overturned.
Craig, a cliff.
Craigis, necks.
Creel, a large basket.
Cringlo, a low straw stool.
Croopan, the trunk of the body of man or animal.
Cubby, a small *cashie*.
Cuist, cast.
Culye, to cuddle.
Curch, curtch, courtch, linen cap for the head.

Da, de, the.

Dael, they will (= they'll).
Daert, dart, arrow.
Daffok, a large wooden dish or tub.
Dang, beat, struck.
Dat's, that is.
Dead, death.
Ded, daddy, father.
Dee, die.
Dem, them.
Dempt, judged.
Der, they are.
Dilait, accuse.
Ding, beat, strike.
Dir, der, their.
Doo. See *Du*.
Doom, judgment.
Door, stubborn.
Doo'r, you are.
Du, doo, thou.
Duff, blunt.
Dul, sorrow.
Dure, door.
Duyning, dwining, wasting away.
Dy, thy.

Edder, either.
Estait, state, condition.
Euse, a large and very hot fire.
Ewerie, every.

Fa', fall.
Faddome, to measure, to encompass with the arms.
Fae, from.
Faem, foam, periphrasis for the sea.
Fand, found.
Fang, anything taken in hunting or fishing.
Fanyeit, feigned.
Fard, favoured.
Farly, wonderful.
Farrel-creel, cake-basket.
Faschioun, fashion.
Fashed, troubled, bothered.
Fats, faults.

Glossary. 273

Fauldseiknes, a disease.
Faus, false.
Feal, turf.
Fedirs o' da tirl, the paddles or blades of the water wheel.
Fenyeit, feigned.
Fey, death doomed.
Filty, filthy.
Flakkit, straw mat for drying corn.
Fleat, fleitt. scolded.
Flech, flea.
Flitting, moving, changing residence.
Flor, floor.
Floughs, flows.
Flüd, flood.
Flyt, scold.
Foill, foal.
Fou, full.
Foy, feast, festival.
Fra, frae, from.
Franisie, frenzy.
Fuman, foaming, streaming.
Furt, forth.
Fusion, strength.
Futh, abundance.
Fyit, vb. tr. feed.
Fyllis, finds guilty.

Ga', gall.
Gae, give.
Gaed, zeid, went.
Gantit, yawned.
Gare, cause, make; *gared*, made.
Gauin-geel, ale-kirn.
Gealding-vat, fermenting-vat.
Ged, went away.
Gers, grass.
Gie, give.
Gif, if.
Gin (*g* hard), if.
Gis, a deep ravine which admits the sea.
Gissing, childbed.
Glaid, a kite.

Glangoir, probably meant for *glamoir*, witchery.
Glowered, (1) scowled, (2) looked earnestly.
Gloy, the straw of oats.
Gluf, a sudden fright.
Goud, gowd, gold.
Graippit, gripped.
Greetin', weeping.
Grumly, gruesome.
Grund, ground.
Gryss, a pig.
Guid, good.
Guidis, guids, live stock.
Gully, a large knife.
Guthaland, the Holy Land, lit. "God's Land."
Gyain, going.
Gyüd, God.

Haaf, deep sea, generally understood as meaning "deep-sea fishing."
Haars, hinges.
Hae, have.
Haif, have.
Hailled, healed.
Hale, haill, whole.
Halflin, a hobbledehoy.
Handshouse, gloves.
Harns, brains.
Hars, neck.
Harskit, cardialgia.
Hart-cake, cardialgia.
Hedder, heather.
Heed, head.
Het, hot.
Hich, high.
Hid, it.
Hide, skin.
His, its; there being no neuter.
Hol', hole.
How o' de head, crown of the head.
Hümeen, hüming, twilight.

I, in.
Illudit, deceived.

Ipo, upon.

Joles, large pieces of meat; figuratively, large and clumsy.
Jubish, to be doubtful of, and yet to suspect the occurrence of the event.

Kail, keall, colewort.
Kebbock, a cheese.
Keist, cast.
Ken, know.
Kens, knows.
Killogie, the vacant space before the fireplace in a malt-kiln.
Kirne, to churn.
Kirnit, churned.
Kivered, covered.
Knet, knit together, tied.
Knoking, husking barley in a large hollow stone.
Kreigs, craigs, rocks.
Ky, cattle, milk cows.

La, law.
Lassie, a young woman or grown girl.
Lathie, lady.
Laughfull, lawful.
Lawman, President of the "Thing" or local parliament.
Lech, low.
Len, loan.
Leukan, looking.
Libed, castrated.
Lift, sky, firmament.
Liknes, likeness, semblance.
Lipenan, expecting.
Livs, palms of the hands.
Lone, a lane.
Looffullis, handfuls; as much as can be lifted in the hollow of the hand.
Look, lock, loik, luik, handful.
Louder-horn, a large horn used by fishermen in foggy weather.
Low, flame.
Lowed, burned, flamed.
Lowing-taand, a burning peat.

Luck, like.
Lug, ear.
Lugged, eared, having ears.
Lughe, laughed.
Luik, handful.
Lum, chimney.

Mad, made.
Maeds, maggots.
Mair, more.
Man, must.
Megs, forepaws or fins of a seal.
Meill, a weight.
Menye-singers, minne-singers.
Merchis, boundaries.
Merefow, achillea millefolium.
Merk, a Scots coin.
Met, measured.
Midden, refuse-heap.
Midder, mother.
Minnie, grandmother; sometimes used for mother.
Minted, insinuated.
Miny, many.
Mirkin, twilight.
Mould, earth.
Muckle, much, large, great.
Müddow, meadow.

Neem, name.
Nippie, biting, frosty.
Noll fa, shall not get.
Nort, north.
Nourris, nurse.
Noust, landing-place for a boat.

O', of.
Onowayis, in no wise.
Ony, any.
Ootmoucht, exhausted by hunger or hard labour.
Or, ere.
Ouk, week.
Owercome, chorus of a song.
Ov, grandchild.

Glossary.

Peerie, pirie, little.
Pellack, porpoise.
Peris, perish.
Fickle, small quantity.
Pig, an earthenware vessel.
Piltacks, coalfish a year old.
Piric, little.
Plack, an old Scots coin, equal to one-third of an English penny.
Pleat, a plate.
Pleuch, pleuche, a plough.
Pobe, foster-father.
Pock, a bag.
Poor, power.
Puik, pluck, pull.
Pussit, pushed.

Quey, a cow of two years old.
Queyoch, queyok, quoyach, same as *quey*.
Quhair, quher, where.
Quhairfra, wherefrom.
Quhais, whose.
Quhilk, which.
Quhill, while, until.
Quholl, whole.
Quhyt, white.
Quite, acquit.

Rae, rare, unusual.
Raif, tore.
Reeve, tore.
Reuf, roof.
Rifts, belches.
Riggie, back.
Rivlins, shoes of undressed hide.
Rock, a distaff.
Rootin, roaring.
Rowed, rolled.
Ruche, rough.
Ryplie, ripely, maturely (*i.e.* fully thought out).

Saban, sobbing.
Sained, blessed or marked with the sign of the cross.
Sair, sore.
Sall, shall.
Saxter-aithe, an oath in testimony of innocence of six honest neighbours.
Sca, scab.
Scattald, open ground for pasture.
Scheek, cheek.
Scheiris, shears, scissors.
Scheret shilling, clipped or cut shilling.
Scho, she.
Schut, push.
Scoom, skim.
Screws, small stacks of hay.
Scrieg, covered with vermin
Seeven, seven.
Seif, siff, siwe, sieve.
Seik, sick.
Sel, self.
Selch, a seal.
Selkie, a seal.
Sen syne, since that time
Senn, soon.
Sett, soot.
Sha, show.
Shaalds, shoals.
Shair, chair.
Shakesem, nice, coy, fastidious.
Sharn, cow dung.
Shilpid, sour.
Shii, scho, she.
Sic, sick, sik, such.
Sicker, severe; not "secure" as in Scottish.
Siff, sieve.
Sillneris, probably a misprint for *silveris*.
Sing, singe.
Sinno, cannot.
Siwe, sieve.
Skailan, scattering.
Skane, skin.
Skeo, a small dry-built stone hut for drying fish.
Slap, an opening through a hedge.
Slockid, extinguished.
Smolie, disdain, haughty contempt.

Snappered, fell.
Sneck, latch of a door.
Sonsie, lucky, fortunate, pleasant.
Soopel, to make flexible.
Sope, a sup.
Spak, spoke.
Speer, to ask.
Stack, a high precipitous rock in the sea.
Staig, a stallion.
Stark, strong.
Steekit, steikit, closed, shut.
Steen, stone.
Steggie, steps in the side of a stone wall.
Stethe, foundation.
Stickit, stabbed.
Stival, stiff; in a loose way, strong.
Stoup, a water bucket.
Strampit, trampled.
Stüns, stones.
Sturtan, congealed.
Sueir, afraid, unwilling.
Swa, "the low prolonged note of waves heard at a distance."
Sweean, smarting.
Syne, afterwards.
Syün, soon.

Tae, to.
Tae side to the tither, one side to the other.
Ta'en, tane, taken.
Tee-name, nick-name.
Teetgong, swift-go.
Tell, count.
Tequhyt, linnet.
Thestreen, yester-eve.
Thing, parliament.
Thoosan, thousand.
Thrapple, windpipe.
Thrave, twenty-four sheaves of corn.
Threachin, threshed.
Thrid, (1) thread, (2) third.
Tiftan, aching.
Timmer, wooden.

Tint, lost,
Tirl, a substitute for the trundle of a mill.
To, though.
Tocher, dower.
Towis, ropes.
Trappit, questioned.
Travellye, a sudden and violent fall.
Tree, three.
Trew, through.
Trowy, trow-like.
Tryit, proved.
Tuiching, touching.
Tulyie, a fight, to fight.
Twal, twelve.

Udaler, one who holds his property by uninterrupted succession, without any charter, and without subjection to feudal service or acknowledgment of any superior.
Umquhile, umquhill, deceased.
Unfeerdie, unwieldy, unable.
Unkirsn, unclean.
Unthreachin, unthreshed.

Viseck, a ballad song.
Vistie, a journey.
Voe, a narrow inlet of the sea.
Voir, seed time.

Wad, wade, would.
Wadin, wedding.
Wad no', would not.
Wae, we.
Waefu' woeful.
Waems, the belly.
Wald, would.
Wale, choose, select.
Walknit, awakened.
Wallie, large, ample.
Waped, flung with violence.
War, were.
War, seaweed.
War, waur, worse.

Glossary.

Ward fire, a fire built on a high hill as a signal or alarm.
Wark, a fatal disease once common in Orkney.
Wasans, windpipes.
Weel, well.
Weyit, weighed.
Whiecked, whisked.
Whiped, snatched.
Whummelled, turned upside down.
Who, how.
Wi' with.
Wid, wud, would.
Winno, will not.
Wiried, worried, strangled.
Withershins, in a direction contrary to the sun.
Witte, to know.
Wod, wood, wud, mad, insane.
Wodrome, madness.
Woll schier, shears for clipping wool.
Wud, would.
Wur, our.
Wyt, blame.

Yarl, earl.
Yeid, went.
Yeir, yeiris, year, years.
Yuk, the itch.
Yull-banket, Christmas feast.

Zeid, went.

[In a short glossary of old Norse words current in Shetland, given by Mr. Laurenson in his paper, are the following: *banehoos*, *büanhoos*, church ; *Kirser*, *fitting*, *venga*, *foodin*, *voaler*, all meaning cat ; *matratla-stilhad*, minister's house ; *upstanda*, *hoydeen*, *prestinvolga*, the minister ; *kirkasucken*, the buried dead in churchyards ; *trulla-scud*, a witch ; *vamm*, to bewitch.— *Proceed. Soc. Ant. Scot.*, vol. x. p. 714.]

The **Folklore Society**, original publishers of this book, was founded in 1878 and was the first learned society in the world to be devoted to the study of folklore. Its expressed aims were to encourage research and collection of traditional culture, and to make the results of this research available to scholars and the public at large.

The Society is still going strong, and organises regular conferences and other events, issues a well-respected journal and members' newsletter, publishes books on folklore topics, and maintains an extensive library and archive service which is based in University College London. Membership is open to anyone interested in furthering the Society's aims.

Information regarding the Society's activities and current subscription rates is available from **The Folklore Society, University College London, Gower Street, London WC1E 6BT** (Tel 071 387 5894).

Also Published by Llanerch Press Ltd

SYMBOLISM OF THE CELTIC CROSS
by Derek Bryce, illus J Romilly Allen & others. Explores the link between pagan standing stones, market crosses and Christian Celtic crosses
ISBN 1 897853 33 5

FLOWERS OF A MYSTIC GARDEN
John Ruysbroeck
ISBN 1 897853 28 9

THE PHYSICIANS OF MYDDFAI
trans. John Pughe
ISBN 1 897853 15 7

THE FOLKLORE OF PLANTS
T F Thistleton Dyer
ISBN 1 897853 46 7

THE WAY AND THE QUEST
rev'd ed. of The Mystical Way and The Arthurian Quest
Derek Bryce
ISBN 1 897853 67 X

THE ANNALS OF CLONMACNOISE BEING ANNALS OF IRELAND FROM THE EARLIEST PERIOD TO 1408
ed. D Murphy. Facs of 1896 edition
ISBN 0 947992 99 5

WILLIAM OF MALMESBURY: A HISTORY OF THE NORMAN KINGS:
Facs. Trans. by J.Stevenson
ISBN 0 947992 30 8

THE DROLLS, TRADITIONS and SUPERSTITIONS OF OLD CORNWALL (Popular Romances of the West of England) In two series
Collected & edited by Robert Hunt
ISBN 1 897853 17 3, 1 897853 18 1

FOLKLORE OF SCOTTISH LOCHS AND SPRINGS
by James M Macinlay
ISBN 1 897853 23 8

THE MEDICINE TREE
Traditional healing in Wales from pre-history to the present
By John Sharkey
ISBN 1 861431 50 9

FOLKLORE OF WEST & MID WALES
By Jonathan Ceredig Davies
ISBN 1 897853 00 9

SHETLAND FOLKLORE
by John Spence
ISBN 1 861430 85 X

THE SECRET VALLEY
By Nicholas Cage
ISBN 1 861430 11 6

A GUIDE TO THE SAINTS OF WALES AND THE WEST COUNTRY
By Ray Spencer
ISBN 0 947992 57 X

**For a complete list of c.250+ titles, please write to:
LLANERCH PRESS LTD
Little Court, 48 Rectory Road
Burnham-on-Sea, Somerset. TA8 2BZ
or visit our website:
www.llanerchpress.com**